CW00521652

# THE DRUMS OF ARMAGEDDON

## BRITISH SOCIALISTS AND THE OUTBREAK OF WAR

*July – December 1914*

By

# Ian Bullock

Copyright © Ian Bullock 2020
This book is sold subject to the condition that it shall not, by way of trade or otherwise, be lent, resold, hired out, or otherwise circulated without the publisher's prior consent in any form of binding or cover other than that in which it is published and without a similar condition including this condition being imposed on the subsequent publisher.
The moral right of Ian Bullock has been asserted in accordance with the Copyright, Designs and Patents Act 1988.
BONCHURCH PRESS
ISBN-13: 978-1-5272-6126-6

A CIP record of this book is available
From the British Library

Information in this book is true and complete to the best of author's knowledge. This book is presented solely for educational purposes. The author disclaims any liability in connection with the use of this information or with respect to any loss or incidental or consequential damages caused, or alleged to have been caused, directly or indirectly, by the information contained herein.

*For Sue, Chloe and Paul*

*and in memory of Alun Howkins*

# ACKNOWLEDGEMENTS

The newspapers used for this book are now available on-line. But when I did the research on which it is based I had to rely on the microfilm collection at the University of Sussex library. I am grateful to the staff and particularly those who, making light of my ineptitude, helped me with the microfilm readers which were much more sophisticated than the ones I had used previously.

Thanks also to my publishing team at Kindle Book Publishing who did a really splendid job in preparing the book for publication.

# CONTENTS

# INTRODUCTION

## 1914: Disaster and Division

The words 'The Drums of Armageddon' first appeared in the
*Clarion*, one of the weekly papers on which this study is based, on 7
August 1914 just three days after the British declaration of war. It
was the title of the editorial by its editor-in-chief, Robert
Blatchford.[1] By the end of the year references to 'Armageddon' had
become quite frequent and by no means confined to the *Clarion*. But
it was again, in that paper on 4 December 1914 that Arthur Laycock
used 'The Drums of Armageddon' as the title of a poem.[2]

The outbreak of the First World War at the beginning of August
1914 was a momentous event – a tragic one in so many cases – in the
lives of all those in the belligerent countries. It was the beginning of
more than four decades unsurpassed in their procession of human

---

[1] Robert Blatchford, 1851-1943, was described by A.J.P. Taylor in his *Essays in
English History*, of 1976, 174, as 'the greatest popular journalist since Cobbett.' Born
into a struggling theatrical family, he spent much of his early years in the army,
eventually as a sergeant major, an experience which was to be crucial in many ways.
Apart from his socialism he was to become a controversial figure in two other ways.
He rejected religious belief in *God and my Neighbour* in 1903 and in *Not Guilty: A
Defence of the Bottom Dog,* 1905 and from 1909 he lost Left-wing support by warning
of the 'German Menace,' initially in a number of *Daily Mail* articles a few weeks
before the general election of January 1910.

[2] I have been able to find little about Arthur Laycock. He seems to have been the
son of the Lancashire dialect poet, Sam Laycock, a member of the ILP and the
author of at least two novels – *Warren of Manchester* and *Steve the Outlander,* the latter
based on his experiences in South Africa. I am indebted to Professor Paul Salveson
for this information.

tragedies. For many, right across the political spectrum, moral and sometimes religious doubts about the justification of the conflict were raised. What made it particularly problematic for those on the Left was that such issues were accentuated by the fact that since the formation of the (Second) Socialist International in 1889 the world-wide movement seemed to be advancing steadily, especially in Europe, bringing hope of a world without armed conflict as well as one moving slowly but unstoppably towards international cooperation and equality. Such hopes and expectations were now dashed. For the political Left in Britain the war would become a parting of the ways. While no one looked at the war as other than a disaster that should never have happened, the Left, even the parliamentary Left, in the shape of the Labour Party, would be divided.

Arthur Henderson became a member of Asquith's coalition government in 1915 and was joined by two other Labour ministers in Lloyd George's government at the end of 1916.[3] But many of its MPs whose primary allegiance was to the Independent Labour Party (ILP) took a more or less pacifist stance opposing British participation in the conflict, in line with the ILP as a whole. They included many of the most prominent Labour figures including the future Chancellor of the Exchequer, Philip Snowden as well as the redoubtable Fred Jowett.[4]

---

[3] Arthur Henderson, 1863-1935, had been elected as a Labour MP in a by-election in 1903 and chaired the parliamentary party between 1908 and 1910 a position he would resume after Ramsay MacDonald's resignation after the outbreak of war. In 1916 he would become the first Labour cabinet minister in Lloyd George's coalition government, a post from which he resigned the following year after the government refused to support his proposal for an international conference to try to end the war. In 1934 he would be awarded the Nobel Peace Prize following his work with the World League of Peace and at the Geneva Disarmament Conference. He was regarded with affection by many Labour MPs among whom he was known as 'Uncle Arthur.'

[4] Philip Snowden, 1864-1937, was a Methodist and Christian socialist and one of the 'quartet' – together with Hardie, MacDonald and Glasier – who were seen by ILP dissidents as dominating the pre-1914 ILP. He was elected MP in 1906, as was Jowett. He was on a lecture tour in Australia when the war broke out and would not

The position of the future first Labour prime minister, Ramsay MacDonald, was a little more equivocal.[5] Writing decades later, long after MacDonald's death, Emanuel Shinwell, never a great fan of Labour's first prime minister, maintained that 'He was neither for the war nor against it.' He presented himself, wrote Shinwell, as one who 'loathed past wars, regarded future wars with abhorrence, but carefully evaded giving his opinion on the basic question of the current one.'[6] It is true that MacDonald's statements on the war were sometimes subtle to the point of confusion for many. But he resigned from the chairmanship of the parliamentary party after the outbreak of war and, along with other notable ILPers, would lose his seat in the House of Commons at the 'khaki election' at the end of 1918 because of his position on the war.

It would be wrong to describe those who reluctantly supported Britain's participation in the conflict as 'pro-war' if by that it is suggested that they relished the conflict, but as long as it is understood that they regarded the whole thing as a tragedy that nevertheless necessitated resistance to what they saw as 'Prussian militarism,' the term can serve as a convenient label though for the

return to Britain until February 1915. Like other ILPers he lost his parliamentary seat at the 'khaki election' in 1918, but returned to the House of Commons in 1922; he would serve as Chancellor of the Exchequer in both the MacDonald governments of the 1924 and 1929-31. He sided with MacDonald in the crisis of 1931 and was given a peerage that year. Viscount Snowden would resign from his government position of Lord Privy Seal in 1932 in protest at the protectionism being adopted by the MacDonald-led 'National' government.

F. W. (Frederick William) Jowett, 1864-1944, was, like Snowden, a founder member of the ILP, and would remain a key figure in the organisation for the rest of his life including after its disaffiliation from the Labour Party. He served briefly in MacDonald's first government in 1924.

[5] James Ramsay MacDonald, 1866-1937, chaired the parliamentary Labour Party from 1911 until his resignation in 1914. He would later be the first Labour prime minister in the minority governments of 1924 and 1929-31 and, of the Conservative-dominated national government of 1931-35.

[6] Emanuel Shinwell, *Conflict Without Malice,* London: Odhams, 1953, 115 Shinwell, 1884-1986 was in 1914 a trade union official in Glasgow. He would later be a Labour MP and a minister in Attlee's post-1945 governments.

most part they preferred to describe themselves as 'pro-Ally.' Both the veteran Hyndman, virtual founder of the Social-Democratic Federation and now a controversial figure in its successor, the British Socialist Party (BSP), and the influential socialist journalist Blatchford, had been heavily criticised from within the socialist ranks for their warnings about the 'German Menace' during the final few pre-war years.

The idea of this book is to take the three long-established socialist weeklies in Britain – *Justice, The Clarion,* and *Labour Leader* – and follow, in some detail, the evolution of their attitudes to a wide range of aspects of the war and the debates and disagreements it generated from the first editions following the murder of the Archduke Franz-Ferdinand and his wife in Sarajevo on 28 June 1914 until the end of that calamitous year. The approach will attempt to be even-handed and non-judgmental. The hope is to contribute to a better understanding of what caused people on the British Left – and by extension similarly-minded people elsewhere – to take such diametrically opposed positions on a war that was from its outset seen as 'Armageddon.' Anyone wishing to try to work out who was 'right' and who was 'wrong' in 1914 is welcome to try and do so. But this is not the purpose of this book which seeks simply to make a contribution to a more inclusive appreciation of the dilemmas faced and positions taken by a wide spectrum of British socialists. By following the reports and debates in the three papers, week by week, over the first crucial months of the war during which the differing views of the war solidified, the hope is to mentally relive, however distantly and inadequately, something of the dilemmas and experience of those who lived through the appalling disaster of 1914.

Subsequent chapters will deal first with the peacetime preoccupations of the three papers during the final weeks of peace. This will give us some idea of the state of the movement during the final peacetime month and help to indicate how much it was fatefully blown off-course by the outbreak of war. Then they will take a

4

mixture of chronological and thematic approaches, following both reactions to the events of the war and the development of arguments and debates about it. The purpose of this introduction is to give a brief account of the three papers, glance at how British socialists were preparing for the coming congress of the Socialist International in Vienna, doomed to be overtaken by the outbreak of war, and to examine the degree of unity – and disunity – that characterised the British Left in that final pre-war summer.

There were of course, other papers and journals catering for the Left – or sections of it. There was George Lansbury's *Daily Herald,* widely seen by many others on the Left as uncritically supporting 'syndicalist' strikers and 'rebels' in general. Indeed when a letter appeared in *Justice* on 24 September under the, very premature, heading 'The Collapse of the "Daily Herald"' its signatory 'Looker On' claimed that the paper had damaged Social-Democracy by successively championing 'Syndicalism, Guildism, Anarchism, Revolt.'[7] Also during some years of the final pre-war decade there had been the monthly publications of small but not insignificant organisations like *The Industrial Syndicalist* and *Plebs*. These were the organs of, respectively, the Industrial Syndicalist Educational League and the Plebs League whose origins went back to a revolt of students at Ruskin College, the Oxford establishment set up to make higher education available to working-class men. The students objected to the 'reformist' bias of the college. *Plebs* was first published in 1909 and *The Industrial Syndicalist* the following year.

There was also the Fabian-orientated *New Statesman* and the organs

---

[7] Syndicalism proposed that social revolution could be achieved by industrial action and industrial democracy without recourse to political parties. Anarcho-syndicalists believed that the abolition of the state would accompany the abolition of capitalism. Guild Socialism, which can be seen as an effort to combine the 'industrial democracy' of syndicalism with political socialism, would become very influential on the British Left in the years immediately before, during and after the First World War. S. G. Hobson's *National Guilds. An Inquiry into the Wages System and the Way Out* had appeared early in 1914 and a National Guilds League would be formed in 1915.

of the two 'impossibilist' parties that had broken away from the – 'reformist' in their view – Social-Democratic Federation (SDF) a decade earlier. These were the Socialist Party of Great Britain (SPGB), still functioning in the 21$^{st}$ century, and the Socialist Labour Party (SLP). They published, respectively, *Socialist Standard* and *The Socialist*. But both were very small groupings even by the not very impressive standards of the socialist Left in Britain. All of these were of very recent origin compared with the three papers that are the sources of this study; The *Herald* began in 1912 and the *Statesman* the following year. *Justice*, the *Clarion* and *Labour Leader* were all much longer established with at least a pedigree of two decades – three in the case of *Justice*.

## The Three Weekly Papers

Between them the three weeklies – *The Clarion*, *Justice* and *Labour Leader* – covered a wide spectrum of Left opinion in relation to the war. Once war broke out on 4 August the *Clarion* quickly came out in support of British participation, while the *Labour Leader* was opposed from the start. The position of *Justice* is more difficult to describe. For the greater part of its existence, from the 1880s until his fatal illness in 1913, *Justice* had been edited by Harry Quelch. He was one of those remarkable nineteenth-century autodidacts who, with little formal education and at work from the age of 10, taught himself both French and German as well as acquiring all the skills necessary to produce a very literate weekly paper. After Quelch's death the editorship was taken over by the long-time SDF and then BSP general secretary, H. W. Lee.[8]

---

[8] H. W. Lee, 1865-1932, had been general secretary of the SDF since the 1880s and of the BSP since its foundation in 1911. He would remain as editor of *Justice* until 1923. At the time of his death he was working on a history of the SDF which,

Although it was the official organ of the British Socialist Party (BSP) *Justice* was actually in the hands not of the party itself but of the group of, mainly older, leaders who often described themselves as the 'Old Guard' or the 'Old Guard of the SDF' of which Quelch had been a leading member. This referred to the forerunner of the BSP, the Social-Democratic Federation, which a few years before had changed its name to Social-Democratic Party (SDP) and then attempted, unsuccessfully, in 1911 to unite the whole socialist Left. The BSP, which emerged from this attempt, now included dissident former ILP branches and other socialist groups as well as younger members joining a political organisation for the first time. Many, especially of the latter, were influenced to a greater or lesser degree by the syndicalist ideas that accompanied the pre-war strike wave. They overlapped with 'internationalists' who objected to Quelch's advocacy of the 'citizen army' and Hyndman's support of 'national defence.'[9] There was no shortage of internal dissent in the ILP, yet many would have agreed with Fenner Brockway's 1911 verdict that the ILP had 'never been divided by such vital differences of opinion as were apparent at [BSP] gatherings.'[10]

Most of the 'Old Guard,' and above all Henry Hyndman, the most prominent of the founders of the SDF, were 'pro-war'.[11] But the majority of the membership was not, as would become increasingly clear. In 1916, finding themselves in a minority, the 'Hyndmanites' would walk out of the BSP annual conference, taking *Justice* with

---

completed by Edward Archbold, would be published in 1935 as *Social-Democracy in Britain: Fifty Years of the Socialist Movement.*

[9] See Walter Kendall, *The Revolutionary Movement in Britain 1900-21. The Origins of British Communism*, London: Weidenfeld and Nicolson, 1969, 52-62.

[10] *Labour Leader*, 6 October 1911.

[11] H. M. (Henry Mayers) Hyndman, 1842-1921, had been the main founder of the Social-Democratic Federation (SDF) in the early 1880s. As we shall see he was already a controversial figure in the BSP before the war and would leave it to help form the unfortunately named National Socialist Party in 1916. In his final years he was a trenchant critic of the Bolsheviks.

them. The BSP then quickly established its own paper, *The Call.* But all this lay ahead in the summer of 1914. In the meantime *Justice* could – and did – claim to be the oldest socialist paper in the UK.

The old SDF – especially its 'Old Guard' – is almost certainly the least well understood of the pre-1914 socialist organisations in Britain. It is so often described as the 'Marxist Social Democratic Federation' that it seems quite likely that some readers may even have concluded that 'Marxist' was part of its title. The supporters of Marxism-Leninism, with the prestige of an apparently victorious revolution behind them, were so successful in presenting their ideology as *the* rather than *a* successor to the Marxism that existed before the war that assumptions based on the notion that the SDF was from the beginning in some sense on its way to eventually forming the British Communist Party tend to distort the reality. That the Communist Party of Great Britain (CPGB) was, at its foundation in 1920, little more than the BSP under a new name reinforces this view. But Marx's name and invocations of Marxism appeared quite infrequently in *Justice.* Yet the SDF was not free of sectarianism and at the level of the local branch it is true that many found the SDF rigid and doctrinaire. From the early 1890s the ILP became a more attractive and less demanding home for many on the Left.

The most determined opponents of any sort of compromise, especially of inclusion of reformist 'palliatives' in the SDF programme, were labelled 'impossibilists' by their opponents. They had left to form respectively the Socialist Labour Party (SLP) whose main inspiration was the American socialist Daniel De Leon, and the Socialist Party of Great Britain in 1903 and 1904. Several times in the early twentieth century regular contributors to *Justice,* J.B. Askew and John E. Ellam were criticised in the paper by Hyndman for what he saw as their tendency to treat Marx's writings with an almost religious reverence.[12]

---

[12] *Justice,* 24, 31 January 1903, 13 August 1905 and 30 June 1906.

For the 'Old Guard,' especially, the SDF/BSP stood at the end of a long tradition of radical plebeian democracy. Former Chartists had been prominent in the early days of the SDF and as late as 1903 *Justice* proclaimed the party as the 'legitimate heirs and successors of Chartism.'[13] It traced the origin of the term Social-Democracy to the Chartist Bronterre O'Brien. In an insightful article in the SDF's journal *The Social-Democrat* in 1897, Hyndman had warned of the danger of 'State or Bureaucratic Socialism' and concluded by endorsing O'Brien's definition of Social-Democracy as the view of those who 'wished to bring about a complete social reconstruction under democratic forms.'[14] The first three 'planks' of the SDF programme were demands notable for their democratic purism if not for their practicality. Adult suffrage was insisted upon for the elections of *all* 'officers and administrators', a democratic 'citizens' army' was to replace the existing force and referendums were to be required for all legislative proposals with, in addition, 'the people to decide on Peace or War'.[15]

All three papers carried a number of paid advertisements including, in *Justice*, ones for Allinson's bread – 'Unadulterated Wholemeal' – the Pioneer Boot Company, and Willmott's 'Reliable Pianos.' Similar ads appeared in the other two weeklies including in one October issue of the *Leader* ones for the City Life Assurance Co, and the Prudential Assurance Co. as well as for 'Lessons in Oratory,' and the Co-operative Boot Society, producers of 'I.L.P. Boots.' The *Clarion* sometimes carried a fairly large advertisement for 'Lipton's Popular Parcel' – which seems to have comprised bags of sugar and blocks of margarine and – in October 1914 – Gamages' Autumn Sale.

All three also had space to promote, as well as review, a wide variety of books. *Labour Leader* on 8 October drew attention to Frederick

---

[13] *Justice,* 1 August 1903.

[14] H. M. Hyndman. 'Social-Democrat or Socialist?' in *The Social-Democrat,* August 1897, 231.

[15] *Justice,* 25 October 1884. See also Logie Barrow and Ian Bullock, *Democratic Ideas and the British Labour Movement, 1880-1914,* CUP, 1996, 18.

Temple's *Interest, Gold and Banking,* and Emil Davies's *The Case for Railway Nationalisation.* The *Clarion* regularly featured Blatchford's considerable back catalogue of books of many sorts as well as other publications of the Clarion Press such as, in October 1914 A. M. Thompson's pamphlet *Prussia's Devilish Creed.* In *Justice* the other publications of the BSP's publishing house, the Twentieth Century Press, were prominent. In October, for example, readers could buy for 1/2d any of the 'Popular Propaganda Pamphlets' such as *Jones's Boy* by Spokeshave, and W. G. Veal's *The Liberals and the Workers.* For 1d they could have Hyndman's *Social-Democracy: The Bases of Its Principles* or his *Tariff Reform and Imperialism: An Alternative Policy.* For 2d, as originally published in 1903, *A New Catechism of Socialism* by E. Belfort Bax and Harry Quelch was available as was, rather tucked away on a back page, Zelda Kahan's *The Principles of Socialism* from 1908.[16] More prominently advertised was Edward Hartley's new book *Rounds with Socialists* on sale for 1s or 6d as a paperback.[17]

Regular features in *Justice* in 1914 included 'The Bookshop' comprising reviews of recent books. These covered a quite a wide range both in terms of subject matter and the political orientation of their authors. Those featured in the October 1914 editions of the paper included Graham Wallas, *The Great Society,* Louis Levine, *Syndicalism in France,* W. English Walling, *Progressivism and After,* A. W. Holland, *The Making of the Nations: Germany,* and L. Cecil Smith, *Clear*

---

[16] Zelda Kahan, 1886-1969, was born in Lithuania into a Jewish family which emigrated to Britain when she was a child. She was in 1914 a leading figure in the 'internationalist' opposition to Hyndman and the 'Old Guard.' Known later, after her marriage to William Peyton Coates as Zelda Coates, she would be prominent in the Communist Party of Great Britain of which they both were founding members. She would be especially active in the promotion of Anglo-Soviet friendship.

[17] Edward Hartley, 1855-1918, was a prominent figure first in the ILP, of which he was a founder member, and later in the SDF and BSP. He had been an – unsuccessful – parliamentary candidate on several occasions. He had been secretary of the Clarion Van movement 1910-1912. He was strongly 'pro-war' and would later join the 'patriotic Labour' British Workers League.

*Thinking or an Englishman's Creed.*[18] Towards the end of the paper would appear official notices from the BSP's head office, reports from local branches under the heading of 'The Movement' and the regular reports of Margaretta Hicks, secretary of the BSP's National Women's Council. Much the same was true of the *Labour Leader* whose back pages regularly featured reports from conferences, ILP divisional meetings and branches and, often, reports from the Women's Labour League.

The first edition of *Justice* had been published in January 1884. The next of the three weekly papers to appear was the *Clarion*. Unlike the other two, which acted as the official organs for the BSP and the ILP, the *Clarion* was an independent socialist paper. Its founder and presiding genius, Robert Blatchford, had from humble beginnings become a well-known journalist and leader writer on the Manchester-based *Sunday Chronicle*. Together with a small group of like-minded colleagues, of whom the most important was Alex (or A.M.) Thompson, he gave up his well-paid job to start the *Clarion* in December 1891. Blatchford was enormously influential during the next two decades via not only the paper but also his advocacies of socialism in pamphlets and books. Above all there was *Merrie England* whose penny edition in 1894 achieved the status of a bestseller. Few would dissent from Stanley Pierson's description of Blatchford as 'by far the most effective recruiter for Socialism in England.'[19] The paper played an important role in the birth of the ILP and especially of one of its main predecessors the Manchester and Salford ILP.

---

[18] Graham Wallas, 1858-1932, was a social psychologist and prominent member of the Fabian Society. He was a co-founder of the London School of Economics (LSE). William English Walling, 1877-1936, was an American socialist who had been prominent in the foundation in 1909 of The National Association for the Advancement of Colored People (NAACP) He would later campaign for the USA's entry into the First World War. Louis Levine had already published *The Development of Syndicalism in America* in 1913.

[19] Stanley Pierson, *Marxism and the Origins of British Socialism; The Struggle for a New Consciousness* Ithaca N Y, Cornell University Press, 1973, 272.

For Blatchford the vital task was 'making socialists' which, as interpreted in the *Clarion,* centred around encouraging the organisation of a wide spectrum of cultural, social and sporting activities intended to provide a present taste of a future society where William Morris's dictum, 'Fellowship is Life' – still the slogan of the National Clarion Cycling Club in the 21$^{st}$ century – would become a reality. In this endeavour the paper achieved remarkable success.

For Blatchford 'making socialists' was the overwhelming priority; mere political activity – contesting local government and parliamentary elections – fell a long way behind and could, he implied, be more or less left to look after itself. Apart from the cycling club there were the, often overlapping, Clarion Scouts who held propaganda meetings often in previously neglected rural locations, and several other Clarion organisations including theatrical groups, choirs, camera clubs and the Cinderella clubs that organised outings for underprivileged children.. There were a number of Clarion (cara) vans which conducted organised outdoor propaganda and the Clarion Fellowship that united these activities and was open to all readers who paid a minimum subscription of one shilling a year. There were also a number of Clarion Club Houses, usually in scenic locations.

The scale of these *Clarion*-oriented organisations and activities is difficult to appreciate today but needs to be borne in mind when considering the state of the British Left in the summer of 1914. Cycling club reports in the issue of 3 July, for example, began with nine from various 'unions' – regional groupings of individual clubs which included ones covering London, Birmingham, Manchester and Scotland. This was followed by 95 very brief reports from the clubs themselves, laid out in alphabetical order from Ashton-under-Lyne to York. The same page also featured three reports from Clarion swimming clubs, one from the Clarion Ramblers in Rochdale, and another from the Clarion Scouts in Glasgow. In addition there was a Clarion Fellowship report from its national secretary, Frederick C. Hagger, announcing a campaign to try to raise the paper's circulation to 100,000.

Yet, in spite of its relatively high circulation, there were clearly some corners of Britain where news of the *Clarion* had still not penetrated. A friendly newsagent, R. M. Scott, reported in a letter to the paper on 3 July that, running short of *Clarions* he had sent his daughter to see if more could be had from other shops. In one of the latter where the paper was unknown she was asked, 'Won't 'Chortles' do?'

Blatchford and the *Clarion* had been less than pleased when Keir Hardie launched the *Labour Leader* in March 1894. A rivalry persisted from then on, with the *Clarion* often more than willing to lend an ear – and give valuable space – to the internal critics of the ILP leadership, who formed a vociferous minority of the ILP's active membership.[20] If the *Clarion* represented an idealistic strain in the broader ILP family, the *Labour Leader* – though it too could wax eloquently about the 'Socialist Commonwealth' – spoke for Keir Hardie's more realistically 'political' approach.[21]

By 1914 this had achieved a remarkable degree of success. Failing totally at the general election of 1895, to the intense disappointment of its members and supporters, the ILP then followed Keir Hardie's 'Labour alliance' strategy of combining with trade unions, which were wealthy in comparison with the ILP. The result was the Labour Representation Committee (LRC) of 1900 that became, officially, the Labour Party in 1906. Its numbers swelled by the previously 'Lib-Lab' MPs supported by the miners' unions, its parliamentary representation came to over forty in the House of Commons in 1914. It had some degree of purchase on the Liberal government that since the indecisive elections of 1910 was partially reliant on its – and the Irish nationalists' – support. There were in 1914 no local Labour parties as we know them today. These did not become part of the Labour Party structure

---

[20] See Barrow and Ian Bullock, especially chapter 4 'Conflicts in the I.L.P.'

[21] James Keir Hardie, 1856-1915, won a parliamentary seat in 1892 as an independent Labour candidate. At that time there were about a dozen Liberal-Labour or 'Lib-Lab' – or Liberal Labour – MPs and independent meant, essentially, independent of the Liberal Party.

until after the war. Individuals could play a part in the national party only as active members of their trade union or other affiliated organisations. For most British socialists in 1914 who supported participation in Labour this meant working in the ILP though the recent decision of the BSP early in the year to seek affiliation promised a significant change in this respect.

*Labour Leader* was owned and edited by Hardie until 1904 when it was taken over by the ILP itself with John Bruce Glasier as editor. But even before this it was widely regarded as the official mouthpiece of the ILP. In 1914 it was edited by Fenner Brockway and described itself as a 'Weekly Journal of Socialism, Trade Unionism & Politics'.[22] The *Leader* was by no means uncritical of the conduct of the Labour Party in the House of Commons. At its annual conference at Easter 1914 the ILP had adopted the 'Bradford Policy,' associated particularly with Fred (or F.W.) Jowett. This demanded that Labour MPs should vote on each issue that came before them 'on its merits' according to party policy without regard to the effect that might have on the future of the precarious Liberal government. *Labour Leader* wanted to see this policy adopted by Labour and, even more important, implemented by Labour MPs in the House of Commons.

*Justice* and the *Leader* were published on Thursdays and the *Clarion* on Fridays. *Justice* usually had a conventional editorial dealing with one current issue, sometimes by Lee, but often by other leading BSP members like Hyndman. The *Clarion's* 'line' on the week's events appeared under A. M. Thompson's name as 'Our Point of View.'[23] It

---

[22] A. Fenner Brockway, 1888-1988, would remain an important figure in the ILP until the end of the Second World War and subsequently in the Labour Party which he then rejoined. A conscientious objector during the 1914-18 war and a founder of the No-Conscription Fellowship he was later the secretary of the ILP after its disaffiliation from the Labour Party in 1932. For Brockway's role in the ILP between the wars see Ian Bullock, *Under Siege. The Independent Labour Party in Interwar Britain*, Edmonton: Athabasca University Press, 2017.

[23] A. M. (Alexander Mattock) Thompson, 1861-1948, was by 1914 the effective editor of the *Clarion* although Blatchford remained 'the Chief.' He was also the librettist for a number of musical comedies including *The Arcadians*, which ran for

featured a number of sections each under an appropriate sub-heading. *Labour Leader's* – unsigned – 'Review of the Week' fulfilled much the same function in the ILP paper.

All three papers included, of course, readers' letters – labelled 'Views of Our Readers' in the *Labour Leader*. These are often at least as interesting and significant as the articles and reports in the rest of the papers. The *Clarion* 'Cockpit' was usually more extensive than the other two, sometimes filling nearly two whole pages. The reader whose letter was signed 'Ney' on 17 July 1914 asked 'if any other weekly paper can print as interesting a page of matter from unpaid contributors.' Plainly, Ney thought the answer was 'no'.

## The International – that never was

In July 1914 British socialists, like their comrades elsewhere, were looking forward to the forthcoming congress of the Socialist International that was scheduled to meet in Vienna from 23 to 29 August. The confidence in the inevitable progress towards socialism is evident in *Labour Leader's* judgement on the importance of the coming meeting.

> Rightly understood, these triennial congresses are the most important assemblies of modern times, for they represent the movement which is destined to rule the world and are themselves an earnest of the day when the workers of all lands shall dwell in harmony and concord. The Labour and Socialist army is now fifty million strong, and every year it increases in strength.

---

809 performances in London and 103 on Broadway.

This appeared in the edition of 2 July. The following week – on 9 July – *Justice* was urging BSP members able to attend to make sure that the BSP's allocation of 25 for the British delegation was fully taken up. So far there were only 12. The list of these BSP delegates reflected the coming schism in the party over the war – and eventually over Bolshevism. Theodore Rothstein was to play an important role in the foundation of the British Communist Party while Albert Inkpin would be its first secretary. He was in 1914 already secretary of the BSP after Lee took over the editorship of the paper. Others intending to make up the BSP party in Vienna were Henry and Rosalind Hyndman, and the notoriously 'anti' votes-for-women Belfort Bax – leading members of the 'Old Guard.'[24]

With the advantages of hindsight, *Justice's* summary of the issues to be debated is surprising. It might be expected that it would be completely dominated by the dangers of war given that in each of the previous two years conflicts in the Balkans had had something of the character of proxy wars contested by the great powers, above all by Austria-Hungary and Russia. But this was far from the case. *Justice's* expectations concerning the congress gave no special prominence to such issues.

> The principal resolutions on the agenda are those dealing with Unemployment, the Cost of Living, Imperialism and Arbitration, Alcoholism and Russian Prisons. The British Section is also responsible for resolutions on political and industrial action, Emigration and Immigration, Suffrage and the Democratic Organisation of Industry

---

[24] Ernest Belfort Bax, 1854-1926, had studied philosophy in Germany. His own philosophical works included a *Handbook of the History of Philosophy*. At the outbreak of war his most recent philosophical work was *Problems of Men, Mind and Morals* published in 1912. He was often seen as the SDF's most accomplished Marxist theoretician. For some in the BSP – especially those outside the ranks of the 'Old Guard' – Bax's anti-feminist views were deeply embarrassing. He believed that women, far from being disadvantaged were over-privileged in relation to men. He had published *The Fraud of Feminism* in 1913 which was his most recent, but by no means only, work of an anti-feminist character.

(Co-operative, Trade Union, Municipal and State).

On 9 July a letter in *Justice* and the following week (17 July) in the *Clarion* from Donald Bruce-Walker, the secretary of the University Socialist Federation, passed on an invitation from the Austrian *Freeier Sozialistischer Studenten* for delegates to attend an informal students' meeting during the International.

## The International scene – the advance of socialism

More generally, a great deal of attention was given, particularly in *Justice* and *Labour Leader* to the activities of socialist parties in other parts of the world. *Justice* had a regular feature called 'The International' while the equivalent in the *Leader* was entitled 'Socialism the World Over. Progress of the movement in other lands.' On 2 July *Justice* reported on the first post-war congress of the 'Bulgarian Centralised (Socialist) Trade Unions' in Sofia and the opposition of French socialists to proposals for taxing those employing foreign workers. The socialists wanted instead to force employers to pay the same wages to all workers. Other items concerned municipal elections in Italy and the growth of the Socialist Party in the USA, which, *Justice* said, had now 104,581 members and 11 daily papers. *Labour Leader's* 'Socialism the World Over' the following week (9 July) included reports from Australia, Bulgaria, France, Germany and the United States.

Naturally enough, in the light of its size and success – with the Social-Democratic Party of Germany (*Sozialdemokratische Partei Deutschlands* – or SPD) now the largest party in the *Reichstag* – the German movement was given much attention in the British socialist press. *Labour Leader* on 9 July headlined as 'An Example from Germany' a report of the speech of a German fraternal delegate to the General Federation of Trade Unions conference in Liverpool that featured details of the successes of the German movement – including its 98 daily newspapers. It also reported that during the recent 'Red Week' the SPD had recruited 148,109 new members of whom 32, 298 were women.[25]

The same day *Justice* reported, under the headings 'Bravo, Rosa!' and 'The Exposure of German Militarism,' the trial of 'our comrade Rosa Luxemburg' who was putting up 'a splendid fight in court on behalf of the rank-and-file victims of militarist jackbootery and cruelty' practised on army conscripts. She had been accused of insulting the Prussian Army in March following the suicide of a soldier in Metz. But, said *Justice,* with 922 witnesses (over 1,000 according to *Labour Leader*) lined up to support her, the War Minister was backing off by asking for an adjournment of the case. But Luxemburg would try to reopen the case or raise the same issues by other means. 'The whole hideous truth about life in the barracks must be brought out whether the authorities like it or not.'

*Labour Leader's* report the same day began:

> Since Comrade Liebknecht's famous revelations of the Armaments scandals, Prussian militarism has been constantly under public trial. Last week the most pernicious and most perverse of Capitalist systems received a blow from the hands of German Socialists from which it will not easily recover.

It went on to say that 'the ill-advised proceedings taken against the well-known Socialist writer and speaker, Dr. Rosa Luxemburg' had

---

[25] The SPD was, and still is, the *Sozialdemokratische Partei Deutschlands* (Social-Democratic Party of Germany). It was formed by a merger of two socialist groups in 1875. Surviving Bismarck's effort to suppress it by the 'Anti-Socialist Law,' the SPD went on to become the party polling the greatest number of votes in 1912. *Vorwärts* (Forward) was its main organ. It would be forced out of Germany after Hitler's accession to power, but was published in Czechoslovakia until 1938, then Paris until 1940, and revived in the 1950s. It is now a monthly.

produced witnesses who were 'were ready to prove, from personal experience that a reign of reckless cruelty that has no parallel in modern history prevails in the German army.'[26]

With what seemed the unstoppable forward momentum of international socialism it is not surprising that so much attention was paid to what was happening beyond British shores. Pressure from the International Socialist Bureau (ISB), which urged socialist unity within each country, seemed, at last, to have succeeded in bringing about something approaching the long-awaited, and much yearned for, unity of the British socialist movement.[27]

## Unity – and Disunity – on the British Left

Actual disunity – starting with the breakaway from the SDF of William Morris's Socialist League in the 1880s – had alternated with campaigns for socialist unity throughout the early decades in the British socialist movement. In the 1890s Blatchford had recommended supporters to join both the SDF and ILP and work for a united party. The *Clarion* had staged a postal referendum in 1898 that came down in favour of 'fusion or federation' of the two parties and convinced many that there were a large number of 'unattached' socialists who were put off making any organisational commitment

---

[26] Rosa Luxemburg and Karl Liebknecht, both 1871-1919, were anti-war members of the SPD who would later found the *Spartakusbund* or Spartacist League. They were murdered by members of the right-wing paramilitary *Freikorps* following the failed Spartacist uprising in January 1919. In December 1918 the Spartacist League had become the German Communist Party. Luxemburg wrote extensively and was well regarded as a Marxist theoretician. Her book *The Russian Revolution* of 1918 was critical of the Bolsheviks' lack of democracy.

[27] The International Socialist Bureau (ISB) had been set up by the Paris Congress of the Socialist International in 1900. There was a permanent secretariat in Brussels and each country was represented by delegates at plenary sessions. By the outbreak of war in 1914 sixteen such meetings had taken place.

by the lack of unity.

The SDF had taken part in the formation of the LRC but left a year later after the new organisation failed to adopt an explicitly socialist objective. At the time this was partly motivated by the desire to keep the 'impossibilists' on board but even after their departure there was strong opposition – notably from the formidable Harry Quelch – to any suggestion that the SDF and later the SDP and BSP should affiliate, though many in the party – including Hyndman – favoured this.

The 'Unity Conference' of 1911 was promoted by the *Clarion* with Victor Grayson, the iconic victor of the 1907 Colne Valley by-election acting as its – short-lived – 'political editor.' [28] The new party failed to attract more than a minority of ILP branches and members. The *Clarion* quickly cooled towards the BSP that emerged from the conference. Divisions in the socialist movement were by no means confined to Britain. The ISB maintained steady pressure for unity and in the immediate pre-war period had some success both in France where a series of mergers resulted a unified movement by 1905 and then in Britain where the BSP took the decision at its 1914 conference to apply for Labour Party affiliation.

This was showing fruit by July 1914. On 2 July *Justice* included an article, 'Meditations on Methods' by Frank H. Edwards. He reminded readers that ten years earlier the Amsterdam congress of the International had urged unity and resolved 'that there could only be one Internationalist Socialist Party'. They were now 'taking steps' but Edwards was critical of the time and opportunities that had been lost.

Had we set to work some years ago, and had we displayed the same magnanimous spirit as that displayed by our comrades in France, then

---

[28] Victor Grayson, was born in 1881 and disappeared mysteriously in 1920. When the Labour Party refused to endorse his candidature for the Colne Valley by-election in 1907 he stood as an independent socialist and won a sensational if narrow victory. He was not a great success as an MP and lost his seat in 1910.

long ere this, we would have had a great consolidated Socialist force in these islands, with a stronger representation in Parliament and that of a pronounced type, with more effective influence on the local bodies, and accomplishing extensive work by reason of the greater membership and because of the greater weight of public support.

The same issue of *Justice* carried reports from five London branches, and others in Greenock, Birkenhead and Kettering, where candidatures for local government were being run jointly with the ILP and the local Trades Councils representing trade union branches in the area. It also included among its 'special notices' news of the 'Northern and Southern Clarion Vans'. The same day the *Leader* reported the results in Kettering where there had been two by-elections for the Urban District Council and the Board of Guardians. The candidates of the 'United Labour Party' had come second to those of the Liberals. They had run as 'I.L.P. and Labour' and 'B.S.P. and Labour.'[29]

The following week's *Justice* (9 July) carried a report, signed 'T.D.H.', of a conference aimed at creating 'A Labour Party for London.' The conference, now adjourned, had rejected the idea of adding 'and Socialist' to its title and T.D.H. complained about the proposal being moved in a 'too antagonistic fashion' – not by BSP delegates but by some of those representing trade unions, concluding that 'My own opinion is that the B.S.P should remain in the London Labour Party, in spite of the decision of last Saturday.' All three papers carried notices appealing for donations to the Harry Quelch Memorial Fund.

If all this suggested a growing degree of unity and willingness to compromise there were also, in the early weeks of that July, no shortage of signs that demonstrated some continued forces of

---

[29] Boards of Guardians administered the Poor Law – including the workhouses – between 1834 and 1930. Urban District Councils were in charge of the local government of, mainly, the smaller towns in England and Wales. They were abolished as part of the local government reorganisation of the early 1970s.

*dis*unity. One of *Justice's* regular features was an 'Answers to Correspondents' column. On 2 July this included a fairly lengthy response addressed to 'J. ANDREWS AND OTHERS (North West Ham)'. It referred to a 'meeting of twelve branches of the B.S.P. held last Sunday, seven of which voted that the Executive Committee of the B.S.P. should refrain from accepting the vote in favour of affiliation to the Labour Party.' Those who objected to the decision made by a ballot of members decided upon by the party's annual conference should accept the decision 'reserving to themselves the right of raising the question at the next Conference, which they have perfect liberty to do', the dissenters were told. To persist in calling further 'conferences' urging withdrawal from the BSP if the executive did not do as they desired was to 'adopt disruptive tactics which the most elementary ideas of organisation beyond mere local groups should cause you to discard.' More would be heard from the North West Ham branch before the end of the year.

Underlying differences were emphasised rather than played down in a *Justice* editorial on 'The Situation' by Belfort Bax on 9 July. It began with words that many, especially younger BSP and ILP members would have found ominous; 'We of the old S.D.P.' Bax complained of the uncritical swallowing of 'reactionary policies' by some on the Left. There were those who advocated puritanical attitudes and policies: 'They will talk unctuously in the style of Methodist parsons of a couple of generations ago. There is no form of canting humbug that is too strong for them.' But that was only one section of the movement that fell short of Bax's exacting standards.

> Another set (not excluding members of the set last mentioned) proclaim Statification or Bureaucratisation to be the only true path to Socialism. For these there is no distinction between the existing class State and a Social-Democratic organised society. The former company of apostles we have referred to more especially affect the Independent Labour Party, the latter clever fellows are the products of the Fabian Society.

The 'Socialist idea' was being 'crucified between the two thieves of Puritan morality on the one side and Fabian bureaucracy on the other.' Consistent socialists must 'oppose any direct augmentation of the police powers of the State over the private lives and affairs of citizens.' Bax also condemned 'the mealy-mouthedness and sycophantic character which has become a characteristic of English political and journalistic life' which was exemplified by what he called the 'grovelling adulation vomited forth by Radical journalists on the subject of the late Joseph Chamberlain.'[30] It seems likely that the superior tone of Bax's diatribe may have alienated more people outside the charmed circle of the 'Old Guard' than the actual substance of his criticisms.

It is always difficult to determine the exact location of the line between constructive criticism and destructive undermining. One person's negativity may be another's lively debate. A sympathetic observer in the early weeks of July 1914 might well have concluded that though there remained many divisive issues in the wider socialist movement, some difficult, perhaps even impossible, to reconcile, both major political entities on the Left – the ILP and the BSP – were, under the umbrella of the Labour Party, gradually moving in the direction of a sustainable level of unity. This would soon be shattered by the outbreak of war but before turning to this it will be as well to consider some of the issues that British socialists were concerned about that July as reflected in the three weekly papers. This should go some way to giving us a better idea of what was about to be lost for the British Left on 4 August.

---

[30] Joseph Chamberlain, 1836-1914, had first come to prominence as mayor of Birmingham. He went on to be instrumental in splitting first the Liberal Party on home rule for Ireland and later the Conservatives on tariff reform. With much justification, many, especially those on the Left, held him responsible for the South African (or Boer) War of 1899-1902. He had died on 2 July 1914.

# CHAPTER 1

# July 1914: War? Surely Not!

## Murder in Sarajevo

Archduke Franz Ferdinand and his wife were killed by Gavrilo Princip in the Bosnian capital on Sunday 28 June. The next editions of *Justice* and *Labour Leader* were both published on Thursday 2 July and of the *Clarion* a day later. *Justice* gave front-page coverage to how socialist papers in mainland Europe had covered this.

> We rejoice to note, not only in "Vorwaerts" but among the journals of our French comrades and elsewhere, that one result of the murder of the heir to the Austrian Imperial throne and his wife is the recognition of the imperative need for a close understanding between England, France and Germany. Such a combination, based upon a genuine democratic policy, can alone ensure peace in Central and Western Europe.

*Justice* went on to say that it had 'never disguised' its opinion that, 'notwithstanding our own infamous and disastrous war against the South African Republics, and France's equally infamous attack upon Morocco, Germany is chiefly to blame for the ruinous armed peace under which all civilised nations are suffering to-day.' [31] The smaller

---

[31] The Second South African War, or Boer War as it was usually known at the time, lasted from 1899 until 1902. The British prevailed but only after a considerable struggle which revealed many of the weaknesses of Britain and the British Empire. The underlying conflict went back to the annexation of Cape Colony – originally

countries of Europe – Belgium, the Netherlands, Switzerland, Denmark – were 'all afraid, not of France or Great Britain but of Germany.' Yet 'that powerful Empire' was destined for continuing success without any 'extension of frontier' and it would be much better if the question and boundaries of Alsace-Lorraine, a major source of conflict between Germany and France, were 'equitably adjusted.'[32]

'We are not mere pacifists or anti-nationalists,' *Justice* declared. 'But Social-Democrats as internationalists are all for peace.' The current situation was very dangerous but meanwhile 'Sir Edward Grey, as usual, carries on his fatuous policy of secret agreements.'[33]

The *Clarion* appeared the following day. The regular editorials of the *Clarion* – 'Our Point of View'– were at this time written by A.M. Thompson who had been Blatchford's journalistic partner since the paper began at the end of 1891. Blatchford still contributed regularly but was now enjoying a sort of semi-retirement in Heacham, a village in north-west Norfolk on the Wash between Hunstanton and Kings Lynn. He spent much of his time cultivating roses. Like *Justice,*

---

Dutch – by the British at the end of the Napoleonic wars. The South African Republics, which were annexed by the British and later became constituents of the Union of South Africa, were the Transvaal and the Orange Free State. They were set up by Afrikaners – descendants of the Dutch colonialists.

As regards Morocco, *Justice* would have had in mind the gradual takeover of Morocco by France which had reached its climax when that country became a full French protectorate under the Treaty of Fez in 1912. The two international 'Moroccan' crises of 1905 ( 'Tangier') and 1911 ('Agadir') had had the effect of bringing Britain and France closer together against the perceived threat from Germany.

[32] Both Lorraine and the more 'Germanic' Alsace had become part of France during the 17th and 18th centuries. The peace treaty imposed on France after its defeat at the hands of Prussia and its German allies in 1871 had transferred virtually the whole of Alsace and a considerable portion of Lorraine, including one of its two major cities, Metz, to the new German Empire. The newly acquired German territory was administered from Berlin as a *Reichsland* and only given a measure of autonomy in 1911.

[33] Sir Edward Grey, 1862-1933, was the British Foreign Secretary in the Liberal government from 1905 to 1916 after which he became Viscount Grey of Fallodon. His 'secret diplomacy' was much criticised by Labour – notably by Fred Jowett MP – and by radical members of his own Liberal party.

Thompson saw the violent events in Sarajevo in the context of the two Balkan Wars of 1912 and 1913 and of the annexation of Bosnia-Herzegovina in 1908 by Austria-Hungary. [34] He blamed 'the greedy intrigues of the Great Powers' for the thousands killed in the Balkan wars to which now 'two more victims have been added.' More specifically, he continued, 'Austria's villainous annexation of Bosnia is the direct cause of the execution of Austria's heir.' He concluded with the hope that, 'If the United States of Europe were established – if the peasants of the Danube could appeal straight to the democracies of Italy, Austria, Germany and Russia, regardless of big financial interests, how different it would all be.'

*Labour Leader* carried no mention of the murder until the following week when an article 'Sarajevo – and After. The Big Powers and Little Peoples' by W.C. Anderson, appeared in the issue of 9 July. [35] Anderson condemned all assassinations. 'No cause is served by murder except the cause of reaction.' He deplored 'the attempt to father the crime on the Servian race, and to punish all Servians with brutal and indiscriminate severity.' [36] The Serbian embassy in Vienna

---

[34] Much to the annoyance of Russia, its rival for power and influence in the Balkans – Austria-Hungary – had been allowed to administer Bosnia-Herzegovina since the Congress of Berlin in 1878. Then as now it had a mixed population of Orthodox Serbs, Catholic Croats and Muslims. But formally it remained part of the Ottoman Empire. In 1908, taking advantage of the distraction caused by the Young Turk revolution, Austria-Hungary had announced the annexation of the territories. Like the two Moroccan crises, this led to one of the diplomatic confrontations that would subsequently be seen as part of the drift towards war in the pre-1914 years. In the First Balkan War of 1912 the Balkan League of four of the independent states that had emerged from the Ottoman Empire in the nineteenth century – Bulgaria, Greece, Montenegro and Serbia – successfully attacked Turkey which lost nearly all its remaining European territories. The Second Balkan War of 1913 saw a struggle over the division of Macedonia. Greece and Serbia defeated Bulgaria which was also attacked by Romania and Turkey.

[35] William Crawford Anderson, 1877-1919, had been chair of the ILP 1910-13. He would be elected as a Labour MP at the end of 1914 losing his seat at the 'khaki election' of December 1918. A few weeks later, in February 1919, he was a victim of the influenza pandemic.

[36] Servia, Servs and Servian were the normal usage in 1914 rather than the current Serbia, Serbs and Serbian.

had warned of the dangers involved in the archduke's visit, he told *Labour Leader* readers. Franz Ferdinand was regarded as mainly responsible for annexation of Bosnia and he wanted to 'widen the bounds of the Dual Monarchy to bring the bulk of the Southern Slav peoples under his sway.' The 'Servs, Croats and Slovenes have a natural racial unity.' It was important to 'watch carefully, lest the Sarajevo murder be made an excuse for destroying the growing national unity of the Southern Slavs.' The Balkan peoples, he concluded, did not want 'more quarrels and more wars.'

## The 'War Trust' and Grey's secret diplomacy

The issue of Sarajevo and what would follow from it did not entirely disappear from the pages of the socialist press and there were also warnings of a more general kind of the danger of war. But the 2 July edition of *Labour Leader's* 'Review of the Week' was almost entirely concerned with controversial aspects of the budget, though it did also include an attack on Grey's conduct of foreign policy.

> Once a year only does His Majesty's House of Commons have the chance of probing the mysteries of our Foreign Relationships. The House has responsibility but lacks alike knowledge and power. Sir Edward Grey does quietly what he pleases, and later on avers that no other action was possible.

Grey had gradually acquired, the *Leader* claimed, a 'well-nigh mesmeric power' over the Commons but his policy was 'viewed by many with misgivings.' Two years previously 'nearly as makes no matter he blundered ... into a war with Germany, and at another time stirred the country into an unreasonable panic about an assumed inferiority of Dreadnoughts.' [37] He was responsible for the Russian alliance and consequent partition of Persia to which that 'disgraceful alliance' had led.

Opposition to the Triple Entente with Russia was general on the British Left. The following week (9 July) *Justice's* 'Critical Chronicle' review of current issues included short piece on the 'Bankruptcy of Russia.' It gave the paper's explanation of how the Entente had come to pass – and why it was thoroughly deplorable.

> France, in despair at finding an ally to support her against German jackbootery, has financed Russia for forty years. This was bad, though possibly excusable. But that Great Britain should even partially do the like is nothing short of infamous. It is as true today as it was in 1874, that the Czar, without loans from Western Europe, cannot finance his Government of butchery.

In the meantime, in 2 July's *Leader,* Harry Snell writing on 'War and Gold', was enlarging on the dangers of secret diplomacy[38]. The ignorance of the British was, he maintained, 'a standing menace to the civilisation of the world'. It allowed 'a small official aristocratic clique to control the foreign policy of their land, to make treaties with other nations, to embark on treacherous methods of diplomacy, and even rush them into war...'

He acknowledged that the socialist movement had 'given a somewhat restricted attention to hammering out a well-considered foreign policy,' but its task would now be 'tremendously lightened by

---

[37] Dreadnoughts were the state of the art battleships named after the original prototype, HMS *Dreadnought,* launched in 1906.

[38] Harry Snell, 1865-1944 was well known as an activist and speaker who had unsuccessfully stood as a Labour candidate in 1910. He would later serve as a Labour MP from 1922 to 1931 and as Baron Snell from the latter year in the House of Lords. Briefly Under Secretary of State for India towards the end of MacDonald's second minority government he would act as Deputy Leader in the Lords during Churchill's wartime coalition. A firm supporter of Zionism, Snell would publish an autobiography, *Men, Movements and Myself,* in 1936.

the publication of Mr. Brailsford's excellent study of the whole question.' This was the well-known journalist's book, *The War of Steel and Gold*, attacking the secret diplomacy and the great power rivalry of recent years. The book had been published earlier in 1914. [39] Brailsford had shown, said Snell, that wars were no longer made to 'assist the trader in his search for new markets.' Snell then invoked Norman Angell's *The Great Illusion*, another fairly recent book. Snell summarised Angell's argument.

He had shown that there is no such thing as the conquest of one nation by another because the internationalisation of capital has developed so that what hurts one nation hurts all. Germany, for example, could not conquer France without injuring herself almost as much as she injured her enemy. All that is true enough, but, as Mr Brailsford shows, what may be folly for a nation as a whole, may be very good business for that portion of a nation that is engaged in the production of war material. These interests deliberately encourage war, and they pour subtle poison into the minds of the people by suborning the press and tampering with every other source of public education.[40]

This theme was renewed the following week (9 July) when *Labour*

---

[39] H. N. (Henry Noel) Brailsford, 1873-1958, had abandoned an academic career in 1897 and joined a volunteer force fighting with the Greeks in their war with Turkey. He became a leader-writer for *The Morning Leader* and later worked for C.P. Scott's *Manchester Guardian*. A member of the ILP since 1907, Brailsford would be a determined opponent of Britain's participation in the war in 1914. After the war he edited the replacement of the ILP's *Labour Leader* – the *New Leader* – from 1922 to 1925, taking a considerable cut in salary to do so. He was one of the authors of the ILP's important report *The Living Wage* in 1926 and opposed ILP disaffiliation from the Labour Party. He supported British participation in the war in 1939 and is widely remembered for his *The Levellers and the English Revolution*. Unfinished at the time of his death, this was completed and edited by Christopher Hill and published in 1961. See F M :Levanthal, *The Last Dissenter: H M Brailsford and His World*, OUP, 1985.

[40] Norman Angell, 1872-1967, is chiefly remembered – as here – for his book *The Great Illusion*. He would later be Labour MP 1929-31 and was awarded the Nobel Peace Prize in 1933.

*Leader* carried adverts for a new ILP pamphlet, *How Asquith Helped the Armour Ring* by J. Walton Newbold.[41] This followed on from his previous offering entitled *The War Trust Exposed.* The new pamphlet had a foreword by Philip Snowden who would still be in Australia when the war broke out and would not return to Britain until February 1915. It showed, said the *Leader,* 'the sordid motives of the Government for their wasteful and insane expenditure of the nation's wealth.' It was 'a scathing exposure of the unprincipled ways of Capitalism and of the Ministers who are the tools of the financial interests.' Some of the arguments used by Newbold in two articles on 16 and 23 July are particularly interesting in the light of the events that were soon to follow and socialist, and especially, ILP, attitudes towards them. At this stage the emphasis was entirely on the waste of resources involved rather than any danger that arms might be used in anger.

The first article addressed the question of what should be the ILP's position on armaments at the coming socialist International. Newbold rejected the idea of a general strike to prevent war. This just would not work. Nor was 'making an end to secret diplomacy' a way of getting to grips with 'the realities of the armaments difficulty.' Changes in foreign policy leading to 'more cordial relations' between the powers need not result in any considerable reduction in naval or military outlay.

The main contributory factors to the armaments problem are, first, the growing fear of the privileged classes that they will not be able, otherwise than by the discipline of the bullet, to continue their authority

---

[41] J Walton Newbold 1888-1943, would have one of those political careers that seem rather startlingly contradictory in retrospect. A conscientious objector during the First World War, he became a leading figure in the 'Left Wing of the I.L.P.'. which campaigned for the party to affiliate to the Third (Communist) International. When this failed in 1921 he joined the Communist Party and was – briefly – an MP, Communist but with Labour endorsement, in 1922-3. He left the CPGB in 1924 and later joined the reconstituted Social-Democratic Federation, editing its journal *Social-Democrat* and then became a supporter of MacDonald's 'National' government in the 1930s.

over the workers, and, second, the colossal vested interests of the military families, and of the labour and capital employed in the industry.

However, he insisted, 'Capitalists Don't Want War.' They had no intention of 'sanctioning the frightfully expensive campaigns which are impractical without their consent.' Nor did 'the makers of war material desire conflict between the great nations. Turkey, Greece, the other Balkan States, and even Mexico, create a pleasant demand for field artillery, explosives, projectiles and small arms when they go to war.' But in order to keep going profitably the armaments industry needed massive orders for ships and weapons from major powers that were never intended to be used.

The intention of Newbold's second article (23 July) was to show how the socialist movement could 'strike at the Armaments Ring, the citadel of Capitalism.' Though it was terrible to think of 'the Universal Death Providers' that modern weapons represented, it was 'in the highest degree improbable' that they would ever be used.

But until we can produce some definite and adequate scheme for providing work for those who would be left unemployed as a result of a naval holiday or a reduction in naval expenditure, all our talk of disarmament will continue, and deserves to continue, empty and vain.

Newbold advocated maintaining resistance to further naval expenditure while demanding the state manufacture of armaments that would 'by competition humble a monopoly which depends for its whole existence on Admiralty orders.' Instead of simply attacking the 'War Trust' the ILP needed to 'go a step further and attack its monopoly of manufacture,' as well as 'diverting expenditure to productive engineering projects.' The Trust was still expanding, he warned. Vickers and Armstrong Whitworth were reported to have interests in a company formed with the Turkish government that would be free of taxes for 30 years and have monopoly of shipbuilding.

## The Tragedy of Bosnia – and the risk of war

W.C. Anderson's well-informed comments on the difficult and dangerous Balkan situation in the *Labour Leader* have already been noted. Before this, on 2 July, *Justice* had published a long article by Rosalind Travers Hyndman on 'The Tragedy of Bosnia.' [42] She had visited Sarajevo in the summer of 1912 and noted how 'astonishingly various' was its population. Development of its abundant natural resources was held back by the fact that absentee landlords – 'begs' and 'agas' – still controlled a third of the country.

There were positive as well as negative aspects to Habsburg rule:

> Thirty four years of Austrian rule have produced peace, prosperity, excellent roads, a wonderful and picturesque system of railways, good clean hotels, watering places, every encouragement of foreign visitors – and fortresses.

It was quite clear that Austria-Hungary meant to keep Bosnia. But no-one 'thought of inquiring whether the people of Bosnia wished to belong to Austria or not. A great power may ask permission of her rivals before annexing a little nation; but the nation itself is never consulted.' Its Slav majority wanted to be part of 'a Slavonic Power' like Serbia while 'the wilder spirits dream of complete independence.'

Unfortunately, she continued, 'every Slavonic race in the Peninsula seems to have been in its turn, for some brief historic period, "head of the Balkan Empire" – since these glories are never quite

---

[42] H. M. Hyndman's first wife, Matilda Hyndman, died on 27 June 1913 after a long illness, and on 14 May 1914 he married Rosalind Caroline Travers, 1874-1923. She was a poet and the only daughter of Major John Amory Travers, the chairman of the North Borneo Trading Company.. After her husband died in November 1921 she published *The Last Years of H M Hyndman,* took an overdose of sleeping tablets and died on 7 April 1923. By her will all her possessions were to go to such causes as would keep alive the memory of her husband.

forgotten.' The 'cynical proverb of their enemies; four Slavs five political opinions' held true. 'Croatians or Catholic Slavs, and Servians or orthodox Slavs – for these terms hold all over the Balkans for distinctions of religion as well as of race, - hate one another even more than "their Muslim fellows" or their "German over-lords."' The 'Trialism' project of Franz Ferdinand – intended to create a 'South Slavonic Monarchy' under the Habsburgs – 'pleased not a single one of the people concerned.' Magyars (ethnic Hungarians) disliked it because it 'would remove the Slavs of Croatia … from the tyranny they have exercised upon them ever since Hungary became a free nation.' Even Jews were opposed because 'the unlucky Crown Prince' had 'openly supported Karl Lueger and "Christsozialen" – the leading Anti-Semitic Party of Vienna' Franz Ferdinand's plan could only work in a vacuum.[43]

The following week (9 July) *Justice* recommended as deserving of 'thoughtful attention' the article 'The Principal lessons of the Balkan Wars' by Sir Max Waechter in the current issue of *The Nineteenth Century*.[44] It said that he had shown that almost half of the

---

[43] Trialism was the idea of reorganising the empire into three rather than the existing two more or less self-governing units with Croatia detached from Hungary forming the third part.

Karl Lueger, 1844-1910, was mayor of Vienna from 1897 until his death. He was both a controversial and, seemingly, a contradictory character. He is widely credited with creating the modern city as it still exists and he supported the federalisation of the empire. But he is chiefly remembered as an anti-Semite and an early inspiration for Hitler who was living in Vienna from 1907. He had founded the anti-Semitic *Christlichsoziale Partei* (Christian Social Party) in the early 1890s. Even Lueger's anti-Semitism was contradictory. When challenged with the fact that many of his friends were Jewish, Lueger famously replied: *'I decide who is a Jew.'*

[44] Waechter, 1837-1924, had been born in Germany but was naturalised British since the 1860s. A businessman and art collector, he had been knighted after serving as High Sheriff of Surrey in 1902. For readers of *Justice*, the interest in Waechter lay in his advocacy of a federal Europe and his foundation in 1913 of the European Federation League.

*The Nineteenth Century* had been *The Nineteenth Century and After* since 1901. It changed its name to *The Twentieth Century* only in 1951 and stopped publication in 1972.

combatants in the two Balkan wars of 1912 and 1913 had been killed or wounded and *Justice* quoted extensively from the article including Waechter's judgement that 'the European Powers have been largely responsible for the carnage.' Active interference in the Balkan Peninsula might lead to 'determined opposition by some other great power and result in an European war.' As, indeed, it did.

Rosalind Travers Hyndman had a second article in the final peacetime issue of *Justice* on 30 July. 'The Rising Tide of Slavdom' was pessimistic about what lay ahead.

> Peasants and workers will hurry out upon a race-war, putting off to some indefinite day the far more important war of class. As with Ireland, we can only shrug our shoulders and wish that all the various believers, all the nationalities small and great, would get over their intolerable differences once for all, grow conscious of their universal slavery, and set to work to make themselves truly free.

Yet the risk of war – at least a war *involving Britain* – still seemed far less serious than it is easy to comprehend a century or more later. It was not only socialists who failed to see what was coming. On 3 July, in a *Clarion* article with the title 'An Educated Democracy,' Fred Henderson made a passing reference to as speech by Viscount Haldane, a leading Liberal who in earlier years as war minister had done much to modernise the British armed forces. As reported by Henderson, Haldane had said that he was not 'in the least afraid of the invasion of German arms but he was very much afraid of the invasion of people who had been trained in German schools.' He meant that the real threat from Germany was an economic one. A reader seeking further reassurance could turn to the previous day's *Labour Leader*. In Snell's article on 'War and Gold' he had quoted Brailsford's assessment of the power of the socialist movement to prevent war.

The Socialist opposition to the war is effective, because under modern conditions on the Continent a war must be the effort of the whole nation... The Socialist deputies in the Reichstag or Chamber may always be voted down... but the Socialist soldiers in the army are indispensable to it. It will win no victories while they are an element of active or even passive discontent.

Such predictions helped to confirm hopes that repetition of earlier tragedies might be avoided. In the same *Clarion* issue as Henderson's article Dora Montefiore wrote, under the title 'Where the "Tommies" Sleep', of her visit in Bloemfontein. There she had visited the graves of British Soldiers killed a little more than a decade previously in the South African war. These words were italicised for emphasis in her article: *'I want the working-class mothers to see to it that never again shall the lives of their men children be thrown away in the cause of a capitalist war.'* [45]

But in all three papers other issues soon came to the fore in July 1914 in reports, articles and readers' letters. In spite of the frequent great power tensions and crises, the two recent wars in the Balkans, and the warnings of Blatchford and Hyndman about the 'German menace,' the assumption in early July seems to have been that, at worst, the Sarajevo assassination might trigger a third Balkan conflict. This should help us to understand the shock that the outbreak of European war at the beginning of the following month caused as should some of the concerns that *were* given prominence that the last month of peace until the end of 1918.

## Darwin, Shaw and Blatchford's 'Gloom'

Scientific topics – especially those related to theories of evolution –

---

[45] Dora Montefiore, 1851-1933, was a prominent feminist, socialist writer and activist in both Australia and Britain.

often appeared in both articles and letters – especially at this time in the *Clarion*. On 3 July there were letters on 'Evolution', 'A New Cosmic Theory' and – with an editorial note saying 'This correspondence is now closed' – the 'Laws of Gravitation.' But the main *Clarion* interest lay in another already on-going debate between Blatchford and George Bernard Shaw. Shaw was already championing Samuel Butler's critique of Darwinism and his own brand of neo-Lamarckian vitalism that would in 1921 be expounded at some length in the preface to *Back to Methuselah*. [46]

Already underway before the beginning of July, the controversy was given front page prominence in the first two editions of the month. Blatchford's defence of Darwin was supported by H. G. Wells[47] who in turn was taken to task by Shaw in a long letter to – for some reason – not the *Clarion* but *Justice* (2 July). Butler was not, as Wells seemed to think, a 'negligible crank', Shaw insisted. The participants were clearly deadly serious, but this did not deter them from engaging in fairly knockabout exchanges. 'Robert must take his orders from me,' Shaw had commanded in a letter to the *Clarion* on 26 June. Blatchford responded on 10 July by signing his latest diatribe against the playwright, in upper-case letters 'THE OTHER INTELLECTUAL LEADER OF THE SOCIALIST MOVEMENT.'

As one would anticipate there was no shortage of readers joining in via the '*Clarion* Cockpit' with advocates for both sides. Buffon, Lamarck and Erasmus Darwin were all cited as well as Butler. One

---

[46] George Bernard Shaw, 1856-1950, had already touched on the theme of 'creative evolution' in his 1903 play, *Man and Superman* – a title inspired by Nietzshe's notion of *Übermensch*. Later Shaw would credit the French philosopher Henri Bergson whose 1907 *L'Évolution créatrice* (Creative Evolution) appeared in English translation in 1911. Bergson argued a neo-Lamarckian view that the mechanism of evolution was not Darwinian natural selection but *élan vital* or vital impetus; the natural creative impulse.

[47] H. G. (Herbert George) Wells, 1856-1946, was a novelist and one of the 'fathers' of science fiction. He described himself as a 'democratic socialist' and was a member of the Fabian Society between 1903 and 1908. He was an important influence on the Universal Declaration of Human Rights, 1948.

*Clarion* reader, signing the letter as 'Coal Shoveller', thought that reading Shaw resembled 'watching an acrobatic turn at the music hall' and asked, 'who wants to wade through pages of wit to get two lines of common sense?' (10 July) In the same issue another reader, H. H. Mytton, even resorted to verse to sum up the debate. Shaw was cast as 'Doctor' and Blatchford as 'Saint'. The last two stanzas read:

> Doctor declares the Saint deserves a smack,
> And, quoting Butler, rushes to attack,
> And perorates: "You'll take commands from Me.
> *I* am the Shavian Superman – quack, quack!"
>
> So CLARION readers one and all rejoice,
> And welcome Wells's intervening voice.
> Object? Not Bernard likely! Daniels all -
> You pay your penny and you take your choice

The following week's *Clarion* (17 July) saw a letter from Shaw making similar points to the one that had appeared earlier in *Justice* and a cartoon showing Blatchford ('Clarion Champion') in a boxing ring with Shaw ('Fabian Lightweight'). It was in the context of this debate about science that concerns about 'Blatchford's Gloom' began to be voiced. It is an episode which throws at least some light on the *Clarion* editor's response to the outbreak of war a few weeks later. In an article on 'Words and Facts' (26 June) he had written:

> Time and experience have moderated my enthusiasm. I no longer believe that the world can be mended with words. I do not think that mere criticism or mere verbal demonstration counts for much in the evolution of society. Words are poor things when confronted with facts.

Blatchford continued:

> I do not believe that war will be abolished by the preaching of sermons, nor by the pleadings or tears of women. I do not believe that the citadel of Capitalism will be reduced by a bombardment of Fabian tracts and Clarion books. I believe that economic and political forces will be changed by facts and not words; that knowledge and invention will do what arguments and criticism have failed to do.
>
> Science will change the world, of that there is abundant evidence; but as to what science will make of it, who is so bold as to risk a guess?

People would say, he predicted, that his writings had had a huge impact but he often asked himself whether 'this is all I have to show for a long and busy life.'

To *Clarion* readers for whom Blatchford had been an inspiration – in some cases for a quarter of a century – these were alarming words. J. F. Horrabin's letter the following week (3 July), headed 'Mr Blatchford's Gloom' accused him of under-estimating his influence and indulging in 'a reckless debauch of self-pity and self-deprecation' and another correspondent was concerned about Blatchford's 'very sombre visage'.[48]

A. M. Thompson clearly felt that an editorial intervention was needed before things got out of hand. 'Are We Downhearted?' he asked. Taking up Horrabin's charge of pessimism he agreed that his friend was surely the only person who failed to recognise his own influence. Evolution might be slow but things were, on the whole, getting better.

Blatchford himself responded the following week (10 July) in a letter addressed to 'The Other Editor of the Clarion' and with the title 'The Pessimism of Robert Blatchford'. He rejected the notion that he was self-pitying; that was something he despised. 'It is not a puling whine over my lack of success; it is the disappointment of a

---

[48] James Francis (or Frank) Horrabin, 1884-1962, was a socialist activist, writer and cartoonist. He had been editor of the Plebs League journal *The Plebs*. In the interwar period he would be well-known for his *Daily News* comic strip *The Adventures of the Noah Family* and serve as a Labour MP between 1929 and 1931.

man who has tried to help others and finds he has largely failed.' People told him he had done wonders but compared to the like of 'such men as Carlyle, Morris, Thackeray, Lyell, Darwin' the results of his labours had been meagre. He did not compare himself to any of these; he simply 'wanted to help the people' and had fallen short. 'And of course, old friend,' he concluded, turning, as it were, to Thompson, 'the times are better than they were, in many ways. But I think the amendment is more due to acts than to words.'

There were more letters from readers the following week (17 July). One correspondent thought Blatchford quite right that speaking and writing were insufficient. 'His Determinist fatalism has hindered *action* and prevented him from defining Socialism as a *Life,* and not a *Theory.*' Another asked 'how many great men ever lived to see the fruits of their achievements? Cheer up, Dad Blatchett!' And indeed, the following week (24 July) saw Blatchford go some way to modify, or at least clarify, his position. Perhaps, he wrote, he had been over emphatic and stressed too much the weakness of the written word. He did not mean that 'words have no influence over social evolution,' he explained in a front page piece rather grandly titled 'A Few Words on European Civilisation.' He simply thought that 'the power of writers and speakers' had always been 'grossly exaggerated.'

## The Servile State, the Single Tax, and the Evils of Drink

In his 26 June article Blatchford had linked his immediate adversary, Shaw, to Belloc and Chesterton. They all, he claimed, 'take pleasure in being rude to the Equator.' He meant by this, he explained, that they enjoyed sneering at science. Belloc's *The Servile State* had had an instant impact among socialists – largely because it chimed with the concerns that many had about what we have seen Bax denounce as

'Statification or Bureaucratisation' in the introduction. In the wider socialist movement it helped to bolster both the syndicalists' demands for self-management and guild socialism. Belloc had insisted that his book 'did not discuss the Socialist State' but rather the inevitable result when 'the Socialist idea, in conflict with and yet informing the body of Capitalism, produces a third thing very different from the Socialist idea, to wit a Servile State.' This would be a society where the 'proletarian masses' would 'lose their present freedom and be subject to compulsory labour.'[49]

The idea, and the phrase, 'the servile state,' quickly became part of the currency of socialist debate. The book had been seriously discussed in all three socialist weeklies but early in 1913 Belloc and Blatchford had clashed over the latter's dismissal of the book as lacking originality. Belloc's reply claimed that recent developments, notably the Insurance Act of 1911, gave 'security for the wage-earner and at the same time for official control over his actions.'[50] This contest was, in essence, re-run in the *Clarion* in July 1914.

It began with the concluding sentences of Thompson's 'Are We Downhearted?' piece on 3 July:

> Science, of course, is the only thing that counts. But is not Socialism a science? If not, we are undone. And the 'written word' may do some service in interpreting the discoveries of Darwin, Huxley, Tyndall and Marx.

The following week Thompson devoted much space in his 'Our Point of View' editorial to Chesterton's assertion that socialism was no more

---

[49] Hilaire Belloc, *The Servile State,* preface to 2nd edition, 1913, 3rd edition, ix-xi. Belloc, 1870-1953, and G. K. Chesterton, 1874-1936, would become the main proponents of the Distributist movement of which *The Servile State* can be regarded as the foundation document – or at very least one of them. Though it had some success in attracting non-Catholics, it was inspired largely by the 1891 encyclical of Pope Pius XI, *Rerum Novarum.*

[50] *Clarion,* 28 February 1913. Barrow and Bullock, 263.

a science than the – then non-existent – Channel Tunnel. Thompson responded with a definition of socialism from Webster's dictionary which began by describing it as 'the science of reconstructing society on an entirely new basis.' He rejected, under the sub-heading 'The Servile State', Chesterton's apparent claim that the 'present state' was worse than the state of affairs before the Factory Acts and quoted copiously from these, commenting that 'Mr Chesterton, like his new master, Mr. Belloc, cannot abide industrial laws.'

Thompson's conclusion included a side-swipe at Chesterton and Belloc, both often regarded as Catholic apologists, though Chesterton would remain an Anglican until after the war. 'The "inefficients",' said Thompson, 'were battledored and harassed and worried and starved before Labour Exchanges or the Insurance Act came into existence; and their servility is not of recent growth. No, Mr Chesterton, the two factors most conducive to servility are very old-established: they are an empty belly and the fear of hell.'

Thompson's onslaught was continued the following week (17 July) with most of 'Our Point of View' devoted to it – including another dig at his adversaries' religious principles.

> We know that the Church did in early times teach the communistic gospel of the Galilean Carpenter. Why has it since adopted and consecrated the principles and methods of Judas Iscariot?

In the same issue he was criticised by a correspondent for giving space to the 'gymnastics' of people like Belloc and Chesterton who could not 'think clearly'.

The distributism of Belloc and Chesterton, founded on Catholic social teaching, was not the only heretical notion that came under attack in the *Clarion* that July. R.B. Suthers, a long-time member of the paper's staff, devoted several articles to refuting 'Single Tax

Delusions'.[51] This generated some correspondence including a letter on 10 July from a reader concerned about the 'revival of Henry Georgism', a reference to American writer and politician who had proposed a (single) land value tax, most famously in *Progress and Poverty* in 1879. On 10 July in an article titled 'Much Virtue in "If"' Suthers rejected the notions of two guild socialists, Vyle and Gibbons. 'If a man can be convinced that industrial unions or guilds are a sane and practical proposal,' he declared, 'he can be convinced that Socialism is IT.'

Another movement of the time that made fairly frequent appearances in the socialist press at this time was temperance. As we have seen. 'Alcoholism' was among the topics that would have been debated at the ill-fated Vienna International. One correspondent in *Justice* on 2 July was vehemently opposed to 'the licensed liquor traffic which deadens, destroys, demoralises and disorganises the democracy. The wealthy brewer is an enemy to the worker.' R. H. Gough concluded that 'The liquor evil is the workers' greatest obstacle,' and signed off, 'Yours for national prohibition and the workers' thorough emancipation.'

But in the same issue appeared a letter from H. B. R. Clark responding to an earlier letter of a similar nature to Gough's. He asked, 'How does your correspondent know that "the public-house on Sundays form the meeting place for a lot of senseless talkers"? If it is because he frequents these very useful institutions, I suggest that he should not judge his fellow-men so harsh.' If not, he was not in a position to express an opinion, Clark concluded.

The correspondent who had triggered this exchange then returned

---

[51] 'A young clerk from the *Sunday Chronicle*. R.B. Suthers was engaged to look after the accounts...' Laurence Thompson, *Robert Blatchford. Portrait of an Englishman,* Gollancz, 1951, 81. This underestimates Suther's role in the *Clarion* and his range of activities. He was the author of a number of the *Clarion's* 'Pass On Pamphlets' such as *John Bull and Doctor Socialism* and – also published by the Clarion Press – novels such as *A Man, a Woman and a Dog,* which the *Westminster Review* called 'One of the most amusing books we have ever read' and its sequel *Jack's Wife.*

on 9 July denying that he was a 'rigid Sabbatarian and teetotaller.' Of his critic of the previous week G. Venables speculated, 'Possibly our friend has never seen Socialist meetings either upset or broken up on Sunday afternoons by his intelligent friends from the "pub" or has tried to speak to them after they have had a good booze overnight.' And Venables concluded, 'Believe me, we shall never get the Social Revolution from the tap-room.' The debate on alcohol was by no means confined to *Justice*. The same day a letter in the *Labour Leader* which concluded, 'I am greatly interested in Socialism, and I have yet to learn that total abstinence is one of its ideals. Socialism stands for liberty and commonsense, whilst total abstinence means restriction of liberty, narrow-mindedness, and intolerance.'

Just how much the issue of drink played not only in the British but also in the wider socialist movement is evident from a report in *Justice* on 16 July. Its coverage of preparations for 'The International Socialist Congress at Vienna' was entirely taken up by the report on 'Alcoholism' drafted by Emile Vandervelde, the chair of the International Socialist Bureau (ISB) and soon to become the first member of the Belgian Labour Party to hold ministerial office after the outbreak of war. The report began, 'Nobody contends any longer that the Social-Democracy can dissociate itself from the problems of alcoholism...' The following week's 'Topical Tattle' in *Justice,* (23 July) was devoted to this issue. 'Tattler' explained that Vandervelde was a 'militant teetotaller'. Was 'alcohol a "poison" in the ordinary everyday sense of the word?' Weren't there other 'poisons' in daily life? 'Tattler' had 'known teetotallers whose hands shake with excessive smoking.' The issue clearly would have loomed large at the ill-fated Vienna Congress. But scarcely a week after 'Tattler's' critique of Valdervelde's report the unity – even the existence – of the international socialist movement would be threatened by the outbreak of European war and the ISB would be struggling – unsuccessfully in the end – to maintain the peace and socialist unity.

## The Liberal Government and Labour in Parliament

The finance bill to implement Lloyd George's 1914 budget was still being debated in parliament in July and there was a good deal of coverage of its progress and the debates it generated in the socialist papers, especially in the *Labour Leader*. All but one of the items in the 'Review of the Week' in that paper on 2 July were concerned with this. It charged that the reduction of tax to be paid on unearned income 'was due to the pressure of rich Liberals' and that Haldane had 'confessed' at a National Liberal Club meeting that 'it is the Labour movement which has forced from the Government the imposition of taxes on unearned and super incomes.' Herbert Morrison was given a box in the middle of the page to berate the Liberals about their failure to appreciate that 'the Labour Party is not a wing of the Liberal Party.' [52] Labour MPs had refused to vote on the second reading of the budget bill 'because the Government had surrendered the interests of the poor to the greed of Liberalism's rich supporters.' The same day *Justice* too gave over most of its 'Parliamentary Notes' to the Finance Bill.

The following day the *Clarion* praised – and headlined – 'The New Labour Spirit.' The parliamentary party had for the first time 'enforced Jowett's Bradford policy.' For his own part, Jowett was critical of the attitude of Philip Snowden, who had already emerged as Labour's chief economic spokesman. In an article in the *Clarion* on 10 July Jowett focussed on a contribution of Snowden to the *Christian Commonwealth*. He charged Snowden with 'associating himself with the millionaires in their objection to being taxed for purposes not previously sanctioned in detail by the House of Commons.'

Snowden had praised the Chancellor, Lloyd George, for his

---

[52] Herbert Morrison, 1888-1965, would become one of the most important figures in the post-1945 Labour government, serving as Home Secretary, Foreign Secretary, and Deputy Prime Minister.

'conciliating of opposition' but Jowett saw him as strengthening 'the hold of vested interests' and establishing new ones. He much preferred the approach of Healy the radical Irish nationalist. Jowett wrote:

> I think the special work of the Treasury mandarins is to strangle every enterprising and promising new thing with red tape, an endless store of which they always keep ready for use. Mr Healy would have the Treasury treated as he says the Chinese treat their officials – i.e., he would have them put in a bamboo cage in the Lobby and, for different reasons to his, so would I.

As for the 'Bradford policy' with which Jowett was so closely associated, having the previous week 'acted on the principle approved by the I.L.P. conference when the Bradford resolution was carried,' Labour had subsequently supported the Liberal government to keep the Tories out. Jowett deplored Lloyd George's conciliation of the shipowners by agreeing to 'loadline regulations which, in effect, paint out the Plimsoll Mark.' *Justice* had the previous day wondered whether the new President of the Board of Trade, John Burns, could 'muster up enough of his old independence to break with the permanent officials and reverse the raising of the Load Line'.[53]

On 16 July with the prospect of a general election in 1915 the *Labour Leader* looked forward to 'The Winter Session.' It wanted to see a Reform Bill 'abolishing the existing anomalies, extending the franchise to all men, and giving the House an opportunity to destroy

---

[53] John Burns, 1858-1943, was a trade union leader who, after being one of the leaders of the London Dock Strike of 1889 – known to the press as 'the man with the red flag' – he became a Liberal MP in 1892. He had been President of the Local Government Board, but would not remain long in the new position at the Board of Trade, resigning from the government over its policy towards the coming war on 2 August 1914.

The load line – often known in Britain as the Plimsoll Line – was designed to prevent to overloading of ships. It was named after the Liberal MP Samuel Plimsoll who, after a long campaign, secured legislation to prevent the over-loading of merchant ships in 1876.

the sex qualification.' About a third of men and all women were excluded from the right to vote in parliamentary elections at this time.

Ever since Dangerfield's *The Strange Death of Liberal England* in 1935 the final pre-war years have been seen as a period when the established order found itself menaced by 'rebels' on all sides. The second part of that book, which takes up the lion's share of its pages, after a short introductory piece, comprises substantial chapters on 'The Tory Rebellion', 'The Women's Rebellion', and 'The Worker's Rebellion'. The first of these culminates in the opposition leader, Bonar Law, making 'one of the most reckless speeches of his whole career' in November 1913. He had compared Asquith's position over Home Rule for Ireland with that of James II in 1689 when civil war had been avoided because 'his own army refused to fight for him.'[54] Dangerfield's final section on 'The Crisis. January-August 1914' deals with the way these 'rebellions' continued up to the outbreak of war. No account of the situation in Britain in July 1914 can neglect any of these.

---

[54] George Dangerfield, *The Strange Death of Liberal England*, 1935, London: MacGibbon and Kee edition, 1966, 120.

# CHAPTER 2

# Rebels All

## Strikes and Disputes – the 'Labour Unrest'

1914 did not see anything on the scale of the transport strikes of 1911 or the miners' strike of the following year. Yet it would be a mistake to conclude that the great 'labour unrest' that had characterised Britain since 1910 was becoming a thing of the past. There was no shortage of disputes and strikes right up to the outbreak of war.

Some of those reported in the three socialist weeklies were untypical of what are normally thought of as industrial disputes. *Justice* on 2 July reported on 'The School Strike in Norfolk.' Children at the Burston and Shimpling County School had been on strike for three months. This, the paper explained, followed the dismissal of 'comrades T G and Mrs Higden, teachers at the school, because of their refusal to give in to the clerical influence that dominates the present school management and their connection with the Agricultural Labourers' Union.' The same issue claimed there were 600 to 700 members of the Agricultural Labourer and General Labourers' Union out on strike in in Norfolk and Essex It called for 'subscriptions' to support the union.[55]

---

[55] Sometimes described as 'the longest running strike in British history', Annie and Tom Higden ran an alternative 'Strike School' until 1939 supported largely by Labour movement donations. The BBC dramatized *The Burston Rebellion* in 1985. The school building now houses a museum dedicated to the strike.

Also that week a *Justice* correspondent reported a meeting of Jewish workers alarmed by the opposition of the Jewish Board of Deputies to the Eight Hours Bill being promoted by the Labour MP, Alex Wilkie. H. Rosner complained that the Board 'never consults the workers on any question.' *Labour Leader* the same day criticised McKenna, the Home Secretary, for failing to intervene in the case of a Burton striker sentenced to seven days imprisonment for assaulting a police officer – an offence denied by witnesses. Keir Hardie had taken up the case. The following week both the *Leader* and *Justice* reported successful Labour pressure bringing about the release of the man in question. According to *Justice:* 'Through Keir Hardie's exertions the second sentence meted out to Mr. Rawlings the Burton trade union leader was remitted.'

Also in that edition of *Justice* (9 July) was an article on 'The Agricultural Labourers' Strike in North West Essex' by Edward G. Maxted, the Vicar of Tilty. He claimed that 95% of the men working in agriculture had come out on strike. There were very few blacklegs. The strike had been going for just over a fortnight and was supported, Maxted emphasised in a sub-heading, by 'Women as Determined as the Men.'

The successful strike at Woolwich Arsenal over the dismissal of a worker also made its appearance in the same issue. *Justice* managed to combine its expression of support with its usual scepticism about the longer-term significance of industrial action. It cordially congratulated the workers on their 'wonderful exhibition of solidarity' while regretting that such 'admirable outbursts of proletarian sympathy' seldom left 'much real or lasting effect behind them.'

An interview with Arthur Harris, secretary of the Labour Protection League, appeared on 16 July, again in *Justice*. The origins of the 'Woolwich Outburst' were explained. A millwright called Entwistle had refused to operate machines placed on 'concrete beds made by blackleg labour.' Eventually, Entwistle was sacked and the strike ensued. Within two days there had been an intervention by

Prime Minister Asquith and an agreement had been reached on terms which 'were regarded as an unconditional surrender on behalf of the Arsenal authorities.' Victory celebrations had continued 'long after midnight' with people 'parading the streets singing songs in recognition of the fact that for the first time in the history of this country the men at a Government factory had taken their stand with the general industrial movement.' Asked whether the strike was the result of union organisation or had been spontaneous, Harris replied, 'Largely spontaneous. Of the 12,000 men who came out only 1,100 were members of the ASE and 7,000 were labourers.'[56]

Meanwhile, another London-centred dispute was escalating. There had been disputes in the building trade for the previous six months, though some employers in the provinces had reached settlements. *Justice* reported (23 July) that the London Master Builders' Association had agreed unanimously on a lockout of their workers and were hoping to secure the necessary two-thirds majority vote in their national body to extend the action to the rest of the country. The following week it reported that there had been an 'overwhelming' vote, well above the two-thirds mark, and as a result more than half a million building workers were likely to be locked out.

The *Clarion* had little to say about the domestic industrial scene that July though there was a letter on 10 July warning readers not to use London Parcels Delivery for contributions to the Carter Paterson strike fund since that business was owned by the delivery firm in question. The same issue also carried an article headed 'Little Pictures of Free America. Fire Hose and Gaol "Solve" California's Unemployed Problem.' This reported the violent breaking up of what was intended to be a march to Washington.

---

[56] The ASE was the Amalgamated Society of Engineers, the original 'New Model' craft union founded in 1851. The Labour Protection League dated from the next great development in British trade unionism – the organisation and recruitment of the (supposedly) unskilled in what became known as the 'new unionism.' It had been founded in 1889 as the South Side Labour Protection League with the SDF's Harry Quelch as secretary.

The United States was also the setting for what Thompson called, two weeks later (24 July), 'the most warlike battle fought in the Labour War since the Paris Commune.' He saw the 'death of the men, women and children slaughtered at Ludlow' in Colorado 'as a warning to workers in Britain and elsewhere.' The same edition of the paper carried a detailed account of 'The Battle of Ludlow.' Workers at the Colorado Fuel and Iron Co. had been on strike since the previous September. On 20 April 1914 the strikers, members of the United Mine Workers of America, were attacked by the Colorado National Guard as well as by guards employed by the company. In what became known as the Ludlow Massacre about two dozen people, including 'two women and eleven children who were sheltering in a tent which was set on fire' were killed. The main owner of the Colorado mine was John Rockefeller Jr.

'The Civil War in South Colorado' also featured in the last peacetime edition of *Labour Leader* on 30 July. In a substantial article with the subtitle 'Miners Harassed by Imported Assassins,' Upton Sinclair told how 'fighting of terrible ferocity broke out with startling suddenness and in a few days the country was appalled by the news that the authority of the State had broken down and that federal intervention was necessary to prevent revolution.'[57]

In the *Clarion* Thompson had asked 'British trade unionists to call the attention of complacent non-unionists to the battle of Ludlow.' It was, he said, 'an example of what happens where Capitalism is strong and Labour weak.' There was no shortage of potential Rockefellers in Britain. He went on:

> Labour's first line of defence against them is trade unionism, the second is Parliamentary representation, and to prepare against the perils that

---

[57] The American socialist Upton Sinclair, 1878-1968, was already famous for his novel *The Jungle,* first published as a book in 1906 having previously appeared serialised in the socialist paper *Appeal to Reason* the previous year. It was based on his own experience and it exposed appalling conditions in the Chicago meat-packing industry.

threaten, both need to be fortified, not only in numbers, but also in spirit…

For here, as in America, capitalistic power is stiffening its back against trade unionism. Here also a professedly democratic Government invoked the help of the soldiers in the case of the last railway strike, and here 250,000 workers now stand practically pledged to fight shoulder to shoulder in each other's quarrels.

This was a reference to the 'Triple Alliance' formed earlier in 1914. A combination of miners', transport and railway workers', unions, it was named after the German-centred military alliance of that country with Austria-Hungary and Italy. The union alliance was seen as having revolutionary potential which was both widely welcomed and feared. Syndicalism, promoted in Britain since 1910 by Tom Mann, already a veteran trade union leader, claimed that 'politics,' including socialist parties, was unnecessary.[58] The revolution would instead arrive via the direct action of the working class in the industrial struggle which would become increasingly militant and bring capitalism to an end with a general strike. This gave an impetus for achieving trade union amalgamations and replacing a confusion of

---

[58] Tom Mann, 1856-1941, had been one of the leaders of the great London Dock Strike of 1889. Briefly, secretary of the ILP and later of the National Democratic League, he emigrated to Australia returning to Britain in 1910. Despairing of parliamentary politics, he formed the Syndicalist Education League which published the monthly *The Industrial Syndicalist.* In the *Clarion* its erstwhile 'political editor,' Victor Grayson, amiably ridiculed this title: 'Fancy a hod-carrier asking his newsagent for "The Industrial Syndicalist." And imagine the newsagent looking it up in the list of horses for the next day's race!' (*Clarion,* 22 July 1910). Mann had led the Liverpool transport strike in 1911 and was convicted of incitement to mutiny for his famous 'Don't Shoot' article (and later pamphlet) urging soldiers not to use military force against strikers. Released after a successful public campaign in his support, Mann would oppose the war, be a founder member of the Communist Party of Great Britain (CPGB) and serve as general secretary of the engineering union (ASE) from 1919 until his retirement in 1921. He remained an influential figure and a unit of the International Brigades in the Spanish Civil War, the Tom Mann Centuria, was named after him.

For syndicalism in the UK see Bob Holton, *British Syndicalism 1900-1914. Myths and Realities,* London: Pluto Press, 1976, 134.

small craft unions squabbling with each other in demarcation disputes by unions recruiting all grades of workers within a specific industry. Many union activists who were hesitant about syndicalism still pressed for 'industrial unionism' in the belief that workers would be greatly strengthened if all the unions in each industry amalgamated and were able to present the employers with a united front. On 30 July *Labour Leader* headlined 'One Union for the Textile Industry.' This was a development it very much welcomed. But the main focus of industrial unionism would be firmly on the Triple Alliance.

At the end of June the *Clarion* (26 June) had carried a substantial article by Vernon Hartshorn, of the South Wales Miners, on 'Labour's Standing Army.' [59] The Miner's Federation, the National Union of Railwaymen and the Transport Workers' Union had all approved the alliance and he looked forward to the joint national conference of delegates that was expected to ratify it. This would 'bring into being the greatest fighting organisation that Labour has ever possessed in this or any other country,' and would 'convert into reality what has been for many years a dream,' wrote Hartshorn. But he warned against those who demanded that it should be 'exclusively industrial and… have nothing to do with politics.'

> These men scorn the idea of any reform by Parliament, and can think of no other means of progress but that of a general strike. They look to use the combine in the way of general strikes and nothing more. As soon as the organisation is complete they want war to be declared. Physical force is the only influence they seem to understand.

Moreover, with Scottish coal owners threatening wage cuts a confrontation seemed inevitable. Dangerfield would later write:

---

[59] Vernon Hartshorn, 1872-1931, would later be president of the South Wales Miners and a Labour MP from 1918 until his death. He would be Postmaster General in MacDonald's 1924 government and Lord Privy Seal 1930-31.

To the miners' rank and file this was the final challenge. It was evident that the Miners' Federation of Great Britain would take issue with the Scottish coal-owners; that the transport workers and railwaymen would join in; and that – in September, or, at latest, October – there would be an appalling national struggle over the question of the living wage.[60]

*Labour Leader* on 9 July featured a report of a speech by the Scottish miners' leader and vice-president of the Miners' Federation of Great Britain (MFGB) Robert Smillie, in which he laid out the aims of the Triple Alliance.[61] It also carried a letter from 'Common Sense, Rhondda Valley' which ended: 'If the miners, railwaymen and transport men will not use their mighty institutions *this time* for the securing of a minimum of £3 a week for every worker they may as well "chuck it" altogether.'

If the revolt of worker 'rebels,' though still far from over, seemed to be in a period of comparative calm, albeit with the cloud identified by Dangerfield already looming over the coming months of 1914, both the other sets of rebels were absolutely in full swing in July 1914. The Home Rule and Ulster question would reach another boiling point in the second half of the month and meanwhile the 'militant' suffrage campaign was at its height.

## Militant Suffragettes

Writing in the *Labour Leader* on 16 July on 'The Russian Reaction' – prompted by reports that Rasputin had been stabbed by a woman – W. C. Anderson denied that 'physical force and terrorism are the

---

[60] Dangerfield, 320.

[61] Robert Smillie, 1857-1940, was the vice-president of the Miners' Federation of Great Britain and a key figure in its decision to transfer its electoral support to the Labour Party. He chaired the 'Triple Alliance' and would, in 1915, become president of the National Council Against Conscription.

accepted weapons of the Russian reformers.' He went on: 'An attempt at bomb-throwing bears the same relationship to the reform movement in Russia that an attempt to burn down Burns Cottage does to the Suffrage movement in Britain.'

In the early hours of 8 July 1914, Burns Cottage, the birthplace of the poet, had been attacked. According to the *Glasgow Herald*, 9 July 1914, the 'dastardly attempt' made 'by suffragists to fire and blow up Burns' Cottage was frustrated by the night watchman.' One of the perpetrators was arrested and later gaoled. She gave her name as Jean Arthur, but subsequently turned out to be Fanny Parker, a niece of Lord Kitchener. Kitchener would soon be appearing all over the country in the now-famous recruiting poster.

Blatchford's daughter Winifred and Hilda Thompson both worked on the *Clarion*. The latter's regular feature, 'The Passing Show' on 3 July told how she had gone with a female friend and 'our Mr Wilkinson' to the trial at the Old Bailey (the Central Criminal Court). The defendants were the printers of *The Suffragette*, the paper of the Women's Social and Political Union (WSPU). Wilkinson was an important witness.[62]

The two women had great trouble getting in. Protesting indignantly Hilda gave her word of honour 'that we have no intention of creating a disturbance' only to be told by an official 'We have had titled ladies' making such promises who had 'gone upstairs and smashed the windows.' She resented, Hilda said, the insinuation that 'the word of honour of a titled lady is better worth accepting than mine or any other woman's.' The trial, in the end, did not proceed that day and she took her friend to the National Gallery – only to be

---

[62] W.T. Wilkinson was another of the original *Clarion* team. He had left the Manchester *City News* to become the 'advertising representative' of the new paper. Laurence Thompson, *Portrait of an Englishman. A Life of Robert Blatchford*, London: Golllancz, 1951, 81.

*The Suffragette* had been the WSPU newspaper since 1912 after that organisation lost control of *Votes for Women* when its owners and editors, Emmeline and Frederick Pethick-Lawrence, broke with the suffragette organisation over the arson campaign.

told by a policeman at the entrance 'that it was closed because of the Suffragettes.'

It would suddenly come to an end with the outbreak of war but July 1914 was still the era of the arson campaign, the slashing of the Rokeby Venus, hunger strikes, forcible feeding and the notorious 'Cat and Mouse Act.' Blatchford had summed up the situation as he saw it on 26 June:

> The Suffragettes are not being tortured for destroying property; they are being tortured because Right Honourable and Honourable gentlemen have broken their promises and because the mass of the people do not care: Mr Asquith knows it.

In spite of Blatchford's pessimism about support for the suffrage campaign there was in fact much correspondence broadly supportive in all three papers including a letter from 'A.S.' in the *Clarion* on 3 July which asserted that the 'real object of the militant Suffragettes in damaging works of art is to cause galleries to be closed and consequently (this is the point) to scare away wealthy American and foreign tourists.' There was, A.S. concluded, 'method in the Suffragette madness.'

On 17 July the *Clarion* editorial by A.M. Thompson appealed for the 'entire Press' to protest against the conviction and imprisonment of Drew, the manager of the Victoria House Printing Co. which printed *The Suffragette*. As a result of an earlier legal action he had been forced to give an undertaking not to publish or print any 'incitement to violence.' The *Clarion* had agreed to 'compose' the paper. When Wilkinson, the *Clarion's* manager, had stated all this to the earlier preliminary hearing he was warned by the magistrate that he was incriminating himself but said that this was 'no reason not to speak the truth.' Thompson said that he had tried to carry out the undertaking by 'a weekly censorship' so 'if there has been any criminal offence I am the culprit.' The press should demand Drew's immediate release. He concluded, 'I do not absolutely insist that they shall also demand my summary consignment to his dungeon in his stead, but I would naturally prefer that physical discomfort to the moral inconvenience of my present position.'

In the same issue Hilda Thompson was attacking 'The Farce of English Justice' in the case of four militant suffragettes on trial at the Central Criminal Court. She had observed the proceedings from the public gallery. She sympathised when, as the judge began his summing up, 'a lady sitting near me rose suddenly and asked "are you a judge or a counsel for the prosecution?"' This protest and others that immediately followed led to all the women in the public gallery, including at least one 'anti-militant,' being ejected. None of the men, some of whom had also protested, were forced to leave, Hilda Thompson reported indignantly.

If there was no support, in the three socialist papers, for the way offending 'militants' were treated there was little support for, as distinct from understanding of, the militants' campaign. The *Labour Leader* 'Review of the Week' on 2 July began: 'We need not say that we have no sympathy with the women who are committing acts of violence and incendiarism in the pathetic belief that they are furthering the ends of the Woman Suffrage movement.' They were the 'greatest enemies of their own cause.' But forcible feeding was always revolting and in the case of 'Miss Nellie Hall ... found guilty of harbouring bombs' it was 'outrageous.' Hall was one of the defendants in the case Hilda Thompson had thought a 'Farce.'[63]

The SDF had called for full adult suffrage from its outset and in 1907 had reminded Keir Hardie that long before he became a proponent of 'women's suffrage' he had refused to take part in an

---

[63] Nellie (or Emmeline) Hall was born in 1895 and named after her godmother Emmeline Pankhurst. Nellie's mother, Martha, was a founder member of the WSPU. In 1913 Nellie had been sentenced to three weeks in prison for throwing a brick through the window of Asquith's car. In 1914 she was tried, together with her mother and sister, for possessing 'window-smashing equipment' and sentenced to three months. She and her husband emigrated to Canada in 1929.

adult suffrage demonstration the SDF had organised with trade union support in 1893. He had, it was reported, criticised the Social-Democrats for aligning themselves with 'mere Radicalism' and 'deserting the cause of Socialism.'[64] The 'limited' women's suffrage supported by suffragettes as well as the 'constitutional' suffrage movement had routinely been dismissed by *Justice* as the 'Fine Lady Suffrage' since the early 1890s.

Not surprisingly, therefore, there was little sympathy for suffragette militancy to be found in the *Justice* editorial on 2 July under the title 'Socialism and the Suffrage.' The pre-suffragette organisations may have been ineffective, the editorial said, and it conceded that the tactics of the WSPU 'did unquestionably bring the question of woman suffrage prominently to the front.' But what might then have become 'a genuine democratic movement for Adult Suffrage, in which all could have taken part, was switched off into a demand for limited suffrage for women which would have ruled out large numbers of working and married women, and thus tended to increase the voting power of the propertied classes.'

Later, extreme forms of militancy had 'practically killed all public opinion and feeling on the subject of the suffrage altogether. Not the faintest general interest is taken in it.' The result was that now it was harder to get up as much 'feeling in favour of Adult Suffrage' than it had been twenty years before. The socialist principle had always been 'complete Adult Suffrage.'

The fundamental principle of Democracy is that that every man or woman that is subject to law should have an equal voice in making the law. And Democracy is the only political system we can imagine for a people who possess even a moderate degree of intelligence, whatever may be its drawbacks under present conditions.

The same position was taken again by 'Tattler' in the regular 'Topical

[64] *Justice*, 19 February 1907; 21 October 1893.

Tattle' column of *Justice* on 16 July. Forcible feeding was, 'a stupid blunder from first to last' but it was 'impossible just now to get up any enthusiasm whatever for the suffrage, and will be increasingly so as long as tactics of personal violence and arson continue.'

Predictably, Keir Hardie took a much more optimistic view of the prospects for suffrage reform than *Justice* – or, indeed, than Blatchford and Hilda Thompson. The latter complained that the response to her letter urging active support a few weeks earlier had been subdued. 'Out of a circulation of 60,000,' she complained on 17 July, she had received 'exactly four letters from readers, who express a desire and willingness to do something.' There had also been half a dozen letters published in the *Clarion*. 'Not a dozen enthusiasts all told.'

In contrast, Hardie was looking forward to the general election expected in 1915 or possibly before. What, he asked, in a *Labour Leader* editorial on 2 July, should Labour make its 'big fighting issue?' What was the topic which, 'next to militarism, the Socialist and Labour Parties of Europe have in the forefront of their programmes?' He concluded, 'I believe an Adult Suffrage Campaign would enlist great masses of the electorate on our side, and would, besides, lead to an early and complete victory.' A fortnight later (16 July) the paper reported that 'Mr Hardie's suggestion that the Party should specially emphasise the need for the enactment of adult suffrage has been accepted, and this demand will be made the battle-cry of the autumn campaign.'

Apart from much head-shaking about the WSPU's campaign, other suffrage organisations made some appearances in the three papers during those July weeks. Tom Gibb had been a Labour candidate in the recent South Lanark by-election. In answer to correspondents he confirmed, in *Labour Leader* on 2 July, that he had no doubts about the 'honesty' of the NUWSS during the campaign. The National Union of Women's Suffrage Societies had been formed in 1897, six years before the WSPU. The NUWSS was the 'constitutional' campaigning organisation – much larger with about

100,000 members than the 'militant' WSPU which had around 2,000. Since 1912, in order to bring pressure to bear on the Liberal government, it had helped to support and finance Labour in a number of by-elections.[65]

Gibb confirmed its 'honesty' during the South Lanark campaign, but said he was not, personally, an enthusiastic supporter of 'limited suffrage.' He was concerned that the 'greater and still clearer aims of adult suffrage are being lost sight of.' An editorial note followed his letter saying that the ILP had 'always stood for Woman Suffrage on the same terms as enjoyed by men, as a stepping-stone towards adult suffrage.'

The *Clarion* of 17 July included letters from the leaders of two suffragette organisations that had at different times broken away from, or in the second case been expelled from, the WSPU. C. Nina Boyle, Head of the Political and Militant Department of the Women's Freedom League (WFL) poured well-merited scorn on the notion of the exclusively male 'breadwinner.'[66] The second letter was from Sylvia Pankhurst whose dramatic hunger strike outside Parliament on 18 June had secured a meeting of working women with Asquith which was credited with shifting his and the government's attitude towards suffrage reform. In her letter she complained that 'certain newspapers' were attempting to place her 'in the position of the little girl who never went astray' and confirmed that her East London Federation of

---

[65] Though its president, Millicent Fawcett, 1847-1929, was the widow of a prominent Liberal politician and seen as a Liberal herself, she was instrumental in 1912 in getting the NUWSS to set up an election fighting fund which was used to support Labour candidates in four by-elections in 1913-14. Labour failed to win any of these contest – but the Liberals lost two of them which was the NUWSS objective in order to bring pressure on the government over the suffrage issue.

[66] Constance Antonina (Nina) Boyle, 1865-1943, had been imprisoned three times as a result of her militant suffrage activities. She would be a pioneer of the Women's Police Service during the war and was the first woman in Britain to stand – for the WFL – as a parliamentary candidate in the Keighley by-election of March 1918 though her nomination was later refused on a technicality. In the 1920s and '30s she wrote a number of popular novels.

Suffragettes had 'no criticism, but only sympathy for other women who are fighting to obtain the franchise.' [67]

There were also letters and reports from socialist women's organisations; from Margaretta Hicks for the BSP's National Women's Council in *Justice* and from Dr Marion Phillips and the Women's Labour League (WLL) in *Labour Leader*. On 2 July the latter included a report that Dr Phillips and Mrs Salter were to be delegates at the Vienna international and of a resolution 'of a very cordial nature' congratulating the Women's Co-operative Guild for resisting pressure from the Co-operative Board to give up its campaign for divorce law reform.[68] But the most interesting and remarkable contribution to the consideration of the position of women that day came from Ellen Wilkinson in the *Labour Leader*.

---

[67] (Estelle) Sylvia Pankhurst, she usually signed herself E. Sylvia Pankhurst, 1882-1960, began as an artist and became a militant suffragette and socialist. She would initially support Communism but oppose its lack of democracy and become an advocate of Ethiopia after Mussolini's 1935 invasion. Her final years would be spent in that country and she would die in Addis Ababa. See Ian Bullock and Richard Pankhurst, *Sylvia Pankhurst. From Artist to Anti-Fascist,* Macmillan, 1992.

[68] The Women's Co-operative Guild was formed in 1884. Its long-time general secretary was Mary Llewellyn Davies, 1861-1944. In 1912 the Guild's annual congress had passed a resolution calling for divorce to be granted after two years' separation. It was this that led the board of the Co-operative Union to withdraw its £400 annual grant. The Guild successfully resisted this pressure.

Marion Phillips, 1881-1932, was born in Melbourne, Australia, and held a doctorate in economics from the London School of Economics. In 1909 and 1910 she had worked as a researcher for Beatrice Webb in her work on the Royal Commission on the Poor Laws. She became secretary of the Women's Labour League (WLL) and would be a member of the War Emergency National Commission. She would be Chief Women's Officer of the Labour Party from 1919 until her death and was a Labour MP, 1929-31.

Ada Salter, 1866-1942, was the president of the WLL, a Quaker and a socialist active in the ILP and Labour Party. Over a very active lifetime she achieved a number of 'firsts.' She was the first woman councillor – and first Labour councillor – in Bermondsey in 1909. Later, in 1922, she would be the first woman mayor (of Bermondsey) in London and one of the first in Britain in 1922. She was married to the equally celebrated Dr Alfred Salter.

# 'WOMAN'S SHARE OF SOCIALISM.
# A CHALLENGING ARTICLE FROM A FEMINIST'

This was the headline in the *Leader* on 2 July. Ellen Wilkinson had, since graduating from the University of Manchester the previous year, worked as an organiser for the NUWSS. She had made her mark by helping to stage the Suffrage Pilgrimage culminating in a 50,000-strong rally in London almost exactly one year previously. Later she would become a national figure as Labour MP for Jarrow and one of the leaders of the famous Jarrow Crusade against unemployment in 1936. After serving in a more junior capacity in Churchill's wartime coalition she would die in office as Minister of Education in 1947. She would be only the second woman in Britain – after Margaret Bondfield – to become a Cabinet minister.

The July 1914 article was preceded by an editorial note saying that the paper endorsed most but not all of her criticisms. 'We print her article because it represents a point of view which all men will do well to face.' Wilkinson's concerns were much wider than the suffrage issue. She believed that even the most revolutionary syndicalist versions of the new society were built 'to suit men's prejudices.' Moreover, the 'practical bricklayers are worse than the theoretical architects.' There had been only three woman delegates to the last TUC while the 'ILP Conference had 20 women delegates of whom only three spoke. The Labour Party had twelve.' She went on:

In how many cases is one woman desperately trying to hammer in the fact that the men's comfortable assumption that the women will fit into things as they have always done – *i.e.* do the dirty work, and then take a back seat when matters of governance and interest are forward – is based on the old dispensation of dependent womanhood, and will not do now.

When the young woman, fully convinced by practical experience that she is the equal of her brother, wants to know what Socialism is going to do for her, the only thinker to have got beyond the glorious-helpmate-of-man state is H.G. Wells, and he, with the honesty which is his finest characteristic, can only say, 'It remains to be worked out'.

The final paragraph of the article ended with this plea:

> The idea that woman is only undeveloped man, and that if given a fair chance she will proceed on his lines, is so widespread because women have very largely, been content to let men do their thinking for them. What the Socialist movement badly needs is a steady determination among its women to set aside for a while the masculine point of view, and by facing the facts that make them different from man, think out what they really want from the Socialist State.

The subsequent readers' letters this article generated showed considerable interest, both supportive and hostile, for the remainder of the month. Chief among the latter was the correspondent who, sheltering behind the rather unlikely title of 'Prometheus', complained (9 July) that Wilkinson offered 'no suggestions for what a woman's place in the new state should be.' He, and we can assume 'Prometheus' was male, believed that the article was written 'from the point of view of the infinitesimally small minority of woman impossibilists, who don't know what they *do* want. The substance of her article is this: What will be the position, in the future Socialist state, of the few man-hating persons who petulantly refuse to be happy until every man sinks his manhood and grovels at the feet of the Amazons?'

But other readers supported Wilkinson including one who congratulated the *Labour Leader* editor on 'his fair mindedness in publishing this most heretical article.' M. Mitchell, went on:

> Not only many rank and filers, but many leaders seem to be possessed by some nebulous idea that under a Socialist state every man would receive sufficient in money or kind to maintain a wife and a fabulous

number of children, who would all dance round the maypole on summer evenings for his delectation.

How surprised they would be to learn that 'we preferred the Egypt of our present bondage to their Canaan. We have now, at least, a fighting chance, and those of us who possess a modicum of brain can hold our own in most walks of life which are open to both sexes.'

The following week (16 July) Rose E. Stokes thought there was not the slightest chance of socialism being 'man made' and that 'Miss Wilkinson fails to understand the I.L.P. view of Socialism *i.e.* that it will be attained as a result of evolution, and not come along suddenly in the night.' Then, on 23 July, A.L. Bacharach defended Wilkinson against 'Prometheus' who he thought was 'old-fashioned enough to believe with Ruskin that in the home lies "the woman's true place and power."'

"Ruskin"!'

He continued:

> Ellen Wilkinson, having stated the problem as it appears to her, has, with true feminism, asked for the equal co-operation of man and woman in facing and settling it, is met with the astoundingly anti-masculinist – not merely feminist – answer of 'That's your job!'

Bacharach did not, he went on 'pretend to understand women (any more than I understand men)', but unlike 'Prometheus' he ventured 'to believe and hope that I may never show such glorious ignorance of what Ellen Wilkinson, with the men and women who support her, is really demanding.'

A final comeuppance for 'Prometheus' came in the final July issue (30 July) less than a week before the outbreak of war. His letter began, fatally, by 'thanking A.L. Bacharach for her charming letter' and attacked women who 'waste their time writing silly letters and inventing such detestable phrases as male *things*,' only to be told in an editorial note which followed that, 'In justice to A.L. Bacarach we should point out that when the term 'male thing' was used, he was denoting his own sex.'

In the meantime (23 July) Wilkinson had returned to the pages of *Labour Leader.* She had not, her letter insisted, intended to suggest 'that we all should indulge in an orgy of prophesying as to the clothes we should wear and the work we should do, in the approved Edward Bellamy style.'[69]

> My whole contention is that the position of women in the general plan has not been thought out, is being ignored at the present time. No one knows what to do or what they want to do with the mass of unskilled, underpaid, discontented woman labour which is on the market at the present time. No one knows what to do for the admittedly overworked mother of the working class house. When someone like 'Prometheus' blandly folds his hands, and gazing heavenward talks about the queen of the home, the modern girl who has seen these queens drudging after children and husband dare not trust herself to speak.

Attention equal to that concerned with 'men's industries' should be given to these issues by the Fabian Research Bureau. She complained that 'Mr Orage of the *New Age* can write a book to solve the social problem and calmly leave the women under the present wages system. It is this cool burking of the women's position that is making advanced women discontented with the Socialist thinking of to-day.'[70]

---

[69] Edward Bellamy, 1850-98, was an American socialist. Best known for his futuristic *Looking Backward* of 1888. William Morris's *News From Nowhere* was the latter's response to what he regarded as the ultra-technological state socialism portrayed and seemingly approved by Bellamy.

[70] Alfred Richard Orage, 1873-1934, edited the influential magazine *The New Age* from 1907 until 1922. He was one of the originators of guild socialism. The book referred to here by Wilkinson would have been *National Guilds. An Enquiry into the*

Meanwhile other 'rebels,' more potentially violent than even the most militant suffragettes were becoming again the centre of attention.

## Ulster and Home Rule

Gladstone had twice attempted to get legislation for devolution, or as it was called at the time 'Home Rule,' for Ireland through the British parliament but the issue had split his Liberal Party and on the second occasion he had been defeated by the unelected House of Lords.[71] After the two elections of 1910, Asquith found his administration dependent on Irish Nationalist votes. The Third Home Rule Bill was successfully passed in 1914 with the Lords prevented by the Parliament Act of 1911 which had limited its powers from again exercising a veto. Home Rule had been a demand of the British socialist movement since the earliest days of the SDF. However, Hyndman, who earlier in 1914 described himself, justifiably, as 'one of the oldest Home Rulers in Great Britain' had taken the view as early as 1886 that it might 'be necessary in order to avoid a conflict to establish a little local Parliament in Belfast, as well as in Dublin.'[72]

With both Irish nationalists and Ulster unionists forming paramilitary forces to ensure or contest the inclusion of the Ulster counties in the Home Rule settlement, the issue took on an extra dimension and urgency. The prominent Unionist lawyer and politician Sir Edward Carson's had signed the Ulster Covenant, which pledged

---

*Wage System and the Way Out* published earlier in 1914.

[71] The Home Rule Bill of 1886 was defeated in the House of Commons. The second, in 1893 was passed by the Commons but defeated in the House of Lords. In 1886 those Liberals opposed to Home Rule broke with Gladstone and – led by Lord Hartington and Joseph Chamberlain – formed the Liberal Unionist Party. They sided with the Conservatives over Home Rule and went on to form coalition governments with them from 1895 until 1905.

[72] *Justice,* 2 April 1914: 17 April 1886.

opposition to Home Rule 'by all means necessary.' This and the formation from local militia groups of the Ulster Volunteer Force (UVF) in January 1914 had ratcheted up the tension.[73]

The spring of 1914 had seen further worrying developments. In March in what became known as the 'Curragh Mutiny' a number of British army officers at the main military base in Ireland, fearing that they would be ordered to use force against the Ulster opponents of Home Rule, threatened to resign their commissions. Blatchford, who had spent many of his early years in the army in the 1870s, had taken a line that hardly added to his popularity in the wider socialist movement. In an article on 'The Honour of the British Army' (13 March) he had offered what he called his 'personal thoughts as a British citizen.' Like Hyndman, he reminded readers of his Home Rule credentials. He had supported it for 27 years 'because I believe in self-government.' But for the same reason he favoured self-government for Ulster.

The Liberal government had believed that Carson and his followers were bluffing, he said, but only armed force could overcome Ulster resistance and that was impossible 'because the British people would not stand for it.' On the same page of the *Clarion,* Jowett presented the issue very differently as 'A Military Victory. A defeat for Parliament.' But both he and Blatchford agreed on one of the implications of the Curragh incident. Blatchford noted the *Daily Telegraph's* view that the army saw its being used for political purposes as a 'slur on its honour.' Did this, he asked, apply equally to use of the army as blacklegs or strike breaking? Jowett saw the 'mutiny' as signalling that the

---

[73] Sir Edward Carson, 1854-1935, had, as a lawyer, played an important role in the 1890s in the downfall of Oscar Wilde, who he knew from their days at Trinity College, Dublin. He had acted as barrister for the Marquess of Queensbury in the action unwisely brought by the playwright for criminal libel. In 1910 Carson became leader of the Ulster Unionist Party, in 1911 he had been the first signatory of the Ulster Covenant, and in 1913 he formed the Ulster Volunteer Force to resist Home Rule. Later he would serve in Asquith's and Lloyd George's wartime governments.

'governing classes' were preparing to use the army in labour disputes independently of the elected government.

Hardly had the flames fanned by Curragh died down a little than the most widely publicised incident of UVF gun-running took place at Larne and other Northern Irish ports in April. A large quantity of weapons and ammunition from Germany was brought in with, apparently, Carson's support. The authorities failed to do anything to prevent it. After this, the Home Rule/Ulster issue retreated from the headlines – a least in the socialist press. But it came back in the second half of July with a loud bang.

Its retreat was only relative in any event. Hilda Thompson's comment in her 'Farce of English Justice' article about the suffragette trial in the Clarion on 17 July makes this clear.

I should like to say, too, that if three people are truly and fairly and lawfully convicted of the serious crimes attributed to them, of having in their possession explosives and other implements with criminal intention… and inciting and aiding and abetting other people to do likewise --- then I say that, according to that law which they have broken and which has convicted them, Sir Edward Carson and his followers should be also tried and convicted.

The 12th July, Orangeman's Day, celebrating the Battle of the Boyne and other late 17th-century victories over the Catholic James II, has been largely peaceful in the 21st since the peace process began but can still generate tension in Northern Ireland. Much trouble was anticipated in 1914 but 'Everything passed off quietly,' reported *Justice* four days later (16 July), under the headline 'The Anxious "Twelfth"'. That trouble was anticipated, the paper said, 'was clear from the attitude of the entire capitalist Press; and the army of special reporters, Press photographers and film operators dispatched to the province.'

The very quietness of the proceedings might be significant, said *Justice*. It suggested 'discipline and control which must not be lightly dismissed as of no moment.' The brief report concluded that there would be a contracting-out arrangement for 'the Protestant counties of Ulster.' If this brought 'even a temporary settlement of the Home Rule question it will be of advantage. Then we can get on with things that really matter.'

*Labour Leader* saw the situation very differently. On the same day (16 July) its 'Review of the Week' bracketed together 'Two Bad Proposals'. One was a Liberal proposal to 'reform' rather than to abolish the House of Lords. The other concerned Ulster. According to the *Leader* the 'Labour and Socialist movement of Ireland, Belfast equally with Dublin, is strongly opposed to the exclusion of Ulster on the ground, first, that it will divide the ranks of the working-class, and, second, that it will perpetuate the antagonism of Catholic and Protestant.'

The following week there was a new and highly controversial development which brought the whole Irish issue back to the forefront. In *Justice* (23 July) an editorial by Hyndman dealt with Home Rule – but it was 'Home Rule for India' rather than Ireland. But the front page of that paper did report George V's Buckingham Palace conference. This brought together Asquith, Lloyd George, Bonar Law, the opposition leader, together with Redmond, the Irish Nationalist parliamentary leader, Carson, and the deputy leaders of both Irish groups.[74] It would soon break up without any definite resolution of the issues involved in Home Rule. But in the meantime its very existence raised important constitutional issues in the view of *Justice*.

---

[74] Andrew Bonar Law, 1858-1923, was born in New Brunswick a few years before the formation of the Canadian Confederation. He came to Britain in 1870 and, after a very successful business career, was elected as a Conservative MP in 1900. He was leader of that party 1911-1921 and would be prime minister briefly between October 1922 and May 1923 after having served in both Asquith's and Lloyd George's wartime governments.

John Redmond, 1865-1918, was an MP from 1891 and led the Irish parliamentary party from 1900 until his death.

Whether the Cabinet are responsible for the Buckingham Palace Conference, or whether they have bowed to the personal 'command' of the King... they have driven another nail into the coffin of our so-called parliamentary government. No one can resent the introduction of the personal power of the monarch in legislative matters more than we Social-Democrats. But, after all, is it not a logical consequence of the gradual development of Cabinet domination? Parliament is becoming more and more a mere machine for registering the desires and designs of Ministers who happen to be in office.

Confidence in the House of Commons was now at a 'low ebb' among 'all intelligent people of no matter what opinion,' it claimed. But all was not necessarily lost.

The Parliamentary Labour Group in conjunction with the Labour Party outside and all genuine democrats and Socialist bodies, have therefore a golden opportunity. Let them take the initiative in summoning a great National Convention for the complete revision, reorganisation and democratisation of our whole effete and chaotic system of Parliamentary government.

It asked whether the Labour group in parliament had the 'vigour and imagination' to seize the opportunity. The demand in *Justice* for a national convention, with its echoes of Chartism went back to the early days of the SDF in the 1880s.

The critique of 'Cabinet government' was also an old SDF one, though now it was reinforced by Fred Jowett's campaign in the ILP and the Labour Party aimed at replacing the Cabinet with a committee system. Jowett had begun his lifelong campaign for this even before he became an MP in 1906. The 'Bradford Policy' of ignoring the effects on the Liberal government and voting always 'on the merits' of each issue was seen by him as the first instalment towards this larger end.[75] Jowett took every opportunity to promote his campaign for the committee system. His *Clarion* article of 13 March on the Curragh incident had ended with another plea for it as a way of restoring accountable parliamentary government.

In its 'Parliamentary Notes' the 23 July issue of *Justice* congratulated Labour MPs on 'their challenge of the King's intervention in party politics and of his removal of the National Council from St. Stephens to a hole-and-corner at Buckingham Palace.' Similar congratulations were also recorded that day in *Labour Leader*. The previous three elections had delivered majorities in support of Irish Home Rule, it noted. When, thanks to the Parliament Act, the Conservatives could no longer use the House of Lords to block the will of the electorate they turned to 'openly organised rebellion.' The Ulster representatives were 'actually the leaders of an armed rebellion.'

It asked readers to imagine that the government had brought in compulsory arbitration of industrial disputes and the union leaders had 'drilled and armed' the miners and railworkers to resist this. Would the King have held a conference at Buckingham Palace to seek a settlement?

> Of course not. The Government would have turned cannon on the Trade Union army and would have ordered the soldiers to shoot in the name of the King. But the example the Conservatives have set, the acquiescence of the Government in their rebellion, the success which has met its efforts, cannot fail to influence the working class.

The same day the *Leader* repeated its total opposition to the exclusion of Ulster on the grounds that it would divide and weaken the socialist and labour movement and help to perpetuate the 'wretched feud'

---

[75] For the critique of cabinet government and Jowett's campaign in the years up to 1914 see Barrow and Bullock, Chapter 10 and for Jowett's continuing campaign after the war see Ian Bullock, *Under Siege*, Chapter 1.

between Protestants and Catholics. It repeated the warning that it had given at the time of 'the revolt of army officers at the Curragh.' Labour, it predicted, would 'have to concern itself with the issue of the monarchy did not the King remain content with the role of harmless political obscurity which is his one justification.'

Hardie was even more outspoken on the role of George V in a piece headed 'Arrogance. A Word to the King.' The affair would, he said, show whether or not his 'prophecy of a General Election this year is going to be realised.' It was the 'most serious constitutional crisis since the days of the Stuarts.' The King had joined his influence with 'the forces that are working against and seeking to destroy the House of Commons and our constitutional forms of Parliamentary Government.' Liberals, Labour and Irish Nationalists were all in support of Home Rule with only the Tories objecting. So, 'the King in interfering can have no other object than to assist his friends the Tories.' He added:

> …we begin to see why the Royal crowd has been visiting Merthyr and many other industrial centres during the past two or three years. They desired to popularise themselves with the mob so that they can rivet the chains of their iron rule more firmly upon them. King George is not a statesman. He is not the pleasure-loving scapegrace which his father was before him, but, like his father, he is destitute of even ordinary ability. Born in the ranks of the working class his most likely fate would have been that of a street corner loafer.

Democracy·would accept the challenge, Hardie predicted, and 'Once more the Republican slogan will be heard in the land.'

What would turn out to be the final peacetime issues of *Justice* and *Labour Leader* came out on 30 July and of the *Clarion* the following day. In *Justice*, H. W. Lee devoted much of his editorial, 'Drifting into War', to the dangers posed by the Irish crisis, though, as we will see in the next chapter, he did have something to say also about the danger of a general European war as did the rest of the paper. Reiterating the call of the previous week for a 'genuine National Convention' Lee wrote:

The breakdown of Parliamentary government and the dominance of Cabinet rule are unquestionably leading up to a situation wherein people may welcome personal dictatorship whether monarchical or so-called republican.

He also noted that three people had been killed and large numbers injured in Dublin. A statement by the BSP executive followed his editorial. This made an 'indignant protest' against 'the shooting down of men, women and children in Dublin by soldiers of the Crown.' Stone throwing by a crowd did not justify such a response which was 'more outrageous and indefensible' given that the troops had just returned from attempting to prevent gun-running to the Irish Volunteers in the same week that 'the leaders of the successful gun-runners of the North of Ireland, Sir Edward Carson and Captain Craig, were being received by the King in Conference at Buckingham Palace with the full co-operation of the Government.'[76]

The *Clarion* the following day (31 July) was equally aghast at 'the murder of inoffensive women and children.' The Nationalists were simply following the example of the Ulster Loyalists in importing weapons. Thompson wrote:

...the previous day 5,000 Ulster rebels had marched through the main streets of Belfast with rifles and machine-guns, and the only interference by the official representatives of the British Government consisted of keeping the streets clear of traffic for the greater spectacular effectiveness of the warlike parade. On Sunday when the Dublin

---

[76] James Craig, 1871-1940, was Carson's deputy, He would be the first prime minister of Northern Ireland after the war. On 26 July the Irish Volunteers had successfully brought in a consignment of guns at Howth, Dublin. Like the weapons landed at Larne by the UVF earlier in the year these came from Germany. In the protests that followed the return of the troops after the Howth episode four were killed and 38 injured.

Nationalists attempted a precisely similar exhibition soldiers and police were drawn up in battle array to demand the surrender of their arms, and when the men resisted the crowd of volunteers and sightseers was indiscriminately fired upon, with the result that three persons were killed and eighty, including six children, were more or less seriously injured.

Although Thompson led his editorial page with the outbreak of war in the Balkans and the dangers it entailed, he devoted much of it to aspects of the Home Rule crisis. Belfast, he claimed, paid half the taxes and two-thirds of customs receipts for the whole of Ireland which 'is why Mr. Redmond wants Belfast and that is why Belfast revolts.' Belfast capitalists had 'raised a private army of their own in revolt against the State.' Instead, Thompson wanted 'the formation of a Citizens' Army to defend the interests of all the people.' It would 'sweep away this chaos of private war and establish a new peace.'

The main blame for what had happened lay, he insisted, with the government.

> The real cause of the delays and difficulties exasperating the hopes of Irish Nationalists was not the King, nor the Queen, nor King Carson's army, nor had even the Curragh officers but the blundering incapable Government, whose muddling and cowardice invested these elements with the power of intervention. Had the Government been true to its electoral mandate, there could have been no Ulster rebels, no recalcitrant officers, and no Royal interference.

The government's responsibility and its failures went far beyond the Ulster/Home Rule crisis.

> The Liberal Government has established the reign of Anarchy. The militant Suffragettes, King Carson's rebels, the Curragh officers, the Nationalist volunteers, have all been allowed and encouraged to the smashing up of old-fashioned Law and Order.

He ended a section of the editorial 'Our Point of View' on 'Ministerial Responsibility' with an even more dismissive diatribe:

> Government? These forcible-feeding, women bullying, men funking, fight-shirkers, are not brave enough or strong enough to govern a rabbit-hutch.

He was also sceptical about Labour's response; 'the Parliamentary Labour Party put on their sternest Hampden frowns and beneath their clenched teeth muttered dire treasons; but their sudden attack of severe Constitutionalism and symptoms of incipient Republicanism did not at the moment incite us to build barricades.' *Labour Leader* was equally appalled by 'The Outrage of Dublin:'

> The undeniable truth is that the Government has acquiesced in the importation and display of arms by the Ulster 'rebels,' but has treated similar action by the Nationalist 'volunteers' with the utmost rigour.

The previous week (23 July) the *Leader* had seemed surprised by the way the crisis had developed. The Conservative Party was now 'the champion of unconstitutional rebellion;' the Liberal Party had 'acquiesced in unconstitutional rebellion; the Labour Party to-day stands alone as the advocate of constitutionalism. Such surprises does the whirligig of time bring in its train!' Tragically, that whirligig was about to bring a most tragic surprise.

# CHAPTER 3

# The Unexpected Outbreak of War

## The Worst of Surprises

> The war of 1914 came suddenly. Ten days before it started I spoke at Oldham and my audience thought I was an hysterical scaremonger when I said that we were near war.

So begins chapter six of Brockway's *Inside the Left* published in the midst of another war in 1942. He goes on to say that 'Irishmen in the crowd shouted, "talk about Ireland, not Serbia."'[77]

But perhaps the most unexpected, even rather shocking, evidence of how unprepared for the outbreak of war most people in Britain, including those on the Left, were appeared on the front page of the first wartime *Clarion* on 7 August. It was by Hilda Thompson with the title 'A Spoilt Holiday.' It began: 'We had intended making a tour of the Harz Mountains, partly on foot, partly by train; and our intention had been to stay at least a month.' It is not quite clear who exactly the 'we' were, apart from Hilda herself, but they had left Liverpool Street station late on Thursday 30 July and arrived in Hannover at about 1.30 the following day. While having a meal in a café they became aware of people excitedly reading 'printed bills' that were being given out in the street.

---

[77] Fenner Brockway, *Inside the Left. Thirty Years of Platform, Press, Prison and Parliament*, London: Allen and Unwin, 1942, 43.

These, it quickly became apparent, announced 'the Kaiser's decree for the immediate mobilisation of the army.' Still undeterred, they bought train tickets for Hildesheim and continued their journey, though at the station 'the disorganisation caused by war was already felt.' Sometime after midday the next day, Saturday, 1 August, they were advised by the landlord of the place where they were staying to return home immediately. He was himself 'under marching orders.' Reluctantly agreeing, they took a train back to the Hook of Holland hearing *en route* that Germany had declared war on Russia. They worried that they might be marooned in Germany with trains unable to cross the border into the Netherlands. But in spite of such fears they reached home safely. Of their attitude at the start of their aborted journey Hilda Thompson wrote, 'There were rumours of war, as everyone knew but no one in England had taken the matter seriously, and we felt that the excitement would add to the pleasure of our trip.'

A fortnight previously Brockway's editorial 'Review of the Week' on the front page of the *Labour Leader* on 23 July began with 'The Labour Party and Constitutional Crisis.' No doubt Brockway *did* warn of the war danger at Oldham – the meeting would have taken place after the ILP paper was being printed – but his editorial that week was almost entirely devoted to aspects of the Ulster and Home Rule situation with only one paragraph dealing with another subject; not the war but 'Miners' Lives at 1s Each.' So, in spite of his later recollection, his own appreciation of the danger of war must have come only a little sooner than that of his sceptical Oldham audience. The second page of the 'Review' dealt exclusively with domestic issues except for a paragraph on 'Another Revolution in Russia!' which ended with the prediction that 'The day of reckoning cannot long be delayed.' This all reinforces Brockway's point about the unexpected outbreak of war, as do, I hope, the previous two chapters which demonstrate that anticipation of the coming disaster was very low down on the list of socialist preoccupations in July 1914.

In spite of Hyndman's and Blatchford's fears about the 'German menace,' so controversial in socialist circles, *Justice* and the *Clarion* were no more prescient than the *Labour Leader*. As we have seen, the front page of *Justice* on 23 July was mainly concerned with the 'King's conference' on Ulster and the issue of Irish Home Rule, while the editorial by Hyndman returned to one of his long-established themes and demanded 'Home Rule for India.' The *Clarion,* the following day, was equally oblivious to the rapidly developing crisis. Its front page was devoted, as we saw in Chapter 1, to Blatchford's 'A Few Words on European Civilisation' which contained no hint that the war he had long been warning against might be about to break out and threaten to destroy that very civilisation.

## War in the Balkans

Only at the very end of July, with the UK declaration of war just days away, did the picture change. Austria-Hungary had declared war on Serbia on 28 July. The front page of *Justice* had big headlines on 30 July: 'WAR! Austria attacks Servia. Will Europe be Embroiled? Socialist Manifestos.' The focus was firmly on socialist efforts to avoid the war spreading. The International Socialist Bureau (ISB) would meet in Brussels the following week it reported. Meanwhile the SPD had held 27 peace meetings in Berlin alone. The manifestos of the socialist parties of the countries most likely to be drawn into the war were, of course, unanimous that armed conflict should be avoided at all costs. The Austrian – mainly German-speaking – parliamentary deputies of the *Sozialdemokratische Arbeiterpartei Österreichs* (SDAPÖ), repudiated all responsibility for any war while the SPD called on the German government to restrain Austria-Hungary. This was supported by the French socialist party, which in turn called on its own government to restrain Russia to prevent it seeking 'a pretext for aggressive operations under cover of protecting the influence of the Slavs.'

The BSP Executive statement denounced the Austrian-Hungarian ultimatum to Serbia and said that it 'heartily congratulates the Social-Democrats of Vienna, Berlin and Paris' as well as other parties that were trying to defend the peace. But inside the paper was a warning against the more exalted hopes of the international movement.

Writing on 'The French Socialists and the General Strike Against the War,' A.S. Headingley explained that the 'Keir Hardie Vaillant-amendment,'[78] at the coming Vienna International would seek to 'declare that a general strike would be especially effective in the prevention of war.' Many, especially younger members of the French party who 'lean towards Syndicalism and Anarchism,' considered the general strike to be 'a panacea for all evils,' he wrote. But the outbreak of war was, Headingley argued, the worst possible time to attempt to call a strike: 'Let us recall "Mafeking" day!'[79]

He praised Jean Jaurès 'magnificent speech' at the congress of the French party but he concluded that a general strike against war was not practical. The congress's resolution was 'but a sop thrown out to

---

[78] Édouard Vaillant, 1840-1915, had combined with Hardie to move an amendment advocating a general strike to prevent war at the Copenhagen Congress of the Socialist International in 1910. It was decisively rejected by the commission in charge of drafting motions for the relevant part of the agenda but Vandervelde persuaded the congress to refer it to the ISB for further consideration. The ISB was to report on the amendment at the ill-fated Vienna Congress. Following the murder of Jaurès, and the outbreak of war, like most French socialists, Vaillant rallied to the *union sacré* – the political truce.

[79] A. S. Headingley was the author of an article for *The British Socialist*, the BSP journal, on the Balkan War published just after the end of the 1913 conflict. (*The British Socialist*, Vol. 2, No. 5, May 15, 1913, 193-202. www.marxists.org/history/etol/revhist/otherdox/balk/headingley.htm.) Arguing for a socialist policy he concluded: 'We have to prove our superior statesmanship before we can expect communities to entrust us with the reins of government.'

The British garrison in Mafeking was under siege for seven months from the beginning of the South African War of 1899-1902. When the siege was at last lifted in May 1900 it triggered wild rejoicing in Britain – which was viewed with great distaste on the Left.

quieten a brood of half-fledged revolutionaries who may develop into Socialists by-and-by. But what a waste of time for the real Socialists, particularly at a moment when a European war threatens the world's civilisation.'[80]

*Labour Leader* (30 July) had the same fears about the spread of the war. There was still hope that the war might be localised. But if Germany and Russia intervened then 'a general European war would be well-nigh inevitable.' Its 'Review of the Week' thought that though the Balkan conflict might 'amount to little more than a punitive expedition, it may burst into a conflagration sweeping over the entire Continent of Europe.' Like *Justice,* it reported anti-war protests in Austria, France, Italy and Germany. 60,000 had attended meetings in Berlin the previous Tuesday (28 July).

## Stop the War!

*Labour Leader's* emphasis, in this final peacetime issue, was on what must be done at home to prevent the impending disaster. The paper's front page had a mourning-like black box around it announcing in large upper-case letters 'THE WAR MUST BE STOPPED. AND WE MUST STOP IT.'

It was more sanguine than *Justice* – or certainly than Headingley's article – about the prospect of preventing the spread of the conflict. Brockway urged that 'if the Socialist and Labour movement of Europe strikes immediately and strongly, it can, at least, prevent the

---

[80] Jean Jaurès, 1859-1914, taught at the University of Toulouse after graduating from the École Normal Supérieure with a degree in philosophy, to which he later added a doctorate. He was an influential historian of the French Revolution, developing a Marxist interpretation. Beginning as a Republican, he had become a Socialist member of parliament and in 1904 was one of the founders of *L'Humanité*. The following year he had played an important role in the unification of the socialist groupings.

extension of the war.' There were, he said, encouraging precedents.

When Germany, France and Britain were on the verge of war in 1911, one of the most potent factors in preventing the outbreak of hostilities was the simultaneous campaign conducted by the Labour and Socialist movement in the principal cities of each of the three countries...

Now a similar campaign was needed.

There was, he concluded, 'one force which may prove too strong even for the conspiracy of Governments – the international Socialist and Labour movement.' Keir Hardie, for the Labour Party, Bruce Glasier for the ILP, and Dan Irving for the BSP were to attend the ISB meeting in Brussels. In the *Leader,* more than in the case of *Justice,* there was a particular emphasis on at least keeping *Britain* out of the war; 'let the protest of the British Labour and Socialist movement be so strong, in volume and in passion, that the Government will not be able to withstand its demand for peace.'

Thompson's *Clarion* 'Our Point of View' editorial on 31 July started with an emphatic 'War!' His analysis of the conflict in the Balkans was similar to that of Rosalind Travers Hyndman in the articles quoted in Chapter One. Like her, he emphasised 'racial' conflict in the Balkans. Grey's 'well-meant efforts' to preserve the peace had, unhappily, failed.

It is a woeful business, and not one to be thought of without shuddering. But despite Mr. Norman Angell's ingenious proofs of war's total folly and futility, it is hard to see how this calamity was to be avoided. Some international conflicts are caused, truly enough, by financial greed, as ours was in South Africa; some by national ambitions and lust of dominance, as Russia's war against Japan. But others are impelled by irresistible elemental forces, by irreconcilable racial antagonisms as wild and conscienceless as Nature's cruel struggle for the survival of the fittest.

Thompson foresaw the creation of 'a mighty Slav empire.' He was well aware of the danger that the attack on Serbia would trigger general war. Like Headingley in *Justice* he had no faith in the possibility of preventing war by trade union or socialist action.

> If Russia mobilises, Germany, we are told, will attack France; if France is attacked, we are pledged to her defence. To this position we have been brought by the cordial understandings and alliances of two great civilised nations, with the Muscovite Caliban - that our sons may have to die for the honour and glory of Servian assassins. The thought is maddening, yet the contingency may come; and though every man of us abhors the possibility, we are hopelessly impotent to prevent it. Socialists, Syndicalists and Trade Unionists will protest, but their just anger will rage in vain against the iron ring of the capitalistic big legions.

*Justice* did not share Thompson's indulgence towards Grey's 'well-meant efforts.' On 30 July it reported that the previous weekend (24/25 July) the Foreign Office had asked 'the most influential papers' to 'abstain from ventilating in their columns the view that this country was not under any obligation, written or unwritten, to assist her friends of the Triple Entente if it should come to a European war.' It suspected that this was motivated by the desire to keep the public in the dark so the government could 'spring upon it a warlike policy when it suits their purposes.'

*Justice* noted that the 'Imperial Harmsworth Press,' led by the *Times,* was already proclaiming 'the readiness and the determination of this country to see her friends through if the worst comes to the worst.' It hoped that the workers would not be misled and that they would 'take what measures they can in advance to oppose all participation of this country in any war.' Like *Labour Leader* the previous week, *Justice* also optimistically looked forward 'Towards a Revolution in Russia.'

Of the three socialist weeklies the *Clarion* of the 31 July was the last to appear in peacetime – peacetime that is as far as Britain was concerned; Belgrade was already under bombardment on 29 July. Rather strangely, though Thompson had much to say about the war already raging in the Balkans, the last pre-war *Clarion* devoted its front page to Joseph McCabe's book on Shaw and an article by its author on 'Shavian Shibboleths.' Even at this late stage and even for Thompson, soon to become an unequivocal supporter of Britain's participation in the conflict, it was difficult to realise that that Britain was on the verge of war. That evening Jean Jaurès was shot and killed at the *Le Croissant* café by a French nationalist.[81]

## The Murder of Jaurès

By the time the next editions of the papers came out on 6 and 7 August Britain was at war. War had been declared on Tuesday 4 August and by the time the *Clarion* was published that Friday the British Expeditionary Force was arriving in France. The appalling breakdown of peace and its implications naturally predominated, but all three papers also gave space to the shocking murder in Paris with large photos of the victim. Jaurès already occupied a position of enormous prestige throughout the international socialist movement. His murder on the eve of war not only enhanced his iconic standing but also enabled his name to be invoked to justify radically opposed positions on the war.

*Labour Leader* devoted most of a page to an appreciation of Jaurès by W.C. Anderson. It included a photo of the French socialist with the title 'Jean Jaurès – Our Lost Leader.' *Justice* reported that it had sent a telegram of condolence to *Humanité*, the socialist paper founded and edited by Jaurès. It framed its appreciation, written by

---

[81] Since 2011 the renovated café has been called the *Taverne du Croissant*. The plaque commemorating Jaurès, placed there in 1923 by *La Ligue des Droits de l'Homme*, remains in place.

Hyndman, with black borders of mourning. The *Clarion* did likewise with a poem on its front page – 'Jean Jaurès July 31 1914' by John Helston. This had also appeared in *Justice* the previous day.[82] The *Clarion* also included an appreciation of Jaurès' work by Thompson, who having lived as a child in Paris during the Commune and been inspired by the ex-Communard, Jean Allemane in the 1890s, was well-acquainted with the French Left.[83]

All the tributes stressed Jaurès' great powers of oratory, his honesty, dedication to the socialist cause, and statesmanship. Hyndman and Anderson presented him as an advocate and fighter for peace. As the former put it in *Justice*, Jaurès was 'emphatically a man of peace' whose 'removal at such a crisis is a disaster to civilisation.' Hyndman said he agreed with what had been said by one of the other speakers from 'my platform in Trafalgar Square last Sunday' referring to the large demonstration for peace that had taken place on 2 August. The unnamed speaker had said: 'Had every monarch in Europe been assassinated the total injury to the world at large would have been ridiculously insignificant compared with the

---

[82] Helston would later write a poem commemorating the death of Kitchener in 1916. It appeared later, in August 1917, in *A Treasury of War Poetry. British and American Poems of the World War 1914-17* published in Boston, and introduced and edited by George Herbert Clarke.

[83] The Paris Commune of March to May 1871 began when the radical Left took control of the city during the siege by the Prussian Army in the later phases of the Franco-Prussian war. It had ended in the tragic *semaine sanglante*, or 'bloody week', when a deal between the Prussians and the new Third Republic allowed its violent suppression by French troops. The Commune was later described by Marx as having at least some of the characteristics of 'the dictatorship of the proletariat.' Subsequently it was widely seen on the Left as an inspiring example of what the 'revolution' might look like and celebrated every year as a sort of socialist Easter.

Jean Allemane, 1843-1935, who would become a key figure in French socialism was a communard subsequently imprisoned in New Caledonia for most of the 1870s. For Alex Thompson's relationship with him and his effect on *Clarion* thinking see Ian Bullock and Siân Reynolds 'Direct Legislation and Socialism. How British and French Socialists viewed the Referendum in the 1890s' in *History Workshop Journal* 24 Autumn 1987, and Logie Barrow and Ian Bullock, *Democratic Ideas and British Socialism, 1880-1914*, CUP, 1996, 50-51.

death of Jaurès.' For Anderson, he had joined 'our great dead, names like Marx, Lassalle, Engels, Owen, Liebknecht, Bebel, Morris.'

But in the *Clarion* Thompson's stress was quite different. He insisted that the 'madman' who had killed Jaurès believing him to be 'an anti-patriot and an enemy of France' could hardly have got it more wrong. Describing Jaurès as a 'great Socialist patriot' he quoted a long passage from the Frenchman's 1910 book *La Nouvelle Armée* (*The New Army*), generally regarded as his most important work. Thompson insisted that patriotism was not, according to Jaurès 'an exhausted idea.' On the contrary the 'doctrine of abdication and national servitude' was something which 'the proletariat' would never consent to. He quoted the following passage.

> To revolt against the despotism of Kings, against the tyranny of Capitalism, and yet passively to submit to the yoke of conquest, the dominance of a foreign militarism, would be a contradiction so puerile and miserable that it would be swept away at the first alert by all the forces of instinct and reason... Those Frenchmen, if there still are any, who say that it is indifferent to them whether they live under the rule of German militarism or French militarism commit a solecism which baffles refutation by its own absurdity.

Thompson then included another quotation from Jaurès, this time denying that in his younger days he had been 'a Conservative and had only been converted to Socialism in his later life,' as had been asserted in various newspaper articles. Then, as if to make sure that no one had missed the main point he was making, he ended his appreciation of Jaurès as follows:

> It may be suggestive here to note that Jaurès friend, Gustave Hervé, the famous anti-militarist agitator, who has suffered persecution and imprisonment for his campaign against jingo patriotism, has eagerly petitioned the Minister of War to be sent, despite his forty-four years and failing sight, with the first regiment bound for the frontier. Also the

great Syndicalist association, the Confédération Générale du Travail have issued a proclamation calling on all Frenchmen to serve their Fatherland.[84]

This appeared on the same front page as the black-framed poem and Hilda Thompson's account of her 'spoilt holiday.' She added her own view of the attitude Germans at the end of her account.

The Germans do not want to fight, they say; but honour and prestige and national safety demand that Russia's movements shall be checkmated. What is more they guarantee the successful issue of their arms within one month of the commencement of hostilities – that is if one very important factor works in their favour, and this factor is the neutrality of England. They do not want to fight with England. If England keeps out, they say, they have no fears.

This *might* have been interpreted as advocacy of British neutrality, but anyone reading the piece on Jaurès on the same page could have little doubt what the *Clarion's* response to the war was going to be.

There was nothing similar in the obituary pieces on Jaurès in the other two papers. The only hint of a position at all resembling Thompson's came, in *Justice* (6 August) and, as one might expect, it came from Hyndman. Recalling Jaurès' opposition to the Moroccan takeover by France he commented that had the French government listened to him 'the relations of France to Germany would scarcely have resulted in war, and, if they had, a fine French army, which can be very ill-spared, would not now be locked up in North Africa.'

---

[84] The Confédération Générale du Travail (CGT) was – and is – a national trade union centre formed in 1895 by the merger of two earlier organisations. Like the BSP it would become divided during the 1914-18 war between 'nationalists' and 'internationalists' and after the war it became aligned with the French Communist Party, a relationship that continued until the 1990s.

**First reactions to Britain at war:** *Labour Leader*

Of our three papers, it was the contents of Brockway's *Labour Leader* that initially most consistently reflected the outbreak of war. All three papers, of course, gave the war their prime attention but more of the pages of the *Leader* of 6 August were taken up with the war than is the case with the others. True, towards the back of the *Labour Leader* were to be found reports from ILP branches and from 'Our Cycle Scouts' as well as an article by 'Casey' entitled 'Thumb Trouble. More Hints to Fiddlers.' But the proportion of what one might term continued peacetime content was significantly less than in either of the other two papers. And at least one of the branch reports was related to the war. The local ILP complained of being prevented by Blackburn town council from holding a peace demonstration in Corporation Park even though it had been fairly recently used for military parades on Empire Day (24 May).[85]

The front page was taken up with a black box with 'Down With the War!' in large bold letters at both its top and bottom. Workers had no quarrel with each other. It was a 'quarrel between the RULING classes of Europe.' A million Austrian and three million German trade unionists and socialists had protested against the war. The plea was for British workers not to desert them but to join with 'the organised workers of France and Russia in declaring for peace.' What, the appeal asked, had workers gained from 'the last war – the Boer war'. Twenty thousand workers had died on the battlefield and now £12 million each year was being raised by food taxes to pay retrospectively for that war. South African workers were worse off than before; 'The rich mineowners alone benefited.'

The second page of the paper was mainly taken up by the 'Review of the Week' and an 'Appeal to the I.L.P.' by W.C. Anderson. Above

---

[85] Empire Day had been instituted in 1904 and lasted until 1958 when it was replaced by Commonwealth Day.

this was a short extract from Ramsay MacDonald's speech in the House of Commons which rejected Grey's argument for war and concluded that 'this country ought to have remained neutral.'

The 'Review' accused the foreign secretary of throwing himself into the task of engineering 'national passion against Germany' along with 'the devil press 'of Harmsworth and Hulton.[86] It blamed the policy pursued by the British government for the previous ten years.

> The rivalry between Germany and Britain began because Britain refused to concur in her proposal that merchant vessels should be immune from attack in time of hostilities. That decision forced Germany to build a navy to defend her overseas trade, and from that moment the British Government has pursued a policy in opposition to Germany, scheming by secret treaties and understandings to isolate her among the powers of Europe, assisting Russia and France to become strong so that Germany might be correspondingly weakened.

Britain had supported Russia's 'most nefarious deeds' including the 'dismemberment of the Persian nation' and it was now 'plunged in war to enable Russia to realise her greedy ambitions on the Near East.'

Grey and Asquith had more than once denied that Britain had any treaty obligations to France. Yet the arrangement for the British navy to protect the northern and western coasts of France, while the latter concentrated on the Mediterranean meant that Britain would be dragged into any conflict. This agreement was 'forged without consultation with the British Parliament or the British people.'

As for Belgium, it had certainly 'a grievance against Germany' but 'her neutrality was almost certain to be outraged by one side or the

---

[86] Alfred Harmsworth, 1865-1922, had become Lord Northcliffe in 1914. His press empire included the *Daily Mail*, the *Daily Mirror* and the *Times*. Edward Hulton, 1869-1925, succeeded his father as the proprietor of a number of, initially, Manchester-based papers. By 1914 his portfolio included the national papers the *Daily Dispatch* and the *Daily Sketch*.

other.' Britain should have stood aside 'until the Powers of Europe had broken themselves against each other' and then insisted 'upon the maintenance of her independence' for Belgium. By denying Britain this 'noble part of peace-maker' the government had 'disgraced her in the eyes of generations of the future.'

The ILP, the *Leader* editorial went on, had acted 'boldly and nobly', holding meetings protesting against the war and demanding British neutrality in nearly every town and city. There were signs that 'the best forces in the nation' were on the party's side with Radicals and the Free Churches opposing the war, whose 'most damnable feature was the part played by 'the War Trust' which while appealing to the patriotism of the people ensured that 'the German navy will use gunpowder supplied by a firm connected with this same Trust to blow our warships to bits.'

It named three Cabinet members, Runciman,[87] Harcourt and Hobhouse, as shareholders while 'their colleagues in the war business' included six bishops, seven peers and eighteen MPs, several of whom were named. 'When the Jingo crowds hunger to tear the bodies of peace advocates to pieces,' it concluded, 'we wonder whether they will pay any attention to these gentlemen in high places who have helped to arm Germany, Austria and Italy.'

---

[87] Walter Runciman, 1870-1949, was a Liberal politician who had held office in the government first as President of the Board of Education then as President of the Board of Agriculture, and had just taken over the Board of Trade on John Burn's resignation the previous week. There was to be a sequel to the claim about Runciman. The following week, 13 August, *Labour Leader* carried a letter from Runciman denying that he was a shareholder in any armaments company. The paper accepted this and apologised. But the next issue (20 August) devoted its front page to another attack on the 'War Trust' headlined 'A Hellish Conspiracy. Germany and Austria armed by British firms.' Having thus continued the exposure by 'our investigator, Mr. Walton Newbold' of the 'machinations of the Armageddon Ring,' the *Leader* claimed that as regards Runciman 'the full facts are now before us.' Examination of the shareholder lists of armaments firms by 'Special Commissioner,' Newbold, revealed that the minister had held 100 preference shares in 'Cammell, Laird and Co. one of the principal firms in the Armaments Ring' until September 1913, his wife had held some until earlier in 1914 and that his father remained a shareholder.

Anderson's 'Appeal to the I.L.P.' urged 'Stand true, Comrades, whatever comes!' He condemned the 'devilish press' and Grey's speech full of 'anti-German prejudice.'

> The House of Commons was allowed to believe that the Germans were crossing Belgian territory, whereas not a single German soldier had then set foot on Belgian soil. Of Russia, the real villain of the piece, he had not a word to say.

Britain's 'plain duty' was to remain neutral and 'exercise friendly pressure for peace among the warring powers.' He invoked Jaurès in a very different way to the one that, as we have already seen, Thompson would do the next day. As regards treaty obligations, Anderson said, he agreed with Jaurès' statement made two days before his murder. 'Socialists recognise only one treaty – the treaty that binds them in love and peace and service to humanity.' Compromise was out of the question; 'We shall break this evil thing, or be broken ourselves.'

> Our conscript comrades in other countries have gone to the front with the cry on their lips and in their hearts; 'Down with the war.' They look to us to continue the war against war.

Another page of the *Labour Leader* was devoted to 'Labour's War on War' and the protests against British intervention in the war. Framed in the centre was the manifesto of the British Section of the International Socialist Bureau (ISB) in the form of 'An Appeal to the British Working Class.' It was signed by Keir Hardie and Arthur Henderson as chairman and secretary respectively. Clearly composed before Britain's entry into the war, it talked of 'steps being taken which may fling us all into the fray.' Like Anderson and Brockway's 'Review of the Week', it stressed the danger of being committed to 'cooperate with Russian despotism' whose success would be 'a curse to the world.'

Surrounding this manifesto was a report on 'London's Gigantic Protest'; 15,000 had attended the meeting in Trafalgar Square – the same one that Hyndman referred to in his appreciation of Jaurès. This had taken place on the previous Sunday, 2 August – two days before the British declaration of war. The *Manchester Guardian* was quoted as saying that it was 'the biggest Trafalgar Square demonstration held for years, bigger than any of the suffrage rallies.'

Keir Hardie's 'bold and inspiring speech' was fully reported. Paying tribute to Jaurès he 'then passed on to denounce the infamy of war in terms which one could well imagine Jaurès using.' Hardie urged Britain to follow the example of Italy and declare neutrality. He blamed the alliance with 'the foul Government of anti-democratic Russia' for the position Britain found itself in and concluded that 'The only class which can prevent war is the working class.'

Henderson moved the ISB British Section motion calling on the government to 'rigidly decline to engage in war' and try to bring about peace as soon as possible. Other speakers briefly mentioned included Lansbury who, once again, 'paid a noble tribute to M. Jaurès.'[88] There were also other, briefer reports of developments that had taken place that weekend including the formation of a 'National Labour Peace Emergency Committee' by trade unions and the TUC as well as the Labour Party.

Welsh miners were praised for refusing an Admiralty request for them to work two or three days of their holiday 'so that the Government might be well supplied in case war was declared.' The

---

[88] George Lansbury, 1869-1940, was at this time editor of the *Daily Herald* which like *Labour Leader* took an 'anti-war' position. He had joined the SDF in 1892 and unsuccessfully contested elections under its banner in 1895 and 1900. He left the SDF for the ILP in 1903. Elected as a Labour MP in the second general election of 1911, he resigned the following year to stand – unsuccessfully – on the single issue of women's suffrage – in the subsequent by-election. After the war he would be a leading Left wing figure as mayor of Poplar in what became known as 'Poplarism', serve in MacDonald's 1929-31 government and lead the Labour Party 1932-35, resigning when the party supported sanctions against Italy following the invasion of Ethiopia.

miners' executive committee statement demanded British neutrality, while at a Cumberland miners' demonstration Robert Smillie, the president of the MFGB, had supported a general European strike against the war. He 'would be glad to pledge the British miners to such a cause if they could get the others to do it.' The two middle pages of the *Leader* were devoted to a spread under the large heading 'The I.L.P. Leads the Way' and the sub-heading 'Great Demonstrations throughout the Country. Vast Audiences Carry Strong Resolutions.' A large number of meetings and protest demonstrations were reported from many parts of the country.

This was followed by an editorial by Keir Hardie. 'The angel of death with blood-stained wings is hovering over Europe,' this began. Many had hoped that Britain would stay out of the war unless 'our interests as a nation were threatened.' Grey was no doubt sincere in wanting to preserve the peace and working hard to accomplish it, 'but evidently at the back of his mind there was the thought all the time that if there was to be war, this country must take a hand in it.' Both of the reasons for British intervention given by Grey were 'so flimsy that it is difficult to give them a serious consideration,' insisted Hardie. Britain was 'no more bound to protect the coasts of France than the coasts of any other country.' In any case, Grey admitted that the German government had 'offered not to attack the coasts of France with its Navy provided Great Britain would continue its attitude of neutrality.' So, said Hardie, 'this one fact explodes all the contemptible sophistries.'

The same was true of the other reason given by Grey, the need to defend Belgium. 'The Government of that country, speaking officially, has made it clear that they don't ask for armed intervention.' Therefore, 'surely if a Government of a country repudiates in advance, as the Belgian Government has done, all desire for armed help, that should ensure other nations standing aloof unless they have some ulterior motive somewhere at the back of their mind.' Moreover, the German government had 'offered to sign a declaration that at the conclusion of the war they will retire altogether from Belgium even if they should appear nominally to violate the independence… of Belgium by sending troops through the country while the war lasts.' Grey's response 'was equivalent to throwing Germany's offer back in its face.' Grey had 'sounded a high note' on Belgium, yet only three years previously he had signed a solemn agreement with Russia to 'maintain the integrity of Persia' and then 'connived at the destruction of Persian liberties' when Russia invaded and 'shot or hanged' every Persian 'who showed any love for his country.'

Hardie blamed secret diplomacy, and particularly the Triple Entente for the war. It compelled 'freedom-loving France' to go to the aid of 'the most reactionary and blood-stained Government that probably the world has ever known.' He made a plea for the anti-war general strike. 'What a different situation we should have in Europe tonight had the Governments known that the moment they launched their ultimatums all work would cease.' It was still not too late. The 'great outstanding fact,' said Hardie, 'was the impotence of the moral and Labour forces of Europe.' The trade union and socialist movement had been 'contemptuously passed over.' Ten million socialist and Labour votes had been unable to prevent war He predicted that within a week either the British or the German navy would be destroyed. But the ILP should 'stand firm.' He ended with an injunction to 'Keep the Red Flag Flying.'

The *Labour Leader* reported foreign anti-war activities under the banner 'European Socialists Against the War' with smaller, but still quite large, headlines below: 'Governments Declare War: Organised Labour Never! German, French Austrian and Russian Workers Protest.' Inevitably, most of the material, and all of the actual reports of statements made and meetings held went back to the Austrian declaration of war with Serbia rather than the outbreak of the wider conflict. As the report concluded:

The lightning quickness with which recent events have overcome the world have unfortunately prevented the workers from exercising the power which they have secured by years of agitation and organisation.

But if we cannot prevent the outbreak of hostilities, we have still sufficient means to shorten the war and to lighten the lot of those who suffer most from the present calamity.

Another page was shared by 'Labour's Protest in Parliament' and Bruce Glasier's account of the meeting of the ISB.[89] Responding to the foreign secretary's speech on 3 August, MacDonald had challenged Grey and the government, 'both of whom he impeached before the Bar of History.'

> The war they were fostering was wrong and would be considered so by posterity. MacDonald analysed successfully the argument of the Grey speech; denied that this country or Belgium was in danger and poured contempt on the plea of 'National Honour,' the invariable cloak for every national crime.

Hardie had concentrated on 'the consequences rather than the causes of the war' predicting that 'unemployment would spread and, lacking wages, the poor man or woman would be robbed by the manipulator of the various food rings.' A bill to 'help the bankers' had been rushed through parliament: 'Where was the Bill to help the workers?'

The meeting of the ISB had taken place in Brussels on Wednesday 29 July. Already, said Bruce Glasier, that now seemed a very long time ago.

---

[89] John Bruce Glasier, 1859-1920, was the most prominent member of the ILP of this period never to be an MP. He had edited *Labour Leader* before Brockway and would again, briefly, after it became impossible for the latter to continue due to his imprisonments resulting from his resistance to conscription. But Glasier was seriously ill with cancer and his wife, Katharine Bruce Glasier, 1867-1950, soon took over as editor. She had been and would remain a major ILP activist until disaffiliation and for Labour for the rest of her life.

Then we were still living in the twentieth century, as we knew it; to-day we live in the midst of events that might belong to the end of an epoch during which humanity and civilisation had undergone an affrightening change.

The ISB representatives had all had lunch together.

That was our last breaking of bread and drinking of wine with Jean Jaurès. It was the last supper of the International before the crucifixion of our cause by the armies of Europe. It, also, shall rise again!

The resolutions passed at the ISB meeting – to transfer the meeting of the International from Vienna to Paris and to encourage anti-war protests – were quickly overtaken by events. The report ended, 'Down with War!' Long Live the International!' An article by Harry Snell, 'Patriotism that Pays. The War-Mongers Exposed' praised *The War Traders*, a 'shilling manual' by G.H. Perris published by the National Peace Council.[90] Quoting Perris on the co-operation of the ostensible rivals, the Harvey and Whitbread companies, in supplying the admiralty with armour plate, Snell noted that 'the share lists of these armour-plate companies are infested with the names of the high and mighty souls who decorate the benches on both sides of the Houses of Parliament.'

## First reactions: Justice

To a rather greater extent than in the case of the *Labour Leader,* peacetime concerns, both serious and less so, were also to be found

---

[90] G. H. (George Herbert) Perris, 1866-1920, was a prolific writer who had published on a number of subjects ranging from Tolstoy to British foreign policy. In 1914, apart from *The War Traders,* he published *The Industrial History of Modern Britain.* During the war and immediate post-war years he wrote *The Campaign of 1914 in France and Belgium* and *The Battle of the Marne.*

in the issue of *Justice* which came out on the same day (6 August) though naturally war-related material dominated. Among the 'peacetime' content was a piece called 'It Can't Be Done, A History of Impossibilities' which had a – very short – first chapter headed 'Stone Age'. There was an article entitled 'On Socialists' Bad Manners'. There were the regular reviews in 'The Bookshop', and, on an issue touched on in the previous chapter, John Maclean's report on 'The Scottish Coal Crisis'. [91] Only two letters were included that week; neither related to either the threat or the actuality of war.

The front page on 6 August was lined in mourning black with the upper-case headline 'THE WAR: SOCIALIST EFFORTS FOR PEACE'. There had not been in Germany 'a single town of any importance where the workers did not turn out in their thousands and tens of thousands,' it reported. Closer to home, its estimate of 30,000 those attending the ILP/BSP peace demonstration in Trafalgar Square the previous Sunday was twice as high as *Labour Leader's*. The meeting had expressed 'deepest detestation of the international war' that threatened and protested against 'any step that may be taken to support Russia, either directly or indirectly, in consequence of any understanding with France.' Like the *Leader* it included the Hardie/Henderson statement of the British ISB contingent.

But unlike *Labour Leader* it also included the appeal of the Belgian Socialist Labour Party's general council which called for its members

---

[91] John Maclean, 1879-1923, was a Glasgow teacher and, at this time, a BSP activist. He was heavily involved in Marxist controversy and education. Later he would become one of the leading figures in 'Red Clydeside', serve prison sentences for anti-war activities, and be appointed by the Bolsheviks as the soviet consul for Scotland. He did not, however, join the Communist Party when it was formed in 1920. Maclean's daughter, Nan Milton, played the major part in preserving and republishing his writings, founding the John Maclean Society and writing a biography *John Maclean*, published by Pluto in 1973. Walter Kendall devoted Chapter 17 of *The Revolutionary Movement in Britain* to Maclean's relationship with the CPGB. Earlier in the book (89), he describes Maclean's paper the *Vanguard*, as 'the first organ of an anti-war, anti-Hyndmanite opposition within the party' which 'undoubtedly set the pace for the movement which eventually broke the power of the old guard.'

to 'direct efforts to stopping the invasion of our territory.' By doing so, and 'in defending the neutrality and even the existence of our country against militarist barbarians we shall be conscious of serving the cause of democracy and the political liberties of Europe,' the statement concluded. In its own statement the BSP executive protested against the suggested adjournment of Parliament which offered the 'only possibility of obtaining reliable information as to this country's commitments' and the opportunity to 'bring pressure to bear in favour of peace.' The party would be represented at the Labour Peace Conference by Hyndman, Victor Fisher, and Inkpin.[92]

With the declaration of war neutrality was now out of the question, said *Justice,* and maintaining the supply of food must become the most important question. There were 'rings being formed to control and force up food prices.' The government must take all necessary steps to safeguard food supplies and 'frustrate the grossly unjust and unpatriotic action of these persons.'

The theme of 'War and Food' was taken up in H. W. Lee's editorial, which like the front page was lined in black. Lee began:

> Treaties, alliances, ententes, and secret diplomacy, in their efforts to preserve the 'balance of power' in Europe have done their work. The majority of the nations of Europe are plunged into a war which will far exceed the dimensions of the Napoleonic of a century and more ago, though the very devilishness of modern armaments may lessen its duration.

---

[92] (Frederick) Victor Fisher, 1870-1954, was a journalist and active member of the SDF/BSP. His 'pro-war' views would lead him to become one of the founders of the British Workers' League in 1916. In the 1920s he joined the Conservative Party and was a leader of its Conservative Workers' Union.

Albert Inkpin, 1884-1944, had been assistant secretary of the SDF and succeeded H. W. Lee after Quelch's death when Lee took over the editorship of *Justice.* A conscientious objector during the 1914-18 war, he would later be secretary of the Communist Party of Great Britain (CPGB) 1920-1929. Walter Kendall, in a footnote on 336 of *The Revolutionary Movement in Britain,* describes him as 'An honest and able administrative worker but not a political figure.'

Grey's 'lawyer like dexterity' in insisting that Britain had no international commitments meant that the people had 'been driven into war by secret "diplomacy."'

Meanwhile, the government had taken no steps to ensure food supplies. But Lee looked forward to better times.

> For our turn will come when the war is over and the 'balance of power in Europe is so completely upset and 'alliances' and 'ententes' broken that there will be an opportunity for a general democratic understanding of the peoples themselves. Such an understanding between the people of France, Germany and Great Britain will be a solid guarantee for the peace of Europe.

*Justice*, said Lee, had 'never been a peace at any price journal.' But, he insisted that 'The nation should never be committed to war on secret agreements and private understandings.' As noted in the introduction, ever since the earliest days of the SDF the Social-Democrat programme had demanded 'the people to decide on Peace or War.' This was now recalled. 'The least that could have been done,' said Lee, 'was to take a poll of our entire population as to whether they were ready to go into this terrible business without any adequate preparation, and without any knowledge whatever as to what was being done in their name.'

## First reactions: The Clarion

Rather oddly, given that the paper's editor in chief had warned of the 'German menace' for some years, the *Clarion* – which as usual came out a day later than *Justice* and the *Leader* (7 August) – showed the most sign of being taken by surprise by the outbreak of war, though this did not prevent a decisive response to it. Regular features such as

Winifred Blatchford's 'In the Library', Hilda Thompson's theatrically-oriented 'The Passing Show' and the column 'For Children', signed 'Dorothea', appeared as usual, as did an article on 'Education and Freedom', a large batch of reports from cycling clubs, vocal unions, Clarion scouts and the Clarion Fellowship as well as Tom Groom's 'Cyclorama'.[93] Suthers continued his attack on 'The Single Tax Delusion'. The sixteen letters in the 'Clarion Cockpit' covered many of the topics we have seen preoccupying the paper during July including the Darwin versus Butler controversy and Blatchford's contribution to socialism. But not one dealt with a directly war-related issue. Perhaps the advertisements for Blatchford's *My Life in the Army* reflected the situation better.

Apart from the Jaurès poem and Hilda Thompson's account of the spoilt holiday the front page, somewhat oddly, was given over to a leading article by Frederick Temple on 'The Effect of War Upon Credit'. He asked, 'Why is this the first time that any Labour or Socialist paper has ever opened its columns to a brief examination of the subject?' Temple was the author of *Interest, Gold and Banking, A Discourse on Democratic Finance* which was also advertised in *Justice*.

The speed with which everyone was overtaken by events is once more evident in F. W. Jowett's *Clarion* article on 'The Fruits of Secret Diplomacy', which began: 'Secret Diplomacy has done its work. Nothing short of a miracle will save us now. Before the words I now write appear in print Great Britain will, if there is no miracle, be at war.' Jowett repeated the claim made in the previous day's *Leader* that Germany could have been persuaded, in exchange for British neutrality, to give an undertaking not to make naval attacks on north and west coasts of France, and possibly, also, to respect Belgian neutrality too. Belgium, he insisted, had asked only for 'diplomatic support' and treaty obligations did not commit Britain to 'armed

---

[93] The Birmingham-based Tom Groom had written an account of a cycle tour he had led in 1894. This led to the formation of the National Clarion Cycling Club which still, in the 21st century, awards a 'Tom Groom trophy' at its Easter Meets.

intervention.'

Blatchford's own contribution was 'The Drums of Armageddon'. Like Jowett's article, this had been written before war was declared. Blatchford predicted that by the time the paper appeared 'every CLARION reader will know more than I know now.' He had lived the whole of the previous week, he told readers, 'in a kind of waking nightmare.' In Sussex he had seen sentries posted on Newhaven Quay but 'the few English women and men we met seemed so marvellously unconscious of the gathering storm.' The regatta in Rye had seemed to generate greater interest.

Yet there was no escaping.

> The drums of Armageddon are coming nearer, rolling louder. The men are marching steadily to slaughter and death. Do the German people want to fight the French? Do the French people want to fight the Germans? Do the Russian peasants want to fight? Do the British people want to fight? Have any of these peoples a quarrel with any other? No!

He continued in this vein for much of the editorial. Would it always be the case that 'when our bloodthirsty, decadent half idiotic masters set the drums of Armageddon rolling we must march and slay?'

But, as with Thompson's article on the same page and the latter's appreciation of Jaurès, it was clear that the *Clarion* was not going to follow the lead of *Labour Leader* in opposing British intervention in the war.

> In the midst of this devilish tragedy as I can see clearly enough and so can many others, there are two powers against whom no charge of blood-guiltiness or violent threats can be brought, and those two countries are Britain and France. And they are both democracies. I have said before, and said it many times, that it behoves those two democracies to stand together and that while they stand together no power on earth can break them.

He added, 'I hope and trust our people will be true to the French in this crisis.' Having contemplated writing the article 'with much anxiety' and having never before 'approached a subject with so overpowering a sense of responsibility,' Blatchford concluded, that he regarded 'the loyal and firm alliance of the French and the British as the greatest safeguard of peace and democracy in Europe.'

At the time Blatchford wrote war had broken out between Germany and France, the Germans had 'threatened the French frontier' but had not invaded. There had been no fighting. He continued:

Perhaps it is yet possible to prevent the tragedy? Perhaps if our Government stands firm and at the same time offers to Russia and to Germany the mediation of America, of Italy, of Britain, we may come through this awful trial without disaster or dishonour.

Blatchford ended by urging the British government to 'use all means possible to keep the peace of Europe' which, he argued, could succeed only if it made it 'unmistakably plain' that 'the mutual interest and friendship of the British and the French are a solid reality that cannot be shaken by bluster nor broken by the sword.'

Alex Thompson's article, 'War!' was written after the declaration of war. Like Blatchford, he recounted at some length how 'The dread of this awful contingency has appalled and paralysed my faculties for a week.' He recalled the Franco-Prussian War of 1870-71 and the suppression of the Paris Commune during 'Bloody Week' which he had experienced as a child in Paris. 'Forty four years ago my youthful mind received impressions of scenes so deeply grievous and ghastly' that he could not now 'muster philosophic composure to face the prospect of the tale's repetition.' Yet, he concluded, 'It had to be. This war could not be averted.'

It was not a war to defend Serbia; 'Britain would not fire a pea-shooter or kill a cat in defence of Servia.' The war was, as Blatchford had been warning for the last decade, 'premeditated and prearranged.'

It is a war for the domination of Europe by the German War Lords, for the annexation of the Dutch, Danish and Belgium seaboard, and the eventual smash of the British colonial Empire.

Thompson turned to the 'infamous' German 'treachery' in relation to Belgium, quoting the statement made just twelve hours before Germany's ultimatum to that country by the German minister in Brussels which he italicised for emphasis; *'German armies will not cross Belgian territory.'* Britain, he argued, which had 'accepted the moral and material help of French military and naval resources ever since the beginning of the *Entente Cordiale*,' could not 'stand by to see our friends attacked.' And if it deserted 'brave little Belgium' it would have really 'deserved the epithet of "Perfidious Albion" for all eternity.'

To do so, urged Thompson, would have been like the transport workers deserting the miners and railway workers during a dockers' lockout; 'we should have been blacklegs and scabs.' The history of war was 'a tale of hypocrisy and crime which should make every true patriot blush with shame,' but it was not 'an argument against war under any circumstances.' Rather, it argued 'for the awakening of more action and more intelligent interest in British doings and better control of our unprincipled filibusters.'

Further protests were futile. Having been forced into the war the British should 'acquit ourselves as a united and resolute people.' There was no quarrel 'with our brothers in Germany' but with 'the aggressive, arrogant, brutal and domineering War Lords of Berlin.' When they had been 'humiliated and destroyed' and the 'great German Republic' had replaced them 'the three most enlightened democracies in Europe will be able to form an alliance that shall indeed make for peace and progress.'

In the meantime the government had acted quickly 'to protect the bankers and financiers.' They should act equally quickly in the interests of the people. 'The whole of the country's food supply should be nationalised immediately.' The *Clarion* was reduced to eight pages and further changes would take place the following week. By these means it hoped to 'keep going for a period of two months.'

> After that - ? Well we hope and trust that by that time the bloody spectre of war will have been decisively defeated and safely chained up again in the hell that has let him loose.

If anyone had the slightest doubt about the *Clarion's* stance the front page of the following week's issue (14 August) featured not only Blatchford on 'The Strain of Armageddon' but also the large advertisement carrying Kitchener's now famous appeal 'Your King and Country Needs You' which ended with 'God Save the King'. It is not hard to imagine the shock this must have caused to many readers.

## A new divide on the Left begins to open

As we have seen in the two previous chapters there was still far from perfect unity on the British Left in July 1914. Yet with the BSP now seeking Labour Party affiliation and it and the ILP co-operating in many places to run joint candidates in local elections the trend seemed to be in that direction. How long and with what effect that might have continued had the war not intervened it is impossible to say. But the signs were at least encouraging for those who believed that a significant factor in the lack of progress of the socialist cause was the disunity and rivalry of competing organisations. Whether there were really so many 'unattached socialists' as some, particularly some associated with the *Clarion* believed, is questionable, but there is little doubt that disunity had little attraction for those not engaged in factional activities.

By July 1914 there were still divisions, but they were at least as much within parties as between them. There was the division in the ILP between those like MacDonald, dedicated to conducting parliamentary politics on more or less traditional terms and those like Jowett who wanted to see a much more radical approach.[94] In the BSP there were many divisions especially those centring on 'nationalism' and 'internationalism'. But without the advent of war it is difficult to see any of these overpowering the move towards co-operation and effective unity. There were certainly differences of emphasis on important issues such as the suffrage campaign and the future of Home Rule and Ulster, but nothing that would necessarily lead to serious divisions.

The coming of the war reversed all this. No one welcomed the war. All three socialist weeklies expressed their total horror of it. But that is where unity ended. Having played a crucial role in the early ILP the *Clarion* had long been a critic of its leadership and that of the Labour Party, but now the war had produced an unprecedented polarisation with the ILP and its *Labour Leader* totally opposed to British participation in the war and the *Clarion* equally unequivocal in its support.

Only in the case of the BSP's *Justice* could there be any doubt of where it stood. The initial reactions to the unexpected – and massively unwelcome – outbreak of general European war show how divisions that would be very difficult, if not impossible to reconcile were already beginning to open. The manifestos and statements of the ILP and the BSP would continue this. Divides would also open within parties, especially within the BSP.

---

[94] For Jowett's campaign for the reform of parliament see Ian Bullock, *Under Siege,* Chapter 1.

# CHAPTER 4

# The BSP and ILP Manifestos.

# Divisions emerge in the BSP.

### The BSP and ILP Manifestos

The manifestos of the BSP and ILP, both published in their respective papers on 13 August, give us some idea of the emerging differences between the two socialist parties in their response to the war. Both 'War, the Workers and Social-Democracy,' the manifesto of the BSP and the ILP manifesto, 'The War and the I.L.P.' took up all or most of the front pages of *Justice* and *Labour Leader* respectively. Both, of course, deplored the war and predicted many of its horrors. It was not, said the BSP, 'a war of the peoples,' none of whom had been consulted; 'The workers of Germany declared vehemently against war. No-one knows to-day how many German Social-Democrats or trade unionists have been shot down or imprisoned for their opinions since martial law was proclaimed.'

The BSP pleaded for a distinction to be made between 'the mass of the German people and the Prussian military caste which dominates the German Empire.' Similarly, the ILP manifesto included a section under the title 'Our German Comrades' which looked forward to the 'suppression of militarism and the establishment of the United States of Europe.' But there was no reference to specifically *Prussian* militarism in the ILP statement. The

BSP, in contrast, looked forward to seeing 'the power of Prussian militarism' broken and the German people themselves 'freed from a crushing Imperialism.'

The BSP saw as the 'supreme questions of the moment' the 'pressing measures' the government needed to take to ensure food supplies and employment. It listed several demands as did *Labour Leader*, though in its case these appeared in a statement by the ILP's National Administrative Council (NAC) to party members rather than in the manifesto itself. Both manifestos denounced 'secret diplomacy' with the ILP's using it as a sub-title for one of the four sections.

Both parties were more than wary about the alliance with Russia. The BSP feared the war might lead to 'encroachments of Russian despotism.' For the ILP, Britain had 'placed herself behind Russia, the most reactionary, corrupt, and oppressive power in Europe. If Russia is permitted to gratify her territorial ambitions and extend her Cossack rule, civilisation and democracy will be gravely imperilled. Is it for this that Britain has drawn the sword?' it asked.

The ILP devoted a manifesto section to 'The Cause of the War'. It explicitly ruled out trying to apportion an 'exact measure of responsibility' but it was 'just as untrue to say that British policy had been wholly white and German policy wholly black' as it was to maintain the opposite. Secret diplomacy was the villain.

Instead of striving to unite Europe in a federation of States banded together for peace, diplomacy has deliberately aimed at dividing Europe into two armed, antagonistic, camps, the Triple *Entente* and the Triple Alliance. Diplomacy has been underground, secret, deceitful, each Power endeavouring by wile and stratagem to get the better of its neighbours.

The BSP had little to say on the causes of the war but the way it characterised the issue of Belgium, though fleeting, is noticeably different from the ILP manifesto. Summarising what had led to 'the great war long threatened and feared,' the BSP document said that

Britain had been 'drawn into the general struggle by the declaration of war upon Belgium by Germany on account of the refusal of that little state to forego its neutrality in the interest of the attacking power.' This was very different from  the way in which the ILP manifesto dismissed the notion that the German invasion of neutral Belgian justified Britain's involvement in the war. If France had 'invaded Belgium to get at Germany who believes we should have begun hostilities against France?' it asked.

So, though there was much that was common to both manifestos, it is easy to see the beginnings of a rift in the BSP's emphasis on 'Prussian militarism' and the different treatment of the issue of Belgian neutrality in the two manifestos. But while the position of the ILP and *Labour Leader* seemed, to have quickly settled, though not entirely without challenge as a, more or less, 'anti-war' one, for the BSP/*Justice* there would soon emerge fundamental internal disagreements. Soon arguments both for and against British participation in the war would come to feature increasingly in that paper.

### For British participation...

If the differences in the manifestos seemed quite slight, any reader who looked at Fred H. Gorle's short article 'The Battlefields of Belgium', which also appeared on the front page of *Justice* (13 August), would have at least begun to doubt this.[95] Such a reader would already have been likely to conclude that the two socialist

---

[95] Frederick H. (Hunt) Gorle is described on website of the West Watford History Group as 'a human dynamo in the cause of Socialism.' He was an early member of John Trevor's Labour Church movement of which he was elected president in 1908 and a local councillor in Watford. He had been much involved with the organisation of celebrations for Hyndman's 70th birthday in 1912. His candidacy in BSP executive committee elections will feature later in this chapter. Subsequently, he would leave the BSP with Hyndman in 1916. For his attacks on the Bolsheviks see Ian Bullock, *Romancing the Revolution,* Edmonton, Athabasca University Press, 2011, 130-32.

parties were heading in opposite directions.

Gorle recalled a visit to the Belgian industrial areas around Liège. He praised the Belgian socialist movement, especially the co-operatives, and noted that 'among those soldiers and civilians who have been killed or wounded there are many Socialists.' He concluded:

> Our hearts cannot fail to go out to our Belgian comrades of Liège, Visé, Seraing, Waremme etc. What the future will be we know not but we know that the tireless industry and dauntless enthusiasm which have built up the Belgian Socialist movement, which are showing themselves anew in the defence of their liberties will on the ruins of Prussian aggression build up again the structure now shaken to its foundations. Brave Belgian Comrades, we salute you!

The reader's impression of a very different response from that of the ILP could only have been confirmed by Hyndman's editorial, 'The War, Secret Diplomacy and Social-Democracy' on the following page. He began by recalling BSP efforts to maintain the peace. 'We of the B.S.P. ... however completely some of us may have been convinced for years past of the detestable truculence of German militarism were at one with the extremist of pacifists in our determination to avert war.' But the invasion of Belgium, 'that much ill-used and plucky little country,' had changed the situation. Hyndman invoked Emile Vandervelde, the chair of the ISB, who had been compelled by his party to join the Belgian government 'to maintain the independence of his country' and the 'noble Jean Jaurès denouncing the outrage committed by Germany and Austria upon civilisation.' When the German government made 'what Mr Asquith calls the "infamous proposals"' in order to secure British neutrality 'we were bound, not by secret agreements and private understandings, but by the solemn international treaties and agreements at the Hague.' [96]

---

[96] Hyndman was referring to the Hague Conventions of 1899 and 1907, a series of international treaties resulting from the two international peace conferences of

His personal opinion was that had Britain 'kept up an overwhelming navy and established long ago a citizen army on democratic lines' while at the same time refraining from 'secret agreements' the war could have been avoided.[97] Like virtually all on the Left, Hyndman viewed the alliance with Russia with great unease and distaste. Though everyone must 'eagerly desire the final defeat of Germany in view of the crime committed in Belgium, nevertheless the success of Russia, which must inevitably follow, will be a misfortune to the civilised world.' But now the most that could be done was to exert as much influence as possible to bring about 'a reasonable peace as soon as possible; while not hampering in any way the efforts of the Government to win a speedy victory.'

Hyndman believed that the fact that since 1870 Germany had industrialised and become 'bound up in international finance' meant that it was dependent on foreign countries for raw material, and even to a large extent food. Unless it could 'smash the British fleet' this problem would remain. And if the Kaiser and his armies 'fail to win all their tabulated victories, according to their time schedule, which is

---

those years. The Convention for the Pacific Settlement of International Disputes of 1899 which set up the – still existing – International Court of Arbitration was ratified by all the European great powers, though Germany opposed binding international arbitration.

[97] The third point of the SDF programme at its foundation in 1884 was 'The Abolition of Standing Armies and the Establishment of a National Citizen Force.' This was followed by the demand for referendums on 'Peace or War.' A strong advocate of the 'citizen army' had been Harry Quelch, whose pamphlet *Social-Democracy and the Armed Nation*, had appeared in 1900. Will Thorne – a Labour MP but a Social-Democratic Party member – had introduced a private members' bill to promote the citizen army in parliament in 1908. This had much in common with Jaurès' *La Nouvelle Armée*, but, as socialist critics pointed out, in France and continental Europe generally, where conscription was in force this was a demand for the democratisation of the armed forces. In Britain, they argued, it became a dangerous support for those already agitating for conscription in the National Service League. [See Barrow and Bullock 167-69.] Support for the citizen army was not confined to *Justice* and the BSP. Even after the outbreak of 'Armageddon' the *Clarion* published a detailed diagram by George Beckett of a citizen army 'based on the South African system which. in turn, has been adapted from the Swiss' (13 November).

more quickly than they seem likely to win them at the time of writing' – the economic and social repercussions would be severe.

The alliance with Russia was a great problem. Hyndman argued that had the British public been told the truth this could have been avoided by 'a change of policy – by no means more favourable to Germany or less advantageous to France.' He ended on a note of optimism. 'It is even possible that, as the war of 1870-71 gave France a Republic, the war of 1914 may secure England the beginnings of a Co-operative Commonwealth. We sincerely hope so. *That,* at any rate, is worth fighting for. By far our worst enemies are the landlords and capitalists of Britain.'

The final point was reinforced by a short unsigned piece on 'War and the Class War.' It poured scorn on the claim of the *Times* that the war had 'obliterated the class war.' It insisted that Vandervelde's participation in the Belgian government was 'justified under the decisions of all recent International Socialist Congresses.' The 'class struggle' was for the moment 'overshadowed by European war, but it is still here,' it concluded.

The hostility towards the Russian alliance evident in Hyndman's editorial was reflected also in a well-informed article on Poland by his wife on the following week's front page (20 August). 'Our pro-Russian press' delighting at the Russian offer of Polish autonomy to tempt Poles in the German and Austrian parts of the country were, she thought, naïve. She summarised the history of post-partition Poland including the struggles against 'Polish influence' of 'the Ukrainian or Ruthenian race.' Britain could now play a part in bringing about Polish independence by exerting 'strong pressure' on Russia.

At first it looked as though the position of reluctantly supporting British participation in the war, while deploring both the necessity for it and the alliance with reactionary Russia, was becoming the settled view of the BSP. An article on 'Our Duties' on 27 August asked what these were for those not able to fight. The first paragraph denounced 'the infamous German invasion of Belgium,' applauded the 'splendid resistance and self-sacrifice of that noble little people,' and hoped for 'the speedy and total rout of the Prussian military caste.'

On the front page on 3 September, Lee introduced the 'French and Belgian Socialist Manifesto to the German People.' The German people had been told that 'Russia was the enemy' and they had to defend themselves 'against the half-civilised hordes from the East.' But if this was so, asked Lee, why were a few German army corps left to guard the eastern frontier while the bulk of its forces, including the most highly trained and 'most scientifically organised' parts, were 'flung on to France through Belgium?' Why was Luxembourg invaded even before war was declared on Belgium and France?

The Russians, he predicted, would have 'the easiest part of the work to do.' The danger was that at the conclusion of 'this terrible and disastrous business may we not find a beaten Germany, an exhausted France, a crippled England, with Russia fresh and strong and able to dictate whatever terms she likes to impose.' Nor was a *Dreikaiserbund* – like understanding between Russia and Germany at a later stage of the conflict out of the question.[98]

The joint Franco-Belgian manifesto absolved the French government, which 'was sincerely anxious for peace,' from blame for the war. This was placed squarely on the German government. Belgium and France were defending their 'independence and autonomy' and fully respected that of the German people. The same issue carried a long interview with Emile Valdervelde who was 'on a

---

[98] The *Dreikaiserbund* (Three Emperors League) was Bismarck's attempt to avoid the now united Germany being dragged into a war between its Austrian-Hungarian ally and Russia over rival claims in the Balkans while keeping France 'isolated' without a powerful ally. The first version lasted from 1873 to 1875 and the second, more formal version, ran, with a renewal in 1884 from 1881 to 1887. After this Bismarck continued to pursue his aim of maintaining a peace which was to Germany's benefit by means of the 'Reinsurance Treaty' with Russia, but the policy was allowed to lapse after his dismissal in 1890 by the new emperor, Wilhelm II. This contributed to the events leading to the outbreak of war in 1914. Bismarck's dismissal was famously the occasion of John Tennial's *Punch* cartoon, 'Dropping the Pilot'.

special Belgian mission' to Britain and the United States 'to make known some of the brutalities that some of the German troops' had 'committed upon the inhabitants of Belgium.' On the Allied side the war was 'a great fight against militarism' and he told of socialists defending Liège who greeted the German attack by 'singing the International.'

In a similar vein, the *Justice* front page of 10 September featured a statement by the main socialist groups in France approving the entry into the government of 'our friends Jules Guesde and Marcel Sembat' and an interview with the Edouard Vaillant.[99] It will be remembered that Vaillant was the sponsor, along with Hardie, of the Socialist International amendment supporting a pan-European general strike to prevent war. The *Justice* editorial of that week (10 September) was by the German-educated Belfort Bax. He traced the history of German unification and regretted that country's domination by Prussia, 'the least German of all the German States' and its 'accursed militarism.'

## ...and against

No doubt all this reflected the control of *Justice* by the 'Old Guard.' But dissent could not be kept at bay for long. It surfaced on 10 September with a letter in *Justice* from C. H. Norman, whose anti-war and anti-conscription activities would see him imprisoned later in the war. He challenged Hyndman's 'laboured defence of the substitution

---

[99] Jules Guesde, 1845-1922, had been a leader of the *intransigents* who opposed any compromise of Marxist principles and after the unification of the French socialists he remained a critic of the 'reformism' of Jaurès. Though he had earlier opposed any participation in 'bourgeois' governments, he would serve in the French wartime government until late in 1916. Marcel Sembat, 1862-1922, was, like Guesde, a socialist journalist and politician who joined the wartime governments as minister of public works. Married to Georgette Agutte, the fauvist artist, he published a book on Matisse in 1920. He is commemorated in Paris by Place Marcel Sembat and the Marcel Sembat Metro station.

of the Russian Tsar for the Prussian Kaiser.' Britain and France had
been 'manoeuvred into a Continental war' by Russia.[100]

The British Socialists have walked into the trap which I foresaw was
being laid when I wrote in my book 'Essays and Letters on Public
Affairs,' published in 1913, 'It is not a coincidence that the great spread
of Continental jingoism has occurred at a moment when England and
Europe are seething with social unrest. The ruling classes of Europe and
England are ready to resort to any methods to divert the stream of social
discontent and the call to arms is the most artful way of raising a false
issue.' Socialists are now killing each other with the same vigour as
Christians of all denominations. There is nothing like true fraternity.

He deplored Britain finding itself on the same side as Russia whose
record was one of 'unexampled oppression' and where the treatment
of Jews was 'a standing infamy.' Nor did Britain's allies Belgium and
France – and Japan in 'Corea' – have anything but appalling colonial
records. But 'Galicia, which is Austrian Poland, has always been
regarded as a model way of ruling a conquered province.' He believed
that 'Britain should mind her own business, and not send hundreds
of thousands of Englishmen to France to their deaths.' With so many
states ranged against Germany and Austria-Hungary 'Englishmen
might restrain themselves, because the odds are hardly unfavourable
to the Allies.' An editorial note agreed with every critical comment
about Russia but asserted that 'his just hatred of the Russian

---

[100] C. H. (Clarence Henry) Norman, 1886 -1974, was a shorthand writer and court
reporter who had been a member of the SDF and later joined the ILP. During the
war he would be a member of the national committee of the No-Conscription
Fellowship and was imprisoned in 1916. After he organised a strike of detained
conscientious objectors in 1917 he was sentenced to 12 months hard labour. In
1920 Norman was a leading member of the 'Left Wing of the I.L.P.' which sought,
unsuccessfully, to persuade that party to affiliate to the Third (Communist)
International. He chaired the 'Third International gathering' at the ILP's annual
conference in 1920 but unlike many other members of the 'Left Wing' he never
joined the Communist Party. [see Ian Bullock, *Under Siege*, 31-39] Norman was a
lifelong campaigner against capital punishment.

bureaucracy causes him to ignore every other past and present aspect of the European situation.'

Hyndman replied in a letter the following week (17 September). Norman, he said, 'would have allowed Belgium to be destroyed and annexed, France to be finally crushed and annexed, and Europe to be held in tutelage by Germany.' To have failed to declare war on Belgium's behalf 'would have been infamous.' He endorsed Norman's denunciation of imperialism, including that of Belgium's King, but linked this to the most notorious event of the German invasion. 'I know that the late King Leopold's rule in the Congo was abominable. Was Louvain sacked and burnt on that account?'[101] It was 'scarcely necessary,' Hyndman said, to remind readers of *Justice* that for forty years he had 'persistently advocated the emancipation of India from British domination' or that for just as long he had 'vigorously denounced Russian despotism.' But as things stood it was, he said, 'a choice of evils.' A German victory would be far worse for humanity than an Allied one.' In a postscript he added that Norman was 'misinformed concerning Galicia.' The Polish Party in the Austrian *Reichstag* had an agreement to support the government, in return for which the Polish nobility were 'free to rule Galicia as they see fit.' Many of Galicia's inhabitants, Hyndman pointed out, were not Polish.

Fred Gorle also took Norman to task. In a long letter on 24 September he rejected the notion that Russia had 'manoeuvred' the rest of the Triple Entente into war. The war resulted from 'the acts of Austria-Germany' and there was no doubt that 'one word from Germany 'would have prevented the war. The war *was* 'Britain's business.' He continued: 'No one, who is not prejudiced, can ignore the certainty that ultimately Britain would have been drawn in. It is better to lose a hundred thousand lives now and save our national soul than to lose several hundreds of thousand lives in an

---

[101] Louvain (Leuven) and the issue of German 'atrocities' will feature in a later chapter.

immediate future and our soul as well.' Democracy in Europe was 'fighting for its life.' As a Social-Democrat he was 'on the side of Democracy and the right of nations to live their own lives.' Whether they liked it or not, socialists were citizens with no right to 'shuffle off any of their responsibilities,' one of which was 'to uphold justice.' Gorle's quite lengthy letter was followed by a much shorter one. J. Frederick Green[102] said he had had his 'differences of opinion with comrade Hyndman in the past' but now wished to record his support of the latter's reply to Norman. He said that 'nearly all the Russian Socialists and Progressives' he had met 'rejoice that Russia is fighting on the side of England and France' and believed that 'the regeneration of Russia as well as Germany' would follow the war.

On 1 October another letter from Norman, responding to Hyndman, appeared in *Justice*. He was, he wrote, 'not convinced that Germany is such a terrible conspirator as the Anti-German Party here are attempting to make out.' Germany had made every effort to achieve Belgian, French and British neutrality in a Russo-German War.' As proof he quoted two telegrams. The first was from the German ambassador, Prince Lichnowsky, in which he assured Grey that if France declared neutrality it would not be attacked and the second a reply from the German chancellor to similar effect.[103]

---

[102] J. (Joseph) Frederick Green, 1855-1932, had resigned from the BSP in protest against Hyndman's call for a larger navy – the main difference of opinion referred to in his letter. Later he would follow Victor Fisher into the British Workers League and defeat Ramsay MacDonald as a candidate for the National Democratic and Labour Party in the 'khaki election' of 1918. He lost the seat in 1922 and later joined the Conservative Party, working at its headquarters.

[103] Karl Max, Prince Lichnowsky, 1860-1928, the German ambassador to Britain in 1914, had certainly done his best to prevent the outbreak of war. He would later, in 1916, privately publish a pamphlet, *My Mission to London 1912-1914*. It was critical of the German government's failure to prevent war. This was later published in the USA and then in Sweden and Britain. Lichnowsky concluded that 'it is no wonder that the whole of the civilised world outside Germany places the entire responsibility for the world-war upon our shoulders.' He had been quoted by *Justice* on 27 August 1914 as saying – in what the paper said was a private comment

These, Norman emphasised, 'prove definitely *that Germany had no designs on France unless France joined Russia in the Russo-German war.*' Hyndman had admitted that Europe was faced with a choice of evils. It was much worse than that. Three outcomes were possible, stalemate, allied victory with the 'aggrandisement of France and Russia,' or German victory and the 'aggrandisement of Germany and Austria.' All three were 'disastrous to British interests.' He proposed:

> That on the retreat of the Germans from France and Belgium that British participation in the land operations should cease, leaving France to win back Alsace-Lorraine if she can, and leaving Russia to do what she pleases. Britain should continue her sea operations and economic blockade of Germany and the British troops could be stationed on the lines of communication.

To pursue the war until the German and Austrian-Hungarian capitals were in Allied hands would be 'criminal.' It would prolong the conflict, and lead to thousands more deaths. It would not be supported in Britain which had 'no cause of dispute with Austria and has some reason to be grateful to both Austria and Germany for refusing to join the Russo-French move on behalf of the Boers.' Norman dismissed Hyndman's view of Galicia. He could not agree that 'the inevitable results of capitalist domination in all conquered countries should be imputed to the special evils of Austrian rule.'

Norman's was not the only dissident voice in *Justice*. John Maclean in a letter on 17 September rejected Bax's injunction of the previous week to 'hate the present Prussian military and state-system.' 'Our first business,' said Maclean, was 'to hate the British capitalist system' which intended to 'continue the robbery of the workers.' After that he would 'transfer the larger part of my hate to Russian soil.' It was impossible to say for certain who was responsible for the war, he maintained, tracing the development of the crisis from the Sarajevo

---

credibly reported – that 'My countrymen have gone mad.'

assassination onwards. But 'Germany plunged into war undoubtedly because it thought the Allies were weak owing to the Caillaux-Calmette murder drama in France, and the sham Irish situation in the British Isles, as well as the unfolding revolution in Russia'.[104]

Even if Germany was responsible, the blame – 'the motive force' – lay not with the Kaiser or the 'Prussian militarists' but with 'the profit of the plundering class of Germany.' How could Britain condemn militarism when it had 'led the world in the navy business?' The inspiration of German militarism came as much 'from Darwin and Huxley, as applied by British economists and sociologists against us Socialists, as from Bernhardi or any other German apologist of organised murder.' The invasion of Belgium had given Grey a 'moral' excuse for Britain taking up arms' but the 'real reason' was 'that he and his class knew that war between British and German capitalism had to come sooner or later.' He continued: 'Now was the day, and Britain struck. Plunderers versus plunderers, with the workers as pawns doing the murdering with right goodwill. The working class at home is beginning to be starved, and is being buoyed up with the assertion that this is the last great war.'

Maclean then made a number of predictions. The aggressive expansion of Tsarist Russia in Poland, Sweden, Turkey and the Persian Gulf was wide of the mark as events turned out. But about one future development he showed distinct prescience. The commercial rivalry between Japan and the United States, which was similar to that between Britain and Germany 'must lead to war in the Pacific basin. Canada and Australia will side with the States, so that Britain will be dragged in or lose those Colonies.' It was, concluded Maclean, the duty of socialists to develop a 'class patriotism.' The only real enemy of

---

[104] Gaston Calmette, editor of *Le Figaro*, published a private letter of former prime minister Joseph Caillaux which discredited him politically. Fearing further revelations, especially ones which would show, accurately, that she and Caillaux been sexually involved while both were married to other people, Henriette Caillaux shot and killed Calmette in March 1914. The trial was a *cause célèbre* finishing with her unexpected acquittal on the eve of war – on 28 July.

kaiserism and Prussian militarism was German Social-Democracy. 'Let the propertied class, old and young alike, go out and defend their blessed property. When they have been disposed of, we of the working class will have something to defend, and we shall do it.'

F. Mathieson, in a letter on 8 October linked Maclean with MacDonald – 'the two Macs' – as opponents of British participation in the war. Maclean's comments about Russia had 'little bearing on the question.' More might have been expected of Maclean than that he would 'join in a peace crusade while the shells are bursting' and declare his internationalism 'by doing all in his power to thwart the efforts of the French and Belgian Socialists.'

Significantly, the rare voices of dissent appeared in the correspondence columns towards the back of the paper. The 'pro-war' line was pursued, albeit in a rather more nuanced way than by the *Clarion,* in reports, articles and editorials. Hyndman was not alone in contributing letters supporting the justice of participation in the war. But it would be the response of the BSP's executive to recruitment which would begin to show the real extent of 'internationalist' opposition to the 'Old Guard.'

## Recruiting for the European War triggers revolt in the BSP

The government launched a recruitment campaign and urged all political parties to participate in promoting it. Dated 15 September, a statement advising members to accept if invited to take part appeared in *Justice* two days later. It was signed by all eight members of the executive and by Inkpin as general secretary. The signatories included, as well as the future first secretary of the British Communist Party, Inkpin, also E. C. Fairchild who would soon be a leading figure on the 'internationalist' wing of the BSP in opposition to most of his erstwhile executive colleagues.[105]

The advice to participate was contingent on BSP speakers being 'permitted to speak from a common platform in support of the national programme and policy set out above.' The statement began by rehearsing the party's pursuit of peace, and the threat to 'the national freedom and independence of this country' of 'Prussian militarism.' It looked for 'a speedy and successful issue' to the war. But the rest of it was very critical of the government's approach and policies. It must abandon 'methods of cajolery and starvation' to secure recruits. Those enlisting must be 'offered proper rates of pay,' guaranteed employment or insurance against disablement on their return and 'adequate provision' must be made their dependents.

Though it had 'pledged the national credit in aid of the bankers, financiers and capitalists' the government was failing to ensure the 'national control and distribution' of food and other necessities. In line with the government's appeal for support to maintain 'the independence and autonomy of the free States of Europe' the government should 'proclaim' that it would be 'no party to the vindictive crushing of the German people,' that as soon as possible it would seek 'a reasonable and honourable peace,' and work to end militarism, armaments and secret diplomacy. The effect of the statement was to galvanise opposition within the BSP. Under the title of 'The B.S.P. Executive Manifesto' brief reports began to appear such as the one from the Pollokshaws branch on 1 October: which said that it repudiated the manifesto. It was followed by a similar announcement from the Central Hackney branch.

---

[105] E. C. (Edwin Charles) Fairchild, 1874-?1955 would later edit the BSP's replacement for *Justice* – *The Call* – later resigning when he became involved in a dispute with Theodore Rothstein, a key figure in the origins of the CPGB which Fairchild, unlike most of the BSP, did not join. For this episode see Bullock, *Romancing the Revolution*, 137-45. For a letter from Fairchild in *Labour Leader* in August 1920 attacking Communism and accusing its supporters of 'the revival of aristocracy' see *Under Siege*, 35.

In the letter of 8 October already quoted, F. Mathieson called the manifesto 'a clear and lucid statement of a complex situation.' He declared himself unsurprised by the opposition of the North West Ham branch since 'their amendments to all Socialist proposals, their protests against our activities in general' convinced him 'that they cannot be Socialists at all.' The opposition to the manifesto was 'nothing but the last hysterical shrieks from the band of pacifists in the movement who tried to assail Hyndman as a jingo.' Less emotionally on the same page, another correspondent, 'Interested', insisted that the greater part of the manifesto was about BSP policy rather than recruiting and asked the North West Ham branch if its members thought the country was '*not* threatened by Prussian militarism' and whether they thought the BSP should take part in recruiting under any circumstances other than those stated in the party's statement.

The views of Mathieson and 'Interested' were the subject a letter appearing in *Justice* on 5 November. P. Gladding, a member of the North West Ham branch, challenged Mathieson to 'be good enough to give some of the data on which he bases his affirmation that we are not Socialists.' They were not pacifists and their 'knowledge was gained from definite Marxian literature.' Recruiting was 'the business of the capitalist class, and we believe in letting them do their own dirty work.' For Gladding the real business was to make 'class-conscious Socialists' something they did not forget in 'times of peace or panic.' For them Marx's statement 'Workers of the World Unite' had 'more value to us than it appears to have for a great many of our comrades.'

## An Executive Vacancy

On 17 September it was reported that with the resignation of George Moore Bell, 'now on active service,' there was a vacancy on the BSP executive committee to represent the London and Home Counties branches. A letter appeared the following week (24 September) announcing the nomination of Fred Gorle. He was 'anxious to avoid misunderstandings' and to make his position clear. 'I think that the working classes of Belgium and of France had every moral and political right to expect our support,' he declared. He claimed that this position was 'in accordance with the principles of Social-Democracy and the resolutions of International Socialist Congresses.' All socialists should 'have a care in their utterances' and ensure that 'our relations with the trade unions, the Labour Party and other Socialist organisations should be as intimate as possible.'

The next issue of *Justice* (1 October) announced that, with nominations closing on 3 October, there had already been five nominations for the vacant position. In addition to Gorle, J. G. Butler,[106] F. Victor Fisher, P. Petroff,[107] and F. Tanner had been nominated. The following week (8 October) there were letters from Fisher and a new candidate, J. Fineberg.[108] These were followed by an

---

[106] Kendall, in an endnote, lists Butler as one of the speakers – along with Sylvia Pankhurst, Alex Gossip, Joe Fineberg, E. C. Fairchild, Walton Newbold, and Dora Montefiore – at a meeting in March 1917 called by the BSP to celebrate the revolution in Russia. Kendall, 378, note 29.

[107] Peter Petroff, 1884-1947, played a significant role in the revolutionary movement both in Russia and Britain. Associated with both Lenin and Trotsky he was twice wounded in the 1905 Revolution after which he was exiled to Siberia. He escaped to Britain in 1907, and became closely associated with John Maclean for whom he later acted as London agent for his paper, *Vanguard*. Petroff, as evidenced by his candidature, was a prominent member of the BSP. His wartime activities on Clydeside with Maclean and others led to his deportation to Russia where he chaired the Foreign Relation Committee of the All-Russia Congress of Soviets and acted as Under Secretary of Foreign Affairs during the Brest-Litovsk negotiations. He attended the Second Congress of the Communist International (Comintern) in 1920 but left the Communist Party in 1925 by which time he was living in Germany. After Hitler came to power he and his wife and daughters escaped to Britain. In 1934 with his German wife Irma he wrote *The Secret of Hitler's Victory* which gave a Marxist analysis of Hitler's rise to power and the failure of the German Left to prevent it.

[108] According to Kendall, who gives an account of this election and the rising opposition to Hyndman and the 'Old Guard' in the BSP, Fineberg, was an East London tailoring worker whose parents had brought him from Russian Poland at

editorial note apologising for publishing Gorle's letter in a 'weak moment' without realising that other candidates would expect the same publicity. 'On any other occasion,' it joked, 'we shall have to consider whether "election addresses" do not come under advertisement rates.'

The rapidly emerging divisions in the BSP are evident in the two letters. Fineberg was standing, he explained, because 'no provisos or conditions can justify our associating ourselves with those who must be regarded as part authors of the war.' Furthermore 'Gorle supports the action of the Government in declaring war. I condemn that action.' While 'calling upon the people to make the most extreme sacrifices many of the "governing classes" were making fortunes out of the war.' 'With the cry of "Capture Germany's Trade," on their lips, employers are taking advantage of the present situation to force down wages.'

Fisher's letter could hardly have been more different. He declared himself an 'Internationalist' but not an 'Anti-Nationalist' and in agreement with his friend Moore who had resigned from the BSP executive to join the army. 'Despising the spirit of Jingoism, and detesting the buccaneering expeditions of capitalistic Imperialism, I have to declare that at this moment nothing but the British Navy stands between this country and a German invasion, accompanied by all the hideous atrocities inflicted on Belgium and France.' The socialist struggle against secret diplomacy and militarism could only succeed 'if Socialism continues to maintain and increase its influence with the masses of the people.' This would be 'shattered, and rightly so, if at this supreme crisis our movement renders itself suspect of treason to the Commonwealth.'

Another candidate for the BSP executive committee, Frank Tanner, whose letter had appeared in the 1 October edition, was 'convinced that the triumph of Prussia militarism would be a severe

---

the age of eighteen months. Petroff, an ally of Maclean, was to Fineberg's left and Fisher was 'the party's most chauvinistic propagandist'. Kendall, 89.

blow to popular liberty in France, Belgium and Great Britain, as well as in Germany itself.' The issue was one of expediency: 'I desire the defeat of Prussian militarism, not as a patriot, but as a democrat and would cheerfully pray for the defeat of "my" country were I convinced that the cause of Socialism would benefit.'

On 8 October *Justice* announced that the candidates for the Executive vacancy were the six already mentioned plus 'J.W. Wilkinson, M.A' and that voting papers would be sent out to branches within a few days. Inkpin gave the results in *Justice* on 5 November. The clear winner was Fineberg with 25 votes. None of the other candidates achieved even double figures with Butler and Gorle tying for second place each with seven votes while Petroff and Fisher had five, and Tanner four. Wilkinson managed only a single vote. This outcome showed that much of the London membership were already at odds with the 'pro-war' stance of Hyndman and the 'Old Guard.'

The war had almost instantly opened up a gulf between *Labour Leader* and the *Clarion*. The divisions which would eventually bring about a split in the BSP were a little slower to manifest themselves in the pages of *Justice* but were soon all too apparent and quite evident by the end of 1914. However, while there was a fundamental schism on the Left as regards support for the war, there was much more of a consensus about the campaigns that needed to be waged, as a response to wartime conditions, at home.

# CHAPTER 5

## Protecting the People. The Home Front.

The positions taken on British participation in the war were of such fundamental significance and so divisive that this is in danger of obscuring the degree of agreement on the Left. Even on the question of the war itself there were areas of agreement. *No one* was happy with being allied to Tsarist Russia, though many 'anti-war' socialists went further and saw that country as one of the guilty parties in precipitating the conflict, or even, as we have seen, the major villain. For the reluctant supporters of the war, the alliance with Russia was accepted only as a necessary evil.

*No one* had anything to say in favour of 'secret diplomacy.' Those who, like Blatchford and Hyndman, had accepted the 'German menace' as a reality believed that the danger from that quarter should have been recognised and openly prepared against by both military/naval and diplomatic means. Had it been made clear, openly and in public, from early on that Britain would not stand by should Belgium or 'France be invaded, they argued, the war just might have been avoided. At worst, Britain would have been better prepared and in a less perilous position at the start of the conflict. *Justice* (20 August) ridiculed the 'Mania for Secrecy' of the Official Press Bureau in putting out only 'stale and colourless information' concluding that 'Secret diplomacy has landed Europe into a horrible mess, and absolute secrecy as to what is happening is not going to help to clear it up.'

## Food Supply and Citizens' Committees

When it came to the question of what should be done at home and what priorities the government should be pursuing, there was general agreement. An exception, of course, was the key question of recruiting, though even here, as we shall see in a later chapter, there could appear to H. W. Lee to be sufficient common ground to allow for a compromise between the BSP and the ILP. On 6 August *Justice* declared that with neutrality now 'out of the question' the most important issue was food supply. Lee's editorial, though it dealt with much else, was headlined 'War and Food.' He was dismissive of the government's failure to act decisively.

The same heading, and a little later 'War, Food and Unemployment,' would be used in *Justice* during the following weeks (from 13 August) for reports from different areas of the country. In the first issue, there were reports from London, Bradford, Glasgow, Leeds, Manchester and Plymouth, as well as news of the overall national situation. The same page carried a report of shops being attacked.

The formation of a Labour Emergency Committee representing the London Trades Council and the recently-formed London Labour Party together with other Labour parties and trades councils in the wider London area was reported and socialist representation on Citizen Committees urged. A 'rush for food and raising of prices' was reported in Leeds. From Manchester Katie Garrett was able to note with satisfaction that 'A determined effort is being made to curtail the unreasonable raising of prices and a tariff is to be issued to-day; also the laying in of stores by the wealthy members of the community is being stopped.'

But, she noted, 'motor-cars came even to our local shops and bought up the available flour on Thursday and Friday last.' She had spent four hours on the local 'out-relief committee' that morning. The clerk had come in and told the meeting that 'he had had notification from the Government asking Guardians when granting help to consider the rise in prices. It was very curious: he just came in after I had fought the very subject for 20 minutes and been beaten by one vote. However we won for the rest of the morning.'[109]

On the same page of *Justice* appeared a number of brief reports headlined 'Shops Attacked' concerning incidents in different parts of London. Suspicion of profiteering seems always to have been the motive as is evident from the following example:

> On several evenings last week large crowds gathered outside a baker's shop in Chatsworth Road, Clapham. The owner had increased the price of his bread and also given notice that the rents of some small houses he owned would be raised. Indignation meetings were held in the vicinity, and on Thursday night every window in his shop and house was broken. It is understood in the neighbourhood that the rents will not be raised as intended and the price of bread has fallen.

Little wonder than that the next day's *Clarion* (14 August) had a report from the 'London Vans' which concluded that 'The demand for nationalisation of the food supply should prove a tremendous propagandist force.'

By this time, as reported in *Justice* of 13 August, the BSP executive had set up an advisory committee to make recommendations to branches about action to be taken locally. Joint committees should be formed to work in conjunction with the War Emergency Workers' National Committee on which Hyndman was representing the BSP. Every effort should be made to secure places on the Citizens' Committees that were being formed and 'to utilise the propaganda meetings of the B.S.P. for the advocacy of the Party's proposals for

---

[109] Katie Garrett would have been one of the Guardians in her area whose role was to administer both 'indoor relief' in the workhouse and 'outdoor relief' – mainly cash support – for those in need. The latter is the 'out-relief' in Garratt's account. Unlike many other elected bodies, including of course parliament, women were, since 1894, able both to vote and stand for election to Boards of Guardians.

dealing with the distress which the war will entail.'
'KEEP BACK STARVATION. LABOUR ORGANISATIONS
MUST ACT. HINTS FOR CITIZEN COMMITTEES' was a
headline in *Labour Leader* of 20 August. It urged readers to get
involved with the Local Committees for the Prevention and Relief of
Distress, urging them to '*avoid to the last the mere doling out of relief whether
in money or in bread.* Do your utmost to get every applicant taken on at
regular wages at some occupation or other.' It supported municipal
enterprise, insisting that work on schools, hospitals, roads, tramways
and so on must not to be thought of as 'relief work.' The following
week (27 August) Beatrice Webb, in an article that was largely
positive about government action to date, added her own urging.
Labour should concentrate on getting representation on citizens'
committees. She applauded MacDonald's acceptance of a place on
the Central Cabinet Committee. [110]

The following day a letter in the 'Clarion Cockpit' again demanded
nationalisation of food supplies. The government's actions to combat
distress were widely seen as totally inadequate. In a letter to the *Clarion*
(4 September) headlined 'Distress in London,' Sylvia Pankhurst told
readers that the Poplar Distress Committee needed milk and eggs and
barley for babies. Later (2 October) the regular 'Notes to Clarionettes'
included one in which her East London Federation of the Suffragettes
acknowledged contributions for 'relief of distress.'[111]

*Justice's* editorial on 20 August had complained of 'muddle,
incompetency and overlapping' which threatened 'almost every
channel for the relief of the coming distress.' Elsewhere in the paper

---

[110] Beatrice Webb, 1858-1943, was a leading member of the Fabian Society, as was
her husband Sidney. Both were prolific writers, both singly and together, on social
and political issues. She had been a member of the Royal Commission on the Poor
Laws, 1905-9 and the lead author of the celebrated Minority Report.

[111] The East London Federation of Suffragettes (ELFS) originated as part of the
Women's Social and Political Union (WSPU) but became independent of the latter,
and an explicitly socialist organisation after Sylvia Pankhurst's expulsion from the
WSPU earlier in 1914.

the BSP's 'Socialist Proposals for Dealing With Unemployment and Distress' were explained. On 'Local Representative Committees' members should press for increased working class representation while resisting attempts of 'agents of the Charity Organisation Society (COS) to capture' them.[112] In particular COS style 'vexatious investigations into the position of applicants for relief' should be opposed. Work on such things as slum clearance, road-making and the extension of public parks and the renovation of public buildings should be offered to the unemployed on 'trade union wages and conditions.' Full advantage should be taken of such legislation as the Milk and Dairies Act and the Provision of Meals Amending Bill to ensure the availability of free milk to nursing mothers, infants and the sick and the 'feeding of children during seven days of the week.'

A letter from Tom Quelch in the same edition claimed that it was evident that the various 'distress committees' were going to be 'dominated by persons of the Charity Organisation type.'[113] He thought socialists should 'keep clear' of them and instead concentrate on uniting 'all the organised forces of the working-class movement.' An editorial note agreed with his other proposals while rejecting the idea that the distress committees should be 'left severely alone.' The following week (27 August) *Justice* said that 'the Charity Organisation crew,' who were 'so active on the committees, fairly represent the organisation of insult which is general with the upper classes when dealing with the poor.' It urged they be 'resisted to the utmost.' This

---

[112] The Charity Organisation Society had been founded by Helen Bosenquet and Octavia Hill in 1869 to combat 'indiscriminate' alms-giving and focus charitable assistance on the most 'deserving'. It had an enormous impact on the development of social work and, especially, casework, but what was seen as the patronising attitudes of its volunteers and social workers towards poor people, the COS's ideology of 'self-help' and its suspicion of what is now called a 'dependency culture' was much criticised and rejected on the Left.

[113] Tom (or Thomas) Quelch, 1880-1954, was the son of Harry Quelch. He would soon become a leading member of the 'internationalist' opposition to Hyndman and the 'Old Guard' and later play in prominent role in the founding and early years of the British Communist Party.

was vital because 'the Government is doing its utmost to "nobble" all effort on behalf of the people, in the interest of the rich.'

A national relief fund with the Prince of Wales as treasurer had been set up in August. Similar objections to the way this operated came from the left-wing papers. Winifred Blatchford, in the *Clarion* (25 September) cited an incident where a woman 'whose husband and two sons were at the front' was asked to pawn her piano before being deemed eligible for assistance. The insensitive and sometimes prurient invasion of privacy that took place was, she said, appalling; 'to ask for a woman's marriage certificate, and her children's birth certificates, is damnable impertinence and vulgar interference in the private business of private individuals.' If a soldier was not married 'that is his concern and the lady's; it is not your concern or mine.'

Later (10 December), Ada Nield Chew would make similar complaints, under the heading 'A Plague of Prying Women' in the *Labour Leader*.[114] In the article she identified herself as the local representative of the War Emergency Committee and a member of the town's 'Ladies Relief Committee' – which unlike the other bodies she mentioned she put in quotation marks. As a result, she said, she had much experience 'of the methods adopted by "ladies" towards mere women.'

> They look upon the poor as a different species; and though they would not dream of telling any of their private affairs to a total stranger, they resent the fact and hold it up as proof of special depravity that sometimes a person whom they have visited 'has not told all' or has 'kept something back.' It is held to be a good reason to regard them as 'undeserving' and a good excuse for not worrying about them.

---

[114] Ada Nield Chew, 1870-1945, was an ILP activist and suffrage campaigner. Having left school at 11 she worked in a Crewe garment factory until dismissed after she wrote letters to the local paper complaining about working conditions. She was later a leading figure in the Women's Trade Union League. She had worked as organiser for the main women's suffrage organisation, the National Union of Women's Suffrage Societies, since 1911.

All three socialist weeklies found plenty of targets for their criticism in the way that the government and other pillars of the established order approached the very real problems created by or accentuated by the war. Already on 17 September *Labour Leader's* front page had demanded 'STOP STARVATION!' It asked, 'What is the Government doing?' and concluded, 'Workers must demand action.' Only by 'public control of the industries' could 'unemployment and destitution be prevented,' it claimed.

But socialists of all varieties had always found that *some* 'workers' regarded them with great hostility. Never more so than when Britain was at war. But how vulnerable were they to the hostility of those swept away by belligerent enthusiasm? Just how much 'Jingoism' there was in the early months of the war was itself something on which opinions seemed to differ widely within the British Left.

## Jingoes

The more fervent anti-war socialists would soon be accusing their opponents in the movement – above all Hyndman and Blatchford – of 'Jingoism.'[115] But all on the Left, whether 'anti' or 'pro' the war were unanimous in declaring that they had no time for such

---

[115] The term 'Jingoism' to describe the most mindless and belligerent type of patriotic enthusiasm and the designation of 'Jingo' for one carried away by such sentiments went back to a once-famous music-hall song current during the 1877-1878 war crisis when for some time it looked as though Britain might soon be at war with Russia. The key verse went:

> We don't want to fight but *by Jingo* if we do
> We've got the ships, we've got the men, we've got the money too
> We've fought the Bear before, and while we're Britons true
> The Russians shall not have Constantinople.

The wild celebrations that followed the lifting of the siege of Mafeking in 1900 added the possibility of describing Jingoes as 'maffickers.'

chauvinism and no-one, among even the most committed of 'pro-war' socialists regarded *themselves* as Jingoes. Reactions to such a charge illustrate both how much the accusation could sting and how much it was resented. 'Tattler' in *Justice* on 1 October would complain of the 'misapplication of the term' to those who 'genuinely believe that it is necessary to fight over a definite issue. All who feel it necessary to fight are not "jingoes," or the Communards of 1871 could be so termed.'

Much earlier (*Clarion* 14 August), there was a report of one of the Clarion vans – the 'Enid Stacy' van – still carrying out open-air socialist propaganda[116] 'At Walworth we enjoyed Jingo interruptions,' it said. Things were even worse with the 'William Morris' van where 'at East Ham we had to make strategic retreat before "maffickers" who threatened to smash the Van.' This suggests some great initial misunderstanding of the *Clarion's* position on the war. But how widespread was Jingoism anyway?

The previous day *Labour Leader's* 'Review of the Week' had advised that 'Protest meetings will at the moment serve to arouse Jingo feeling rather than suppress it.' But in the same issue it had declared, 'There is no war fever in Glasgow, except in the columns of the Jingo Press.' But the situation was, it appeared, very different in not so distant Edinburgh. Reports from localities in the same issue included one about a peace meeting in the Scottish capital, organised before the outbreak of war, but which took place on the day following the British declaration. It was a large meeting with two speakers' platforms. 'The chairman had barely begun' at one platform, the report said, 'when a steady flow of interruptions commenced, which gradually developed into cheering for the Army and jeers and groans for the Kaiser and Socialists who wanted peace.' Later a speaker was knocked off one of the platforms. A report of this Edinburgh meeting, the same day, in

---

[116] Enid Stacy, 1868-1903, was an early ILP activist and Clarion Vanner based mainly in Bristol.

*Justice* insisted that the disorder had been 'subject to gross exaggeration' by the 'Jingo Press' while in Glasgow, it confirmed, like the *Leader,* that there had been 'no enthusiasm whatever shown for the war.'

A week later (20 August) the *Labour Leader's* weekly review insisted that 'there is still no popular enthusiasm for the war. From all over the country we receive reports denoting an entire absence of Jingoism. The people regard the conflict not as a holy crusade but as a hellish calamity.' Nevertheless, it repeated the warning that 'Hot denunciation of the Government is likely at the moment to arouse Jingo feeling rather than assuage it.' Another week on (27 August) saw the *Leader's* more optimistic assessment confirmed by Katharine Bruce Glasier on the basis of her experience speaking at Burton-on-Trent the previous Sunday. 'There was not a trace of Jingo brutality,' she reported. 'The malignant poison of the *Daily Mail* that would seek to rouse us to mad irrational hatred of every German and set us to fiendish gloating over "the death in haystacks" of the poor conscript soldiers of either Austria or Germany would seem, thank God, to have lost its baleful power.'

Nevertheless, examples of jingoistic attempts to disrupt meetings continued, particularly when the speakers included those regarded as prominent opponents of the war. A report of a public meeting featuring Ramsay MacDonald at the Corn Exchange in Leicester from the *Labour Leader* of 22 October, signed only with the letter 'B', gives a vivid account of one such incident.

The Corn Exchange stands on the spacious Market Square. Before it a crowd of three or four thousand thronged. At its edge men were selling papers which, the contents' bill informed me, indicted Mr. MacDonald as 'a traitor.' Feeling in the crowd was mixed. There was a strong current of feeling for Mr. MacDonald, but the Jingoes were more rowdy. They sang 'Rule Britannia' and coupled Mr. MacDonald's name with the Kaiser. Evidently an exciting meeting was before us.

With some difficulty 'B' managed to get into the meeting. A local councillor chairing the meeting 'spoke with force' but 'it was evident there would be formidable opposition.'

> Mr. MacDonald had a splendid reception from the majority of the audience, but immediately he commenced to speak a group of about fifty at the back of the Hall began to sing 'Rule Britannia' and other 'patriotic' songs. He did not heed them, and by his powerful personality soon dominated the audience. The interruptions were continued throughout his speech and six ringleaders were ejected by the police, but by the end of the meeting Mr. MacDonald had absolutely mastered the opposition. He was able to answer questions practically without interruption.

What of those on the Left seen as 'pro-war'? They were at pains to dissociate themselves from the nastier aspects of 'patriotic' enthusiasm. Blatchford (4 September) gave 'a hint to an excitable British Press.' Telling the truth was not incompatible with dignity and it was not dignified to call the German emperor a 'mad dog, nor to speak of the German people as Huns.' He called for 'a little moderation' as regards recruitment appeals. It was not surprising if having been 'told for years that only the Navy is necessary for defence' young men were not rushing to enlist. To call them 'slackers' was 'an impertinence.' They had been 'deceived from their cradles.' To girls, 'so full of loyalty and spirit,' he wanted to gently hint 'that white feathers do not grow in British wings, but that a Briton fights best when he understands the cause for which he is fighting'.[117] Others, as we have seen in the case of *Justice's* 'Tattler' were equally keen to deny any suggestion of 'Jingoism' on their part.

---

[117] The notion that a white feather indicated cowardice originated in cock-fighting in the 18th century or earlier. An Order of the White Feather, aimed at shaming men into enlisting in the forces, was founded in August 1914 by Admiral Fitzgerald with the support of Mrs Humphrey Ward, the popular novelist and anti-suffragist. There would be instances of members of the armed forces – sometimes wounded ones – in civilian clothes being handed white feathers.

## The Class War of the Rich

There was much hostile comment about the unequal treatment given to the working class. *Justice* (27 August) asserted that 'the class war of the rich upon the poor goes steadily on every day.' In the *Labour Leader* on 3 September Fred Jowett, chair of the ILP, complained that the Chancellor of the Exchequer had been responsible for 'many daring innovations the object of which is to keep the profiteer on his feet during the war.' But when 'a small measure of protection was proposed to save the homes of the poor from being sold up for arrears of rent and for failure to meet payments under hire and purchase agreements, and to prevent the lapsing of insurance policies, vigorous opposition was met with.'

This was a theme that continued to attract the attention of the socialist weeklies for the rest of the year – and beyond. On 3 December *Justice* recommended an article in the current *New Statesmen* to the 'attention of all Social-Democrats and Labour men.' It quoted from the article at some length. The BSP paper particularly commended the statement that that in spite of changes in recent years 'the wage-earner still pays to the State a much heavier tax in proportion to his income than does the wealthy property-owner or even the middle class professional.' It was, *Justice* said, a statement 'that should be put up in every trade union hall and working-class clubroom.'

The same page carried an editorial by Hyndman on 'The Parliamentary Conspiracy against the Working Class.' He criticised Labour MPs for their passive acceptance of the 'unprecedented transactions' of Lloyd George. The Liberal chancellor was very anxious indeed to impress upon the Labour Party the fact that all his operations were directed, not to helping the rich, but were entered upon mainly in the interest of the poor.

That, of course, is unscrupulous nonsense. Private credit, the credit of merchants, jobbers, speculators, gamble-supporting bank shareholders, &c., is of no direct importance to the mass of the producers. It is all used in order to disguise, and at the same time perpetuate, the series of swindles by which the wealthy classes fleece the wage-earning class.

Inequitable taxation also featured in the following day's *Clarion*. A letter from Edward Hartley attacking 'The Unfairness of the Budget' demanded that 'When war is over all indirect taxes should be replaced by graduated income tax.' Another letter, from R.C. Smith of the Royal Colonial Institute claimed that the great burden of tax fell on those who were not 'exchangers' able to offset any increases by raising prices. These were 'the proletariat – the 82 per centum … who are not the owners of any of the accumulated wealth.'

## Servicemen and their Dependents

But the issue of unequal treatment that caused the most anger throughout the British Left –even among those vehemently opposed to British participation in the war – concerned the conditions of servicemen and their dependents. On 3 September, having denounced the Labour Party for supporting enlistment, *Labour Leader's* 'Review of the Week' asked: 'And has the Labour Party secured pledges guaranteeing a living standard of pay, and pensions for the wounded and the dependents of the killed? If not, in what sense is it acting as the representative of Labour?' The following week (10 September) it added, 'Had the Labour Party made provision of a living wage to soldiers and their dependents a condition of their support in the recruiting campaign, we should have had less to say in criticism of its action.'

The next day (11 September) A.M. Thompson noted in a *Clarion* editorial that the paper had received a letter demanding 'a Living Wage' of £1 a week for soldiers. Thompson endorsed this call, adding:

The duty that calls men to arms is the duty of protecting their hearths and homes, their womenfolk and children. No man performs that duty who heedlessly risks his life, leaving his babes, his wife, and his home to suffer in his absence. The root of true patriotism is in men's devotion to their families. All other kinds are swank and bluster. If the nation asks for patriotism, its first duty is to provide the cause.

The people who have shown most contemptibly in this emergency are the fools who have proposed to decorate with white feathers the men who took thought before enlisting, and the wealthy profiteers who have enforced the cowardly coercion of 'the sack' to drive their chattel slaves to bleed for them.

In the same issue Hilda Thompson took up the theme awarding 'White Feathers for the Government' which had, she said 'funked one of its biggest responsibilities' in failing to take care of the 'welfare and financial security of the women and children of soldiers and sailors.'

Blatchford was not far behind his *Clarion* colleagues devoting a front page article on 25 September to the question. He began by contrasting the pay of MPs and ministers to that of servicemen.

Members of Parliament are paid nearly eight pounds a week.[118] Cabinet Ministers are paid from forty pounds a week to a hundred pounds a week, and they expect the wife of a man who is working night and day and risking life and limb into the bargain to live on twelve and sixpence a week.

We pay experienced, highly-trained scientific petty officers in the Navy twenty nine shillings a week. We pay the able-bodied seaman, the finest

---

[118] MPs had been paid only since 1911 when an annual salary of £400 – deemed to include allowance for expenses – was introduced. It was generous by the standards of a century later and pay remained at the same level until 1937.

sailor in the world, fourteen shillings and sevenpence halfpenny a week. We pay the pick and flower of youth who volunteer as soldiers eighteenpence a day: ten and sixpence a week. We pay our City of London dustmen thirty shillings a week.

He then turned to the plight of dependents.

We ask young married men to leave good situations and face the danger and fatigue of a long campaign, and we offer them eighteenpence a day and ask their wives to live on twelve and sixpence a week
What would a Cabinet Minister think if we asked his wife to live on twelve and sixpence a week, and told her she could earn money by sewing or washing?

Blatchford than went on to draw what he saw as the unavoidable conclusion. He continued:

Now I put it to my readers in my blunt and rude way, that if twelve and sixpence a week is thought by these gentlemen enough for the wife of a soldier or sailor, but would be regarded as an insult if offered to the wife of a Minister, or a squire, or a judge, are we not obliged to come to the conclusion that the gentlemen who fix the allowances look upon the wife of a soldier as an inferior person, and hold her husband's services in very low esteem?

In Blatchford's view the 'very lowest' figure for a separation allowance or widow's pension should be £1 a week. 'An extra shilling on income tax would cover the whole cost,' he claimed. He believed that 'In a war like this it is the duty of every able-bodied man to serve; and it is equally the duty of every prosperous citizen to pay.' He was prepared to 'give up everything I have and to live on very little till the war is over, and I look upon every rich or well-to-do citizen who is not prepared to do the same as the meanest kind of "slacker."' And, as so often, he was dismissive about the 'official' Labour movement; 'If we had a Labour Party worth its bread and treacle, if our Trade Union leaders had any steel in them, the Government would be compelled to make the slackers pay.'

The following week (2 October) – in the *Clarion's* 'Cyclorama' – Tom Groom announced that 'the Club' had had 20,000 copies of Blatchford's article printed, adding, 'If there are any non-cycling readers who would like to pay for a few thousand I will see they go to sections of the Clarion C.C. that will do the work.' Meanwhile, in *Justice* (1 October) Will Crooks, MP, was denounced as 'the buffoon of the Labour Party' for 'begging' for charity support for soldiers at a recent meeting.[119] The Parliamentary Labour Party, had, *Justice* charged, 'failed miserably to secure anything like proper treatment for the soldiers and sailors who are risking their lives.'

On 8 October both *Labour Leader* and *Justice* praised G. N. Barnes, the Labour MP who had taken up the £1 a week demand.[120] *Justice* noted that Barnes was 'on strike,' refusing to take any further part in the recruiting campaign until the government made 'adequate pensions' for disabled soldiers and the dependents of those killed. *Justice* asked why this had not been pressed by the parliamentary party as a whole. Why had not Labour and the TUC insisted on this before agreeing to join the recruitment campaign?

On 12 November *Labour Leader's* 'Review of the Week' quoted from a speech by Barnes in Birmingham in which he compared the

---

[119] Will Crooks, 1852-1921, was elected as a Labour MP for Woolwich in 1902 and continued in that role until a few months before his death – apart from a gap between the two elections of 1910. A supporter of Britain's participation in the war in 1914, he is said to have led the House of Commons in singing the national anthem at one point.

[120] G. N. (George Nicoll) Barnes, 1859-1940, was an MP from 1906 until 1922. He had chaired the parliamentary Labour Party for a year, 1910/1911. During the war he would serve in Lloyd George's coalition government and became a controversial figure when he refused to resign as a minister when Labour left the coalition in 1918. He was expelled from the Labour Party but returned to parliament at the December 1918 election on a 'Coalition Labour' ticket.

treatment given to officers to that of ordinary servicemen. It had been made at a conference – one of twelve regional meetings – organised by the Workers' National Emergency Committee. Barnes had gone into some detail.

> The gratuity payable on disablement to officers range from £3,500 for a field marshal to £100 for a second lieutenant. A captain losing the use of one limb or eye might receive £250, or for two limbs or eyes £500, and he would be entitled in those respective cases to a pension of £100 or £200 a year for life. The widow of a captain killed in battle or dying while on active service would get a sum of money dependent largely on the circumstances of his death, and would be entitled to a pension of £100.

Yet the government, which, said the *Labour Leader,* treated officers and their dependants comparatively generously, 'had the audacity to offer the wives of soldiers killed whilst on service 7s 6d only – the rent money only!' A letter in the *Clarion* of 27 November evoking Olive Schreiner on 'the parasitism of women' argued that a proper socialist response would be to insist on permanent work paying 30s a week for a seven hour day for widows without children.[121] Of course the £1 a week should be supported if it was the only possibility but, wrote A. Ringe, 'I consider it an insult to offer such a paltry sum as a consolation, or compensation, for the loss of a husband.'

On 26 November the *Leader's* 'Parliament Day by Day' praised Barnes' 'really excellent speech.' It applauded his insistence that the 'determinants of "pensionability" should be the same for men as for officers.' An officer was entitled to compensation for the loss of an eye; a private suffering the same fate had to demonstrate loss of earning power. 'He is regarded, that is, not as a man, but as a receiver of wages.' There were similar differences with regard to the support

---

[121] Olive Schreiner, 1855-1920, was a South African novelist, feminist and peace campaigner now best remembered for her 1883 novel *The Story of an African Farm.* Her *Woman and Labour* in 1911 had addressed issues of feminism and socialism.

given to dependents.

Other aspects of the conditions of army life were sometimes featured. A *Justice* editorial by H. W. Lee, also on 26 November, considered 'The Expansion of the Contractor in War-Time.' It began by stating that 'Contractors are the jackals and hyenas of the capitalist system.' Lee cited a *Daily Chronicle* report of contractors charging £2 more a ton for metal products supplied to the armed forces, and a Birmingham price-ring operating via an accountant. 'Scamped work,' concluded Lee, endangered soldiers' health.

Lee's response was mild compared with that of A.M. Thompson in the *Clarion* (27 November). Responding to reports that volunteers were being supplied with 'khaki tunics little better than blotting paper,' Thompson attacked the 'scoundrels who are exploiting the nation's needs to pile up fraudulent fortunes,' under the sub-heading 'Work for the Hangman.' They were, he complained, not even prosecuted. He asked whether the German spy recently shot at the Tower of London was 'as vile a villain as the Englishman who enriches himself by clothing English soldiers in shoddy which invites pleurisy and pneumonia?'

*Labour Leader* and the ILP may have abstained from the recruitment campaign, but this did not mean that they were indifferent to what became of the volunteers. On 8 October the *Leader's* 'Review of the Week' drew attention to disturbing reports of conditions in the training camps. 'Dirt, drunkenness, disease, and vice appear to be general,' it said, and 'the character of the towns' in which the recruits were stationed was 'becoming besmirched and degraded.' It concluded that 'It is well that mothers should know that their sons who join the army are going to camps swarming with diseased prostitutes.' This concern did not stop the paper a fortnight later (22 October) ridiculing the proposal of the Plymouth town council for the re-enactment of the Contagious Diseases Acts.[122] In

---

[122] The Contagious Diseases Acts of 1864, 1866 and 1869 sought to combat the spread of sexually transmitted diseases in the armed forces by introducing –

December (10 and 17) *Justice* carried two articles by 'Ubique' on 'Camp Scandals and How to Avoid Them'. But there was, in the consciously anti-Puritan BSP paper, no mention of the 'vice' that had played such a prominent part in the *Leader's* account of the training camps. Instead 'Ubique' claimed:

> It is not disputed that recruits have had their health shattered:-
> - By lack of proper sleeping accommodation in the camps;
> - By improper feeding and partial starvation;
> - By inadequate clothing and lack of facilities for maintaining personal cleanliness;
> - By inadequate medical attention.
>
> There are also contract scandals with regard to the construction of wooden huts, the supply of boots and clothing, and the management of canteens.

One other, related, issue which would continue to cause indignation and outrage until the end the year – and long after – were the attempts to impose police supervision on working-class women.

## Drunken Wives?

On 22 October *Justice* commented on the introduction of a 10 p.m. closing time for London pubs. 'The alleged reason... is recruits, soldiers and territorials are being treated to such an extent by their friends and the public as to be a danger to their efficiency.' There might, it said, be 'some truth in this contention,' perhaps even a case

---

initially in a few army towns and naval ports, like Plymouth – compulsory medical inspection of prostitutes and the virtual imprisonment of those found to be infected in a 'lock hospital' for – from 1869 – up to a year. Josephine Butler led the Ladies National Association for the Repeal of the Contagious Diseases Acts which, after a prolonged campaign, succeeded in getting the Acts repealed in 1886.

for restricting sales to soldiers, but it was clear that 'the Puritans are on top again and have seized upon the cry that soldiers are being treated far too much to restrict the sale of liquor to all.'

If that was objectionable, even worse examples of 'Puritanism' were to follow. A. Neil Lyons a regular *Clarion* contributor, had two articles (20 and 27 November) under the title 'On Kindness to Cats in War-Time.'[123] The strange title is explained by his contention that women were looked upon 'as so many stray cats who are required to be "kept in order."' His first article began, 'Have you heard the latest disgusting fact about our soldiers' wives? These abandoned women drink beer! What is more they drink it openly as a result of which inexpedience it has become impossible for liberal-minded persons any longer to conceal from themselves the existence of this obvious alcoholic fact.'

Lyons mocked the irrational nature of the restrictions that had been introduced. 'No woman can now enter any house of public entertainment until 11.30 a.m. From that hour onwards until 10 p.m. (Sundays and Christmas Day, of course, excepted), any woman can enter any inn and drink herself blind.' Moreover, enforcement was not even 'fair and impartial,' A lady of his acquaintance, he said, having been refused a glass of beer in the Mile End Road at 11.15, had had no problem on another occasion in the West End in 'obtaining a biscuit and some champagne at 10 a.m.'

Even worse was to follow. On 10 December *Labour Leader's* 'Review of the Week' declared itself 'disgusted' with a Home Office order 'imposing upon the police the duty of supervising the wives of all soldiers and sailors.' The War Emergency National Workers' Committee, now with F. W. Jowett and H. Dubery representing the

---

[123] A. (Albert) Neil Lyons, 1880-1940, was a journalist and writer. His book *Arthur's: the Romance of a Coffee Stall,* first published in 1908, ran through four editions. In 1910 the Clarion Press published his biography of its founder and editor, *Robert Blatchford. The Sketch of a Personality; an Estimate of Some Achievements.* In 1915 he would publish *Kitchener's Chaps.*

ILP, had 'carried a strong resolution of protest.' The Committee dismissed the order as 'a document full of gratuitous insult to all British women and to every man fighting for the country.' It also held 'the women of Great Britain up to the contempt of all other nations.' The order, which made it compulsory for the wives of servicemen to register with the police and gave the police the right of entry into their houses, the Committee declared, placed 'a sinister power in their hands – a power which the order leaves entirely without regulation.'

The same issue carried a letter from Marion Phillips, the secretary of the Women's Labour League, demanding complete withdrawal of the order imposing 'the shameful insult of police supervision.' There could be 'no greater barrier to recruiting' than 'for every man to feel that when he leaves the country he leaves his wife to be watched over by the police as a person open to suspicion.' The following week (17 December) *Justice* devoted its editorial page to 'The Wives of Soldiers' and Sailors' by Caroline S Ganley.[124] She questioned the suitability of the police for the task they had been given.

> We have to remember that the police are in such a position as to know the very worst of womankind, and their opinions naturally fall into the lines of their experiences.
>
> Anyone who has taken note of the opinions expressed by policemen will acknowledge that they are surely the last body to be charged with 'gently admonishing' the erring wife of a soldier or a sailor.

The need to 'protect' married woman arose, Ganley wrote, from their supposed inexperience in dealing with larger sums of money than they were accustomed to.

> They have in many cases never handled so much money before, we are

---

[124] Caroline Selina Ganley, 1879-1966, had joined the SDF in 1906. She would become one of the first female JPs (magistrates) in the 1920s and a Labour MP between 1945 and 1951.

told; and consequently they lose their heads and are not capable of spending the allowances they receive in a thrifty and proper manner. What an indictment of the pre-war system of society that a married woman having to keep a home, and in most cases to rear a family, has never handled so much as 20s. to 30s. per week.

The class-bound nature of the official approach was clearly evident and it was time that the government 'withdrew the line of demarcation between classes in its employ.'

> We never have heard of any of the officers' wives being told to 'sell up their homes or take in lodgers as, of course, they could not expect to have as much to spend as when their husbands were at home.' Yet officers' wives give this counsel to the wives of 'soldiers and sailors' and associations and societies formed for the purpose of giving such counsel are recognised by the Government.

The Home Office order was the 'crowning insult to the womanhood of Britain.' It was framed against the poor, especially as regards drunkenness. 'The rich woman can always be sent home in a "taxi" if she has not her motor-car, or she may have a well-stocked wine cellar to supply her needs.'

A letter from Ellen Phoebe Wright in the following day's *Clarion* (18 December) made the point that 'no such condition as police supervision was mentioned,' when the recruitment campaign began and that 'if it had been, no man worthy of the name would have joined to leave their women, hitherto respected and respectable, to the tender mercies of police supervision.'

In the final *Clarion* of 1914, which came out on Christmas Day, Thompson's editorial included a section with the title 'Our Soldiers' Drunken Wises.' He noted the 'Temperance Campaign' begun in Manchester by Mrs. Frances Parker, the sister of Lord Kitchener, the Secretary of State for War. She had said that 'many of the women did not know how what to do or how to spend their money properly.'

Thompson acknowledged Kitchener's 'tremendous services' but wished he would stop his 'campaign against the liberties of the soldiers' wives.' He added:

> I have seen a British Minister's wife staking very large sums on baccarat at the Villa des Fleurs at Aix-les-Bains – on a Sunday night too – but no one suggested that guardians should be appointed to check her improper expenditure. I have seen a British peeress staggering to her box in a theatre in such a condition that the management were sorely troubled as to the decency of admitting her; yet it was not publicly suggested that a committee should be appointed to control her money, which, by the way, her husband had not earned.

## Unity on the Home Front?

On 5 November *Labour Leader,* following a series of regional conferences at which the National Workers' War Emergency Committee, on which both BSP and ILP were represented, had unveiled its charter, commending the result as 'an excellent programme and one on which the I.L.P. will whole-heartedly unite in proclaiming.' The *Leader* listed some of the demands including Labour representation on all committees connected to the war, '£1 a week for disabled soldiers,' and pensions for dependents, maternity centres, productive work for the unemployed, meals for school children, protection from 'exorbitant' prices and 'continuance of national control of railways, docks and similar enterprises.'

The same day *Justice* issued 'A Call to Vigorous Effort' in support of the five demands of the BSP's winter campaign, all of which, except for the 'complete suspension of all contributions by the workers under the Insurance Act' were already part of the Emergency Committee's programme. It urged the widest possible support for 'these stepping stones to a better social system.' So, on most domestic issues there was something very close to unanimity between the two main socialist parties in Britain. But this was far from true, as we will see in the next chapter, when it came to questions concerning the responsibility for the war.

# CHAPTER 6

## Responsibility for the War

### Secret Diplomacy and the 'German Menace' in Retrospect

Though socialists were deeply divided about the causes of the war, the justification, or lack of it, for British participation and the question of responsibility for the conflict, there were, as already noted, *some* areas of agreement even here. No one had a good word to say about 'secret diplomacy.' Hyndman in a *Justice* editorial with the title 'The War, Secret Diplomacy and Social-Democracy' (13 August) reviewed the sequence of events that had culminated in the outbreak of war. 'And that is the result of the triumphant secret diplomacy of England!' he concluded. 'High time it should be put to an end for ever. This we British Social-Democrats have claimed since 1881.'

In the *Clarion* (21 August) Thompson, similarly, looked forward to a time after the war when the 'rule of Prussian militarism and of immoral secret diplomacy, the wasteful progress-stifling competition of armaments' would be no more. Few, if any, British socialists, whether BSP, ILP, 'Clarionette' or 'unattached', would have found much to disagree with in either of these statements. But there consensus ended.

When it came to what course should have been pursued *instead* of Grey's secret diplomacy there were very different ideas. For Blatchford, Hyndman and those who shared their views the answer was clear. Imperial Germany had long posed a real threat. As we saw in Chapter 4, according to Hyndman in the *Justice* editorial of 13 August a 'citizen army on democratic lines' should have been created together with an 'overwhelming navy.' Had this been done 'offensive and defensive war in co-operation with Russia' would have been avoided and Britain put in 'a much better position than we are today to uphold our treaties, to defend the small Powers and prevent France from being crushed.'

Blatchford (4 September) had much the same thing to say. He had warned five years previously that the government needed to spend £50 million on defence. 'Had the Government raised the fifty million, laid down two keels for one,[125] and formed an army of a million men, and had they stated frankly that any violation of Belgian or French territory would be regarded as sufficient cause for this Empire to appeal to arms it is just possible that this war might have been averted.'

At the time Asquith had attacked him, while Winston Churchill had been one of his 'most cocksure critics' claiming that nothing could hurt Britain as long as it maintained the 'two-power standard of the navy.'[126]

The Government have not been honest. They knew that the very existence of the Empire depended upon the integrity of Britain and France. They knew that if Germany made war upon France Britain would be obliged to fight in self-defence. They knew that the Expeditionary Force was being specially organised for use in France or

---

[125] This is the reference to the 'naval race' between the UK and Germany from 1906. In fact by 1914 while Germany had built 24 dreadnoughts and dreadnought battle cruisers Britain had built 38.

[126] Churchill had been First Lord of the Admiralty, the political head of the Royal Navy, since 1911, having previously been elected as a Liberal MP in 1908 and served as President of the Board of Trade. The 'two power standard' attempted to maintain the British navy at a strength equal to the next two largest navies combined. It had been adopted after the Naval Defence Act, 1889. At that time the states with the next largest navies were France and Russia, both still then seen as potential colonial rivals rather than, as in the early 20th century, potential allies.

Belgium, they knew that the probable scene of operations in Belgium had been inspected by officers of the British Army.

Military experts who knew Britain had to defend Belgium thought that it would require 500,000 men. The Government knew that, but they only prepared a force of 160,000.

For some readers the war seemed to justify those who had warned of the 'German menace'. One *Clarion* correspondent (28 August) wrote in to say that he had stopped taking the paper four years previously because he believed the it 'was exciting feeling between England and Germany.' He added, 'I now see that you and Mr. Hyndman were right.' The letter by M. Dale was published on the front page under the heading 'An Apology.' But some, even among *Clarion* readers who now agreed with him about the necessity of taking part in the war, thought that Blatchford was making too much of proclaiming how right his 'German menace' warnings had been. One correspondent on 18 September wrote: 'A good many of us were perfectly willing to admit that you had been right and we were wrong; that all the time there had been indeed a German menace and we had been blind. Need you insist on rubbing that in indefinitely?'

But the vehemence with which the 'German Menace' warnings had been attacked had wounded. Hostile comments from Liberal politicians were to be expected but what must have irked Blatchford and those who shared his view much more was the dismissive tone that had often characterised the criticisms of fellow socialists. Thompson, in the same issue as the letter quoted above appeared (18 September), dug out a quotation from *Labour Leader* in 1910. It read 'Blatchford's recent Yellow Press articles put him outside the pale of sane politics… He has only himself to blame when he finds the whole movement rippling with laughter and struggling in vain endeavour to stifle its mirth.' As for the Liberal government, 'They buttoned their pockets when we urged them in bygone years to form a Citizen Army capable of defending the nation's rights. They preferred the alternative of an alliance with Russia!'

Meanwhile the *Clarion* was in no doubt about the responsibility for the war. Thompson, who had been born in Germany and regarded German as his first language, expressed amazement in the edition of 4 September at the attitudes of some correspondents. They thought the war was something to do with Serbia or a quarrel between Russia and Germany or a dispute about 'the balance of power.' Even after all that had occurred, they did not understand that the war was 'the effect of an attack, long premeditated and deliberately organised by the greed and envy of the ruling caste in Germany upon the British Empire, Britain's world position, and British trade.'

For Thompson the cause of the war was simple. It was:

> ...the Prussian Juncker Idea – the Idea that beams superciliously through the gold-rimmed spectacles of the Jena professor, and glares arrogant and brutal through the monocle of the Potsdam lieutenant – the Idea governing the Prussian governing class. The founders of the Idea are Clausewitz, Bismarck, and Professor Treitschke, and it inspires and pervades the most popular German literature of recent years. You will find a complete exposition of the Idea in the famous book on 'Germany and the Next War' by General Friedrich von Bernhardi, an eminent officer in the German Army and a standard writer on German tactics.[127]

Much would be made of Bernhardi in the *Clarion* subsequently. Even in the same issue Lyons claimed that 'The worst and most malignant and most ignorant kind of British swashbuckler has never expressed himself in terms one quarter so offensive to our sense of civilisation as are the published pronouncements of such foreign "patriots;" as, for instance, General Bernhardi.'

---

[127] Frederic von Bernhardi, 1849-1930, was a Prussian general noted for his book, written after retirement in 1911, *Deutschland und der Nächstse Krieg* (*Germany and the Next War*) in which he advocated ruthless pursuit of aggression and justified war in a social-Darwinian way as a 'biological necessity.'

## The *Labour Leader* View

The socialist opponents of British participation in the war would have agreed with Hyndman about the desirability in the pre-war years of avoiding an alliance with Russia and his condemnation of secret diplomacy – but that was as far as agreement went apart from a general rejection of pre-war foreign policy. But whereas all this did not stop those of the Blatchford/Hyndman persuasion from supporting Britain's going to the aid of Belgium and France, for most of the ILP the conclusions were very different. For them the *major* villain was British foreign policy. On 10 September *Labour Leader's* 'Review of the Week' denied the paper was 'pro-German.' It was simply that the paper did not feature 'extreme militarist writers' who were the British equivalents of Bernhardi.

The responsibility of British foreign policy was to remain a central theme of the *Labour Leader* in its editorial 'Review of the Week' feature and in articles by leading ILPers. 'Is Germany the Aggressor?' asked the 'Review' on 20 August. Rejecting the arguments of Shaw and H. G. Wells that, though there was no quarrel with German people, 'the Kaiser and his War Lords must be crushed,' it pointed out that the same argument was made by their counterparts in Germany with the Tsar substituted for the Kaiser. It was not fair to blame Germany which may have 'held a pistol to the head of Europe, but is there not some justification for a man whipping out his pistol when he is surrounded by enemies plotting his downfall?'

For ten years Britain, France and Russia had 'deliberately schemed to isolate and degrade Germany.' Germany's 'military arrogance' was matched by Britain's 'naval arrogance.' And, as we saw earlier, the *Leader* argued that the British failure to agree on immunity for merchant shipping during war at the Hague Conference of 1907 made it inevitable that Germany would build a strong navy to protect its overseas trade. Britain was not fighting Germany for democracy or other high ideals but only because it was 'jealous and afraid of her increasing power.' Defeat of Germany would mean victory for Russia 'and a Europe under the heel of Russia would be worse tenfold that Europe under the heel of Germany.'

In the same issue appeared an article by Philip Snowden who, still abroad, now in Montana, had concluded in one of his *Christian Commonwealth* articles that Britain could not possibly have found herself at war had 'the old policy of neutrality in Continental affairs been maintained.' It was the *Christian Commonwealth*'s editorial conclusion that there was 'no alternative' to participation in the war because otherwise it would mean the destruction of Belgium and France and 'a hostile and inimical Power at our very doors' that triggered a vigorous response from Fenner Brockway, the *Leader's* editor. He denied that it was 'a war of liberation.' Britain's position was hypocritical. Germany was 'hemmed in on both sides' with Russia waiting to 'descend upon her historic Teuton rival' and France to regain Alsace and Lorraine. Britain became 'a partner in the conspiracy against her' and inevitably Germany had armed to defend herself.

Not for the last time, the exact position taken by the British foreign secretary on the eve of the war was cited as the crucial factor in what was to follow. Brockway quoted from the government document *Correspondence Respecting the European Crisis,* usually known as the 'White Paper.' Grey had refused to give a guarantee of British neutrality in return for either a guarantee of Belgian neutrality or of the 'integrity of France and her Colonies,' insisting on keeping 'a free hand.' Dismissing Grey's subsequent claim that the German government did not support the offers made by its ambassador as irrelevant, Brockway concluded that 'no pledges given by Germany could have kept us out of the war.' The editor of the *Christian Commonwealth* had claimed not to 'believe in war' while holding that Britain had no other choice. Brockway ended his article by asking, 'Can one imagine the Carpenter of Nazareth supporting the war – in *any* sense?'

The view that the war, or at least British participation in it, could and should have been avoided had the country's policy had been to reject the Franco-Russian alliance and pursue an even-handed approach towards both France and Germany was now the settled ILP view. As the *Labour Leader's* 'Review of the Week' put it on 24 September; 'The incontestable fact is that Britain is engaged in the present war not because Belgium has been invaded by Germany, not because our Government is imbued with a lofty desire to overthrow Kaiserism, Kruppism or Nietzschism, but as a direct result of the foreign policy it has pursued during all the period it has been in office.' As a result the ILP could 'not declare the fruit of the evil tree to be good.'

The position of the *Leader* was amplified in the same issue by Clement J. Bundock.[128] He rehearsed the ILP's opposition to Grey's policy with quotations from the paper from 1911 and 1912 including some from Hardie, MacDonald and Snowden. The latter, in the *Christian Commonwealth* of 6 December 1911, had declared, 'Sir Edward Grey is undoubtedly anti-German, and his foreign policy is dominated by that idea.' Snowden went on to say that the only possibility of avoiding war was a better understanding with Germany. Bundock concluded: 'The I.L.P. cannot say that Britain's hands are clean. All nations' Governments are to be blamed. It is not a righteous war; it is a war of blundering diplomats.'

## But what about Belgium?

For those supporting British participation, however reluctantly, the German breach of Belgian neutrality and the invasion of that country

---

[128] Clement J. (James) Bundock, 1892-1961, was an ILP activist and journalist, originally with the *Christian Commonwealth* and later with *Labour Leader*. He would be a contributor to the ILP pamphlet 'Why I Am A Conscientious Objector', editor of the *Leicester Pioneer* in 1919, a full-time official of the National Union of Journalists [NUJ] and its general secretary 1937-1952.

clearly justified their position. The subsequent atrocities inflicted on the civilian population – above all in Louvain (nowadays known by its Flemish name of Leuven) – simply reinforced their conviction. In the *Justice* editorial of 20 August already quoted, Hyndman had taken the view that once invasion had happened the issue of secret diplomacy had become irrelevant. He insisted that 'we were bound, not by secret agreements and private understandings, but by the solemn international treaties and agreements at the Hague (which have never yet been denounced or condemned even by those Parliamentary pacifists who are now most vehement for neutrality) to declare war against the disturber of Europe and the deliberate violater of his own undertakings.'

The following day (21 August) Thompson in the *Clarion* declared, rather prematurely to put it mildly, that the only note of discord came from 'Mr. Ramsay MacDonald, who still thinks – amazing man – that it is Sir Edward Grey who made war in Europe inevitable.' On the contrary, said Thompson, 'The only fault that can be charged against Sir Edward Grey is that he did not openly and boldly proclaim Britain's fixed resolve.' Such a proclamation *might* have averted the war, though he doubted it.

*Justice* was to take a much more severe view of Grey and the government. The following appeared under the heading 'British Betrayal of Belgium' in the 8 October issue.

It now appears, from Mr. Asquith's speech at Cardiff, that the Prime Minister and the Foreign Secretary, probably also his entire Administration, were completely convinced some years ago that Prussian-dominated Germany aimed at the virtual conquest of Europe, and were also aware that she would not respect the neutrality of Belgium. Yet they upheld precisely the contrary in the House of Commons, and they took no steps whatever to put Britain into such a position as to be able to help Belgium defend herself. That was and is criminal on their part. They are largely responsible for the horrors wreaked upon the unfortunate Belgians by the brigands of Berlin.

Whatever can be said about France and Russia, no one can allege other than Belgium has behaved most loyally and nobly and courageously throughout.

The details of Grey's foreign policy and in particular of his role in the immediate crisis that had culminated in Britain joining the war on 4 August continued to play a major part in the analyses and debates about the country's participation. For Fred Knee in *Justice* (15 October) in an article titled 'Could We Have Kept Out of It?' the picture was a simple one. 'We will suppose that on August Bank Holiday Sir Edward Grey had accepted the German proposal that we should content ourselves with holding the North Sea so that the western coast of France should not be harried; and that we should turn a blind eye and deaf ear to Belgium.[129] I do not see how Sir Edward Grey could have accepted the proposal; and no one in his position – Socialist or Tory or Liberal could have accepted it.'

The British guarantee of Belgian neutrality under the Treaty of London of 1839 had an emotional relevance for many, including many on the Left. This was particularly the case with those like Fred Gorle who had strong personal links with that country. In his long response to Norman's *Justice* letter, quoted in an earlier chapter, he claimed that the latter had 'no sympathy for Belgium (nor, incidentally, our national word to Belgium). Murder, outrage, burning and mutilation in Belgium is retribution for the Congo!!' Norman knew perfectly well that the Congo atrocities had been the doing not of the Belgian people, he said, but of 'King Leopold and a section of Belgian and other cosmopolitan capitalists.'[130]

---

[129] The August Bank Holiday, on the first Monday in the month, fell on 3 August in 1914 – the day before the British declaration of war against Germany.

[130] Aided by the famous journalist and explorer, Henry Morton Stanley, Leopold II, King of the Belgians, had established a private empire in central Africa known as the Congo Free State. Recognised internationally by the Congress of Berlin, it survived from 1885 until 1908. By the beginning of the 20th century it had become notorious for the horrific treatment of indigenous workers and inhabitants which

But for most of the ILP, or at least for its *Labour Leader,* the argument that the war was to defend Belgian independence was totally unconvincing while for supporters of the war the facts of German aggression were sufficient justification, whatever mistakes the British government might have made prior to 4 August. *Labour Leader* contributors and correspondents continued to question the details of British diplomacy and the account given by the government of the reasons for the declaration of war.

For example, John Darbyshire's letter, headlined 'Britain's Obligation to Belgium,' on 26 November took up an entire column and about a third of another. It comprised twelve numbered points which began with the declaration of war and Grey's statement that it was made in order to 'uphold the neutrality of Belgium.' The following points centred on the Treaty of 1839 and one of its clauses that Darbyshire interpreted as meaning that there was no obligation on its signatories to defend Belgian's neutrality by force. The ninth point concluded that Britain's obligation to Belgium 'did not exist in any treaty, but was created by Sir Edward Grey in his telegram of August 4 (No. 155 White Paper).'

The final point insisted that Belgian neutrality was Grey's excuse for declaring war and that this was illustrated by what occurred subsequently. 'Belgium, by obeying our almost pre-emptory injunction to defend her neutrality, practically put herself in the way of an on-rushing juggernaut in order that we, France and Britain, might have a little more time to get ready to defend ourselves. And then we have the nerve to talk our going into the war to defend the rights of small nations. *Poor Belgium: the Futile Martyr of the West!'* If, for

---

was verging on genocide. Joseph Conrad's *Heart of Darkness* was influential in drawing wider attention to the Congo atrocities as was Arthur Conan Doyle's *The Crime of the Congo.* An early campaigner was E.D. Morel who founded the Congo Reform Association after the report of British consul Roger Casement confirmed many of the worst fears of critics. Under pressure from, especially, Emile Vandervelde, a Belgian parliamentary enquiry endorsed the Casement report and eventually, and reluctantly, the Belgian state took over the Congo in 1908.

socialist supporters of the war, the villain of the piece was 'Prussian militarism,' for its opponents it was Sir Edward Grey.

## Grey's Persistent Critics

We have seen in Chapter 3 how Keir Hardie in the *Labour Leader* two days after the British declaration of war had claimed that Belgium had not wanted 'armed intervention' and Fred Jowett in the following day's *Clarion* had insisted such action was not required under Britain's treaty obligations and that Belgium only wished for 'diplomatic support.' Jowett, in addition to being the guiding force behind the ILP's 'Bradford Policy' had been one of the most sceptical questioners of Grey in the House of Commons during the pre-war years. He was not alone. Some Liberal MPs on the Radical wing of the party were equally alarmed at the direction of foreign policy and the unfolding of events. A political realignment was beginning.

On 3 September the *Leader's* 'Gallery Correspondent' identified as 'Homeless Radicals' the Liberal MPs Ponsonby and Morrell.[131] 'The cup of these men is now full of bitterness to overflowing. That culpability for the war rests at the door of Grey is a belief that most of them hold as profoundly as MacDonald, and they also share the latter's view that the Foreign Minister must at any cost be got rid of.'

---

[131] Arthur Ponsonby, 1871-1946, was the son of Queen Victoria's private secretary. He was a royal page in the 1880s and after Eton and Balliol became a diplomat. He was elected as a Liberal in a by-election in 1908. After the war he was active in the ILP and the Labour Party. He would be given a peerage by MacDonald in 1930 and act as Labour leader in the House of Lords from 1931 until 1935, resigning over the party's support of sanctions against Italy after Mussolini's invasion of Abyssinia. His daughter Elizabeth was a leading member of the 'Bright Young People' and inspired the fictional Agatha Runcible in Evelyn Waugh's novel *Vile Bodies*.

Philip Morell, 1870-43, was also educated at Eton and Balliol and became a Liberal MP in 1906. He was married to Lady Ottoline Morrell, who was well known in literary and artistic circles and associated with the Bloomsbury Group.

The writer went on to predict, accurately enough particularly in the case of Ponsonby, that they would become friends, 'adherents even,' of Labour in the near future. Both Morrell and Ponsonby were soon to be active members of the Union of Democratic Control [UDC], together with ILPers such as MacDonald, Snowden and Jowett. Ponsonby was later heavily involved in the ILP and the Labour Party and served as a minister in both Ramsay MacDonald's minority governments of 1924 and 1929-31.

A little over a month later (8 October) the *Leader* published an article by E.D. Morel with the title 'Was Germany Wholly Responsible. Points in Need of Inquiry.'[132] By this time Morel was already involved in founding the UDC, together with others, notably those mentioned above. But he was introduced to readers as the author of *Morocco in Diplomacy*, his 1912 attack on secret diplomacy. He began by complaining that while discussion of the immediate origins of the war was often regarded as 'out of place' yet 'hardly a day passes without some eminent author or historian contributing his quota to the subject, the conclusion invariably being that Germany and Germany alone is to blame.'

Much of Morel's argument was based on his close study of a despatch by Sir Maurice de Bunsen, the British ambassador to Austria-Hungary until the outbreak of war.[133] Morel took issue with the diplomat's implication that Austria-Hungary had ordered a general mobilisation before Russia's when another government publication – 'the White Book' – had Russian mobilisation taking

---

[132] E.D. (Edmund Dene) Morel, 1873-1924, had, as already noted, founded the Congo Reform Association in 1904. His *Morocco in Diplomacy* would be reissued in 1915 as *Ten Years of Secret Diplomacy*. A founder of the Union of Democratic Control, he became its secretary and treasurer. He would join the ILP in 1918 and defeated Winston Churchill in the general election of 1922. He died of a heart attack soon after being re-elected in 1924. the NAC Report to the following annual ILP conference described Morel's standing in the party as 'one of its heroes.'

[133] Sir Maurice de Bunsen, 1852-1932, was the Rugby and Oxford educated son of the Prussian ambassador to Britain who had been a British diplomat since 1877.

place on 31 July the day before Austria-Hungary mobilised. Which was right? Morel rejected de Bunsen's 'main implication, viz. a German determination to drag Austria into war.' On 28 July *The Times* Berlin correspondent, 'who can hardly be suspected of German sympathies' had reported that Germany was 'sincerely working for peace' while three days earlier the *New Statesman* had claimed that, contrary to rumours that the German government was suppressing the peace campaigning of the SPD, it 'hoped that the Socialists would continue their peace agitation with the utmost energy.'

Then, Morel continued, on 1 August, the *Westminster Gazette* correspondent Crozier Long had reported a German government dispatch to its ambassador in Vienna in which the Austrian-Hungarian government was urged to 'exchange views with St. Petersburg' and told that Germany would 'refuse to be drawn into a world conflagration through Austria-Hungary not respecting our advice.' Was *The Times* 'misinformed, the German Socialists – but to what purpose, if so? – purposely misled, and the telegram of July 30 communicated to Mr. Crozier Long a forgery?' Morel asked. The article ended, under the sub-heading 'An Appeal to British Fair-Play,' with conceding the importance of 'Germany's blunders and Germany's faults' but asking whether de Brunsen's 'main implication' could be sustained. It suggested 'a perfidiousness which, in the absence of conclusively-collaborative evidence and in the face of contradictory evidence is not credible as now presented.'

The same issue of the *Labour Leader* also included a piece from MacDonald in which he took the view that 'To force open a discussion of the origins of the war at present is useless.' Better to look ahead and try to ensure that the peace would be guided by a 'strong public opinion in favour of small nationalities and open honest diplomacy.' Meanwhile it was vital to 'do justice to our soldiers and their dependents' by ensuring adequate pay and pensions and 'take them off charity altogether.'

The following week (15 October) the *Leader* reported the speech of ILP chair F. W. Jowett at Accrington. In it he had 'examined the foreign policy of this country since 1904' and demonstrated how Sir Edward Grey had 'secretly pledged Britain to support France and Russia against Germany, although he had more than once stated in the House of Commons that we were not so pledged.' Jowett was, he said, not going to apologise for voting against increased armaments. 'If our foreign policy had been different that increase in armaments would not have been necessary.'

In the same issue appeared an article by M. Philips Price, who was in the process of publishing a book on the diplomacy that had preceded the war. Like Morel he asked whether Germany was 'Wholly Responsible' for the war.[134] After considering the dealings between Grey and the German ambassador, Prince Lichnowsky, in some detail he concluded that 'All these points show that Germany, stupid and even criminally negligent as she was in her support of Austria during the early stages of the negotiations, made desperate efforts to prevent the war from spreading to Western Europe at the eleventh hour.'

Morel returned to the *Labour Leader,* indeed to its front page, on 22 October, asking, 'Could Belgium Have Been Saved?' This was part of a letter to the Birkenhead Liberal Association resigning as its prospective parliamentary candidate. He denounced Germany's breach of Belgian neutrality and its subsequent conduct in that country but reiterated his case that Grey's secret diplomacy had made a definite contribution to the disaster. Morel conceded that it was possible that public opinion would have 'supported a case for military and naval understanding with France, frankly placed before

---

[134] Morgan Philips Price, 1885-1973, was a member of the UDC whose book *The Diplomatic History of the War* was published in 1914. Sometimes referred to as the 'Squire of Tiverton' on account of his ownership of a substantial estate, the Harrow and Cambridge educated Philips Price would become a war correspondent for the *Manchester Guardian* and, initially, an enthusiastic supporter of the Bolsheviks. Later he would be a Labour MP, 1929-31, and 1935-1950. His memoir, *My Three Revolutions,* was published in 1969.

Parliament' but he judged that it would have 'been limited to sanctioning the defence of France if wantonly attacked by Germany.' But public opinion would have refused to extend this to 'contingencies arising out of France's relationship with Russia, the one power which had nothing to lose and everything to gain from a general European war.'

As to Belgium, the British government had 'maintained a doubtful attitude until the position had become hopelessly compromised and until the opportunity of saving Belgium was lost.' Churchill had said that 'Belgium's peril' had been evident for three years. But 'a glance at the White Book' would show that 'the Belgian question was never raised until July 31st last. On that day we asked Germany, whom for three years we had been aware would *not* respect Belgian neutrality in the event of a war with Russia and France, whether she would respect it!' Even then the issue was not presented as 'a question of vital British national policy.' The answer to the question of what had been done to '*prevent* that outrage' inflicted on Belgium lay for Morel in 'an autocratic and secret foreign policy to which I have been consistently opposed, and which I intend to help in rooting out of our national life.'

There were a number of other *Labour Leader* contributors who took a similar line. One was E.G. Jellicoe – introduced as 'Liberal opponent of Mr. F. E Smith,' the controversial Conservative politician. [135] Jellicoe's articles appeared in the paper for three successive weeks beginning with the 22 October edition. In the second of these (29 October) he proposed to show 'how grievously the King and British people' had been 'misled and forced into war by meddlesome diplomacy.' In his interpretation, the failure of Britain and France to pressure Russia to 'suspend her mobilisation for some definite reasonable period' following the German ultimatum showed that 'The Government of each nation wanted war.' On 5 November he asked if

---

[135] E. G. (Edwin George) Jellicoe would continue his critique after the war in his 1924 book *Playing The Game. What Mr. Asquith in his book "The Genesis of the War" does not tell us.*

'Sir Edward Grey's diplomacy rendered war by Germany against Russia and France inevitable?' The same day a *Justice* contributor remarked that 'Our friends of the "Labour Leader" seem to think that the war, the greatest in mankind's memory, was engineered by some half-a-dozen diplomats. A more absurd view it is difficult to find.'

On 12 November MacDonald reviewed Philip Price's *The Diplomatic History of the War,* in the *Leader.* It contained, he said, 'page after page of the impartial narrative.' When the following week (19 November) Professor R. S. Conway attempted a detailed rebuttal of Morel's case, Brockway, added an editorial note.[136] Though Morel was, he said, quite capable of defending himself, his, Brockway's, intervention was justified because the *Leader* had made similar statements to those Conway criticised. 'The fact that the Foreign Secretary gave France a pledge before a German soldier had entered Belgium, and without consulting Parliament, that the British fleet would protect her shipping and her shores shows that the arrangements into which he had entered with France, whatever had been his original intentions, had assumed the nature of liabilities.'

Morel gave his own response to Conway's criticisms in the *Labour Leader* on 4 December reiterating that House of Commons and the country had been 'solemnly assured on four occasions' in 1913 and 1914 that there were no secret agreements. In the same issue Philips Price traced the origin of the breach of Belgian neutrality to 'the first Morocco crisis of 1905 and the conversion of the Anglo-French *entente* into a secret strategic understanding.' He concluded: 'If England had not entered this Continental alliance, she would have been in a position, as she was in 1870, to bargain with France and Germany and to insist on Belgian neutrality as her price for keeping out of any possible European war.'

Many in the ILP found such arguments convincing but for some

---

[136] R. S. (Robert Seymour) Conway, 1864-1933, was, from 1903 Hulme Professor of Latin Literature at Victoria University, Manchester. He would later, in 1929, stand, unsuccessfully, as a Liberal candidate for the Combined English Universities.

others on the Left they were never going to cut much ice. Hyndman, in his *Justice* editorial 'The Great War and the National Dignity' (1 October) had declared that he would have wanted Britain to defend both Belgium and France even had no treaties or guarantees existed. Writing to the *Clarion* about 'Our Duty to France' on 20 November, W. Wheeler maintained that Britain 'would and should' have gone to Belgium's aid and to France's even if the former's territory had not been violated. 'We should not have repeated the terrible and costly mistakes of 1864 and 1871.'[137]

## A Capitalist War?

For some on the Left, as elsewhere in the political spectrum, the question of responsibility was a matter of how to allocate the blame for the disaster. Was 'Prussian militarism' to blame? Was it the blundering secret diplomacy of Grey and others? Or both? But there was the larger question of the nature of the war. Being 'pro-war' did not necessarily mean taking a less hostile view of capitalism. Hyndman's *Justice* editorial of 20 August, had, as we saw earlier, been unequivocal in accepting that Germany must be opposed and defeated. But it ended by asserting that 'By far our worst enemies are the landlords and capitalists of Britain.'

For those, like John Mclean, whose interpretation of Marxism meant that capitalism lay at the base of everything that happened, the nature of the war was not at issue. But for others it was. The question

---

[137] These were the dates of the first and third of 'Bismarck's wars' which led to the unification of Germany under Prussian leadership in 1871. 1864 saw war between Denmark and the two leading powers of the German Confederation, Prussia and Austria, 1866 the war between the latter for the leadership of Germany, and 1871 the Franco-Prussian war after the overthrow of Napoleon III. Britain remained neutral throughout, though Wheeler clearly believed that it should have supported Denmark and France.

of whether the war was 'capitalist' was raised in *Justice's* regular 'Topical Tattle' column on 24 September. Was the war capitalist? 'Tattler' – presumably the editor, H. W. Lee – conceded that there had been capitalist wars – colonial 'expeditions' to promote concessions to business interests or the South African (Boer) War. But he did not believe the capitalists of any country wanted *this* war. It was more like 'a volcanic irruption of militarist States.' He returned to the theme the following week (1 October). Clearly it was true that the armament manufactures had been 'piling up huge profits,' but did not necessarily follow that they were 'delighted at the outbreak of war.' They probably would not see much increase in profits compared to 'ordinary times.' And in any case armaments firms were 'only a small section of the capitalist class.'

But 'Tattler's' view was not long to remain unchallenged. On 8 October a reader, W. H. Powell, quoted the views of the late Harry Quelch and an earlier letter of his own. 'In my letter which appeared in "Justice" in January, 1913, on the German Menace, I think I pointed out very fairly how capitalism, operating in Germany, would eventually lead to a conflict for the world's markets. I suppose "Tattler" is aware of the fact that it is a condition of capitalism that it must expand or burst.'

Fred Knee, who was to die in December, joined the debate the following week (15 October).[138] Yes, there was commercial rivalry between Britain and Germany but he doubted that the 'commercial classes' of either country wanted war. Peace was more profitable. The faction immediately responsible for the war was the Prussian 'military caste' and the 'Pre-Capitalist Junkers'.

But another correspondent, Robert Lowe, asked in evident

---

[138] Fred Knee, 1868-1914, was a veteran of the SDF/BSP and secretary of the London Trades Council since 1913. He was also a councillor and later alderman in Battersea. The *Clarion* announcing his death on 18 December said that 'his life was a constant struggle for the higher interests of his class' and that 'Not many officers in the Labour movement could so ill be spared.'

exasperation in the same edition 'If the present war is not a capitalist war then what is it?' A lot was now heard of the 'Marxian method' as if 'all events could be put into a sort of crucible, resolved into their separate elements, or weighed like salts with scientific exactness.' Yet 'the most surprising results' seemed to flow from this method. He listed the alternative interpretations.

- This is a capitalists' war, and was inevitable;
- it is a capitalists' war which the working class could and should have prevented;
- capitalism was so interwoven and international that the war must be a 'great illusion' – like the atrocities Belgians are said to have imagined themselves to have suffered;
- the workers have no concern in the war or its fortunes.

The nature of the war was also something that concerned some *Labour Leader* contributors. One of Jellicoe's articles (22 October) had the title 'Why Britain is at War. Is There Commercial Rivalry Behind It?' He denounced 'the Tariff Reform League and their political champions as the primary propagators of Britain's ill-will to Germany.'[139] They had 'flooded the country with political speakers and literature denouncing Germany's trade and prosperity to the workers of this country, but they only succeeded in stirring up a jealousy and bitterness towards Germany on the part of the most ignorant and petty-minded of the British public.'

In *Justice* more readers joined the debate that week (22 October). F. P. Sylvester cited the journal of the Birmingham Chamber of Commerce whose editorial talked of the growth of the 'commercial threat' from Germany and now hoped that the war would enable it to

---

[139] The Tariff Reform League had been formed in 1903 to promote Joseph Chamberlain's idea of turning the British Empire into a united trading bloc able to compete with Germany and the USA. It favoured 'Imperial Preference' and duties on foreign imports to protect British industry.

capture German trade. J. Campbell expressed severe scepticism over Powell's claim that the war was 'capitalist'. The latter, he charged, had 'made a running jump at the ready-made conclusion he desired to reach.' It was said that Germany aimed to take over Belgium and northern France preparatory to attacking Britain. Yet he could 'conceive those countries under the German flag without the German capitalist class selling a mouth harmonium the more.'

Debate continued in *Justice* with, on 29 October, Rosalind Travers Hyndman questioning whether the war served capitalists interests and W. K. De Swart begging to differ from 'some comrades' who were trying to persuade him that 'the war was only a capitalist war and no concern of mine.' The only warfare that should interest him as a socialist, they said, was 'the class struggle.' S. F. Whitlock's letter the following week (5 November) seemed at first to be heading in the direction of the 'comrades' arguing with De Swart. 'That this is a capitalist war,' it began, 'will be admitted by the general body of Socialists, for all wars under capitalism must necessarily be capitalist.' But if wars were always caused by capitalism it would be difficult to explain those that had preceded the birth of that economic system. The common factor in all wars was surely the 'hunger and thirst after power.'

'Tattler' returned to the topic on 12 November. He defined capitalist wars as 'wars that were undertaken with the object of either gaining new and undeveloped territory to exploit, or of forcing concessions from unwilling and less developed States or of gaining control of new markets.' He believed he was right in saying that Britain had had 'more of such wars during the last half century than any other country.' He was not prepared to admit that since the 'method of production' was capitalist 'therefore everything that happened' was 'due to the method of production.' Even if he admitted that, it would not affect his contention 'that the present European war is not a capitalist war, is not a war brought about intentionally by the capitalist classes.' On the contrary 'all this militarism and all this navalism' was due to 'the remains of pre-capitalist days adapted, of course, to modern conditions.' He ended by pointing out that a few years previously 'when the "German Menace" was heatedly being discussed, those who sought to prove there was nothing in it pointed to the way in which Germany was peacefully competing us out of one market after another as incontestable evidence of the soundness of their position.'

Much the same argument was deployed in *Justice* by L. E. Quelch on 19 November and by Victor Fisher the following week.[140] The former thought that though all Marxists held that 'the economic was the determining factor' it was not the only factor and that in Germany militarism had achieved such a strong position as to become 'a real vested interest' and 'almost as powerful as capitalism itself.' Fisher (26 November) agreed. Prior to the war Germany's position had been 'magnificent' from a capitalist point of view. 'The war was made by the Junker and militarist sections of the community against the better sense of the capitalist classes properly so called.' But whatever view British socialists took of the intrinsic nature of the war questions about one of Britain's allies and its main enemy inevitably generated much debate.

---

[140] Lorenzo ('Len') Edward Quelch, b. 1862, was the brother of the more prominent BSPer Harry Quelch. The wartime split in the Quelch family with Len's nephew Tom playing a prominent role in the 'anti-war' movement of the BSP – and later in the Communist Party – suggests, once again, that generational factors played some significant role in the divisions on the Left during this period.

# CHAPTER 7

# An Unwelcome Ally.

# Russia and the British Left.

## The *Russian* Menace

As we have already seen, the alliance with Russia was, for 'anti-war' people on the Left, a major reason to oppose British involvement. For those who supported British participation in the war, with varying degrees of reluctance, it was – at its very best – a grave embarrassment. Indeed, it went beyond that. With Tsarist Russia notorious for reactionary dictatorship and violent suppression of dissent, alignment with it against Germany was not something anyone of even mildly liberal views could contemplate without deep disquiet. Only the revolution of February/March 1917 would change this. Yet the advent to power of the Bolsheviks by the end of that year would open up an even greater gulf on the Left – across the world – than the war had done.

The publication by the Bolsheviks of the secret treaties made with its 'Entente' allies would give substance to the view that the war had been simply a struggle between rival imperialisms and suggest that those socialists who had supported the war in order to defend Belgium and France against German aggression had been appallingly naïve. It also gave further grist to the mill of all opponents of secret diplomacy. It is not surprising that the alliance with Russia should trigger a major debate in the socialist press from the beginning of the war.

'Russia. For Whom We Fight' was the *Labour Leader* headline of an article by Clement J. Bundock on 13 August 1914. He had no doubt that Russia was 'responsible for the European conflagration' and that Britain was 'fighting to support that tyranny.' The Tsarist regime had acted tyrannically in Finland and in Persia without British opposition.

Persia is broken.[141] When Russia crushes a small nation under her heel Britain has no word to say, though Britain is solemnly pledged to guarantee integrity and independence. When Germany marches her troops across the soil of a small nation and promises to acknowledge its independence at the conclusion of the war Britain must strike 'in defence of principles the maintenance of which is vital to the civilisation of the world.'

With such an ally how could Asquith maintain that 'no nation ever entered upon a great conflict with a clearer conscience?'

Yet, if there was implacable hostility in the pages of *Labour Leader,* Russia got no more support from the more-or-less 'pro-war' *Justice.* The week following Bundock's piece saw Rosaland Travers Hyndman, in the lead article of *Justice's* front page – now firmly established as devoted to 'The War' She attacked what she called 'Our pro-Russian Press.' which was, she wrote, 'naïvely expressing delight at the bribe of autonomous government which the Tsar offers to the three Polands (Austrian, German and Russian) if the two first will rise and throw of the Teutonic yoke in order to bear the Slavonic one.' She recalled the 'powerful and rather sinister part played in the government of Austria' by the 'Polish Club' of representatives in the

---

[141] When the Russians had brutally intervened in Persia, as Iran was then generally known, in 1911, Radical MPs Ponsonby and Morrell were prominent in questioning Grey as to whether their action was compatible with the Anglo-Russian agreement of 1907 which was supposed to guarantee Persian independence. The foreign secretary insisted that Russian demands involved 'no new departure in practice.' See *Hansard HC Deb 07 December 1911 vol 32 cc1558-60.*

Viennese Reichstag and the 'successful struggle against Polish influence of the Ruthenians or Ukrainians in the eastern part of Galicia.' The latter might identify more with the Russians than with the Poles but would 'think twice of joining the Tsar's empire' in the light of the oppression of the Ukrainians under Russian rule. As for the current Tsarist offer. 'Look at Finland if you would see how imperial promises are kept!'

This last point that she made was bound to resonate with anyone with a knowledge of the recent history of that part of Europe. Finland could very plausibly seen as a good test of Russian intentions. Compared with other parts of the Russian Empire, the Grand Duchy of Finland had enjoyed considerable autonomy. As a result of Finnish participation in the 1905 Revolution the *Eduskunta*, a unicameral parliament, was introduced with universal and equal suffrage. Finland became the first European country where women achieved the right to vote. Earlier the Tsarist regime had pursued a policy of Russification from 1899-1905. After 1908 this policy returned.

'Bad News from Finland' was a sub-heading in *Labour Leader's* 'Review of the Week' on 19 November. Hundreds of socialists and radicals had been arrested. Some had been taken to Russia. Some had been tortured. The practice of fining Finnish newspapers had been 'developed to a ridiculous extreme.' A very conservative paper had been heavily fined 'because it has mentioned, "out of sheer loyalty" the Tsar's manifesto to the Poles. (if Finns learn of the Tsar's promises to the Poles they may expect freedom for themselves!)' Officials were no longer being appointed 'in the legal way the Constitution demands' but appointed by the Russian governor-general. All those appointed had been 'without exception, either Russians or Finns who have sold themselves, body and soul to the Tsar.' Yet the British press was 'still praising the generosity of the Russian Government in the treatment of the Finns, the Poles and other unfortunate peoples under its sway!' Where did it get such ideas, the *Leader* asked and concluded 'unless we are on the alert, the war which Britain is supposed to be fighting on behalf of the liberty of small nations will end in the permanent tightening of the fetters with which Russia has bound every small nation over whom she has had power.'

Then on 3 December 1914 another headline in *Labour Leader's* 'Review of the Week' announced 'Russia crushes Finland' while in the final *Justice* of the year Rosalind Travers Hyndman returned to the subject once more. In the course of a wider survey of Tsarist repression and criticism of the naïve credence given to the assurance given by the Russian rulers by 'our English Russophiles,' she gave details of the 'Complete Russification' of Finland. She concluded with a plea for Social-Democrats to 'speak for the Finns' and not allow 'the most Social-Democratic nation in the world' to be 'overwhelmed by Muscovite barbarism once again.'

Exempted, of course, from all taint of 'Muscovite barbarism' by all segments of the British Left was the Russian Left. On 27 August the *Leader* quoted from the 'Manifesto of Russian Socialists' which asked whether it was possible to 'Imagine the intervention of the Tsar on behalf of poor Servia whilst he martyrises Poland, Finland and the Jews.' Was 'Prussian militarism' to be replaced with Tsarism, asked Keir Hardie on the front page of the same issue.

> Let anybody take a map of Europe and look at the position of Germany: on the one side Russia with her millions of trained soldiers and unlimited population to draw upon (its traditional policy for over a hundred years has been to reduce Prussia to impotence so that the Slav can reign supreme), on the other side France, smarting under her defeat and the loss of her two provinces, Alsace and Lorraine. For a number of years past these two militarisms have had a close and cordial alliance.

The two unlikely allies had been brought together by one object 'to crush Germany between them.' The building up of German armaments and navy was primarily intended 'to protect herself and her interests against these two open enemies.'

## Vernon Lee versus H. G. Wells

The same edition of the *Leader* (27 August) included a response by Vernon Lee 'to' H. G. Wells's article 'The Sword of Peace'.[142] This had appeared in the *Daily Chronicle* on 7 August.[143] Lee was introduced to readers as the well-known author of *Vital Lies*, the *Gospel of Anarchy* and other works. She had 'asked for an opportunity to express ... the opinions of those Liberals who at present are refused publication in Liberal papers.' Wells, Lee said, had hitherto been 'a denouncer of war' and 'his apostasy' was 'all the worse because it is sincere.' The sub-title of his article had been *'Every sword that is drawn against Germany now is a sword drawn for peace'* and now, said Lee, the allies were 'engaged in exterminating Germany and bringing her and Europe under Russia's predominance.' She quoted Wells's contention that 'The defeat of Germany may open the way to peace and disarmament throughout the earth.' That was what was always said by all sides in a war, she concluded.

The next edition of *Labour Leader* (3 September) devoted half a page to 'The Russian Menace' with the subtitle 'H.G. Wells Says It Is A Bogey. Is It?' This began with Wells's reply to Lee. 'No one who remains sane can suppose we have any other alternative before us now but victory or destruction,' wrote Wells. He accused MacDonald and Hardie of 'misrepresenting the negotiations that preceded the war' and 'suggesting that we are in some way cheats in defending the neutrality of Belgium.' What did they want Britain to do – sue for

---

[142] Vernon Lee was the pseudonym of the writer Violet Paget, 1856-1935. She was a pacifist and soon to be a member of the UDC.

[143] The *Daily Chronicle* was a paper broadly supportive of the radical wing of the Liberal Party. Its most distinguished editor was Henry Massingham, 1860-1924, who was forced out due to his opposition to the South African (or Boer) War. He became editor of *The Nation* the leading Liberal/Radical journal in 1907 but left the year before his death when he joined the Labour Party.

peace? They should answer this question. But instead all they offered was a 'whining criticism of the acts of Sir Edward Grey.' His own position on Russia had been made clear in a *Nation* article that had been published immediately before the *Leader* issue in which Vernon Lee's 'reply' appeared. This, Wells claimed, 'knocks the bottom out of all this nonsense which represents Russia as a kind of worst devil and Kaiser-Krupp Prussian system as the clean white fabric of a delightful yet disciplined civilisation, which not only aspires but deserves to dominate the world.'

This was followed by Bundock's critique of Wells's *Nation* article. He quoted Wells's contention that 'the day of the unintelligent, common soldier' was past and consequently 'Russia can only become powerful enough to overcome any highly-civilised European country by raising its own average of education,' a process which could only be done by *'liberalising* on the Western European model.' But how seriously could such an argument be taken, asked Bundock. 'Why should we believe that Russia, if it can be effective in hurling Prussian militarism from its seat, will, when the work is done, be stricken suddenly with ineffectiveness?' Fear of Russian despotism, concluded Bundock, was well-grounded.

But – apart from Wells's own letter – Bundock was not to have it all his own way. In the *Labour Leader* of 3 September was a letter from R.C.K. Ensor, at this time a journalist on the *Daily Chronicle*.[144] He protested against Hardie's 'ill-timed attempt to revive anti-Russian prejudice.' The Russian 'democratic and constitutional movements' had seen in the war 'a unique opportunity of securing at once two things that can only be secured together – the liberalising of Russia and the creation of a permanent Anglo-Russian friendship.' Nothing could be further from the truth than Hardie's contention that it had

---

[144] R.C.K.(Robert Charles Kirkwood) Ensor, 1877-1951, was a Fabian socialist whose *Modern Socialism as set forth by Socialists in their Speeches, Programmes and Writings* had appeared in 1902. Later he would become best known for the volume of the *Oxford History of England* covering the period 1870-1914 published in 1936.

been a century-long Russian policy 'to reduce Prussia to impotence so that the Slav can reign supreme.'

The current war was the first one between Prussia and Russia for 152 years, since when relations had been mostly friendly with 'the influence of the former on the latter almost uniformly bad.' It had been Prussia which had instigated the partitions of Poland. It had been Austria and Prussia which had turned the Holy Alliance, conceived by Alexander I 'in a spirit of genuine, if quixotic, humanitarianism' into 'an instrument of tyranny.' It had been Bismarck who had encouraged 'Russian reaction' under Alexander III and the Kaiser's influence that had 'induced Russia to make the disastrous war on Japan.' The Russian bureaucracy had long been modelled on that of Prussia and 'staffed to still quite an appreciable extent with German heads.' He felt sorry, on opening *Labour Leader*, 'to see every reference to Russia in a key of stale and sterile carping.'

The 'carping' may have been less but front page of the same day's *Justice* was barely less apprehensive about Russia than its ILP rival. It claimed that Russia would have the 'easier part' in the war with the danger that war might end with 'a beaten Germany, an exhausted France, a crippled England, with Russia fresh and strong' and able to impose its terms. Nor could an eventual realignment in the form of a deal with Germany be ruled out. 'It would not be the first time that there has been a Drei Kaiser Bund.'

The same page reported that 'The reply of the Russian Government to the general demand for political amnesty' had been 'more in keeping with its general policy than the recent wonderful manifesto of the Grand Duke Nicholas to the Poles.' The secret police had been active and among the arrested was the lawyer 'who defended the workers prosecuted in connection with the Lena massacres.'[145]

---

[145] In April 1912 workers at the goldfields near the Lena River in Siberia took strike action over their harsh working conditions. When there were protests against the arrest of the strike committee, government troops fired on the crowd killing 270 and wounding nearly as many more. Alexander Kerensky, who would later head the

On 10 September, saying that the *Daily Chronicle* had refused to publish her letter, Vernon Lee returned to her attack on Wells's defence of Russia in the *Labour Leader*. There was freedom of press in Germany, she argued. The Jews, in spite of being 'sneered at and excluded from smart society only a little less than in democratic France' formed in Germany 'one of the most influential factors on public life.' They were not confined to ghettos as in Russia. The freedom of German socialists was in marked contrast to the suppression in Russia of their comrades. There were reasonable hopes that better relations with Britain and France would lead to a decline of Prussian militarism while the present war was more likely to strengthen its dominance. Her dismissal of Wells's 'self-justificatory arguments' was answered in like manner the following week (17 September) when Wells concluded that he was 'forced to declare my conviction that Miss Paget knows nothing whatever about Russia.' Vernon Lee's real name was, of course, Violet Paget.

That same week Hardie made 'A Strong and Uncompromising Reply' to 'Critics of the I.L.P.' Only 'a couple of professing Socialists had been able to muster sufficient courage' to say that Russia was 'fighting for Democracy.' This seems to have been how he interpreted the letters of Wells and Ensor in the previous week's *Leader*. Saying that he was 'away from all books and papers,' Hardie questioned the accuracy of Ensor's 'reading of history' but even if it was correct it would 'only show the ruling class in Russia to be set of nincompoops' who had 'allowed themselves to be driven hither and thither at the will of their Prussian masters.' But it was very difficult, he said, to attribute the pogroms or Bloody Sunday to German influence.[146]

---

ill-fated provisional government in 1917, came to prominence as chair of the Duma commission enquiring into the massacre.

[146] From the 1880s there had been a number of violent attacks on Jews – or pogroms – in several parts of the Russian Empire. Bloody Sunday here refers to the violent suppression of a peaceful demonstration in January 1905 which was one of the key events in triggering the revolutionary risings of that year. Even the Tsarist official figures admitted that 96 were killed and some estimates range from 1,000 to 4,000.

## German Fear of Russia

On 8 October *Labour Leader* devoted a page to 'The Menace of Russia' featuring sections on 'Facts from Finland', 'Ruthenians and the Russian Yoke', 'How Russia Treats Socialists', and 'How Russia Treats Jews.' On the same day *Justice* devoted its front page to reports from the *New York Call* saying that the socialist papers *Pravda* and *Nasha Rabotchaya* and some trade union and cooperative movement journals in Russia had been shut down at start of the war. The following week (15 October) the *Leader* devoted its front page to 'Germany's Fear of Russia. Germans might dislike Prussian militarism but were 'ready to die with Prussia rather than endure a Russian conquest.'

It quoted from a 1913 book by the French socialist politician, Marcel Sembat. He argued that German fear of Russia was of a quite different order to that of France's hostility to Germany which had been unknown before 1870.

> This other thing is different. Every German has grown up under the unceasing threat of a terrific avalanche hanging over his head; of an avalanche ready to loosen and drop and roll upon him; an avalanche of multitudinous savagery, of brutal and barbarous hordes which will spread over his German soil and bury his civilisation and his ways.

As early as 3 September in *Labour Leader,* Jowett had noted that 'Faced with the awful fact of a Cossack invasion, even a German Socialist may well conclude that there is nothing for it but to fight. If it is argued against him that he is striking France and not Russia, the answer is that France had bound itself to Russia, and war with one involved war with the other.'

The fear of Russia in Germany was widely acknowledged on the British Left – even by those who supported the war. In the *Clarion* on 27 November Thompson's editorial focussed on the responsibility of

German socialists. He had, he wrote, never shared the view of 'enthusiastic internationalists, bitterly disappointed by the failure of the German Socialists to stop the war.' Among other factors that explained this apparent failing on the part of the SPD and its supporters he noted that 'there really was a risk of a Russian invasion, and the German Socialists are intensely bitter against Russia.'

## Russian Socialists

A very different note was struck in *Justice* on 15 October in 'A Message from Comrade Plechanoff.'[147] Plekhanov was quoted as saying that Wilhelm II had been the 'strongest supporter of his brother, Nicholas II' and that even after the outbreak of war the 'extreme reactionary party' favoured the German emperor and its organ *The Russian Flag*, known in Russia, Plekhanov said, as 'The Prussian Flag' was 'doing its best to exonerate the Germans from the atrocities which have called forth the just indignation of the entire civilised world.'

If *Justice* was giving front-page prominence to Plekhanov, *Labour Leader* would a few weeks later (19 November) do the same for a very different statement from Russian socialists, which appeared in an article on 'Russian Socialists and the War' by S. Dalin, who was identified as a 'Russian Socialist journalist.' Vandervelde had appealed to Russian socialists for support for the Allied cause. Dalin included in his article the statement in reply by 'the Central Committee of the

---

[147] Georgi Plekhanov, 1856-1918, was a founder of the social-democratic movement in Russia and a Marxist theoretician. By 1914 the split in the Social-Democratic Labour Party which began in 1903 between the Mensheviks, including Plekhanov, and the Bolsheviks, had hardened into permanency. Plekhanov supported the Allied cause during the war and opposed the Bolshevik seizure of power at the end of his life.

Social-Democratic Party (Majority Group)[148] The Bolshevik leadership stated that there was no possibility of an 'armistice,' even a temporary one, with the Russian government. After the war, it predicted, 'a further development of European democracy' would take place, but a Russian government 'having gained a new influence and authority from the war' would be the 'strongest check' on this.

Dalin added that 'both sections of the Russian Social-Democratic Party' were 'united and unanimous on this issue.' Until there was a change of regime there was no possibility that Russian socialists would support the war. He quoted Larin, of 'the Minority Group' (i.e. the Mensheviks), warning 'comrades of other countries' to pay no attention to 'the declarations of people like Bourtzeff and Kropotkin 'who have taken no part in the Russian working-class movement for decades.'[149] *Labour Leader's* editorial 'Review of the Week' that week

---

[148] In spite of its name the Bolsheviks – a Bolshevik was literally 'one of the majority' – did not have a settled majority in the larger party at this time. The Bolsheviks would later become the Communist Party.

[149] Iurii Aleksandrovich Larin, 1882-1932, an economist, would return to Russia in 1917 and join the Bolshevik Party. He subsequently played some part in economic administration serving in the delegation to the Brest-Litovsk negotiations with Germany in early 1918.

Vladimir Bourtzeff, (or Burtsev) 1862-1942, had played an important role in the Russian revolutionary movement by exposing Tsarist agents provocateurs. He returned to Russia after the outbreak of war intending to attempt to enlist in the armed forces but was sentenced early in 1915 to deportation to Siberia. In 1934 in a legal case in Switzerland he was a key witness demonstrating that the so-called 'Protocols of the Elders of Zion' which was used as evidence by anti-Semites of a Jewish conspiracy for world power – and still is sometimes in the 21st century – was a forgery. In 1938 in Paris he published, *The Protocols of the Elders of Zion: A Proved Forgery*, based on his testimony at the trial.

Prince Pyotr Alexeyevich Kropotkin, 1842-1921, was a prominent anarchist best known for books such as *The Conquest of Bread* and his critique of Darwinism in *Mutual Aid: A Factor in Evolution*. He lived for many years in exile in London and later in Brighton and returned to Russia after the February Revolution of 1917. An opponent of Bolshevism, his funeral in 1921 is said to be the last public demonstration of the Russian anarchists. His opposition to Communism did not prevent the soviet regime in renaming a Moscow Metro station after him in the 1950s.

praised 'The Brave Russian Socialists,' agreeing with them 'entirely' that 'the best service they can render European democracy at this moment is to endeavour to democratise the Russian State. The darkest menace that faces Europe is the unprincipled ambition of Russia.' Meanwhile, the earlier message in *Justice* – quite innocently as far as Plekhanov was concerned – would trigger a response that led to important concerns about anti-Semitism.

## 'Real' Russians?

*Justice* on 5 November included an article on 'Russia and the War' signed 'Le Vin'. The latter claimed to summarise the views of 'a considerable body of democratic and Socialist opinion' in Britain which were 'ventilated in the "Labour Leader" and are shared by many political refugees from Russia.' These pointed out that, apart from the promise of Polish autonomy forced by the military situation the Russian government had not shown 'the slightest inclination of making peace with its own country.' There had been no amnesty for political prisoners and the oppression of Jews, Finns and other minorities continued. The result was that the defeat of Germany by Russia was viewed as 'tantamount to a victory for Russian reaction and a setback to the cause of freedom.' But, Le Vin insisted, it was 'nothing of the kind' and in any case it was the 'painful duty' of socialists to 'disregard the call of local interests', in this case of the 'internal Russian situation – and rise to the higher demands' of the overall European situation.

What was at stake was the independence and integrity of Belgium and France and the safety of Britain. It was necessary to choose between them, the 'hope of European democracy,' and 'militarist Germany.' Of course there were plenty of things wrong with them, but 'in this capitalist world one always had to choose the least of several evils. The defeat of Germany would pave the way for 'a German Republic.' Turning to 'my own country – Russia,' Le Vin conceded that a Russian victory over Germany 'without any outside help or assistance' would be 'a great blow to the cause of freedom in Russia. But in the current situation where victory would mean first of all the triumph of the western democratic Powers,' Russia would find itself both dependent on financial support from Britain and France and, if 'expectations of the coming liberalisation' were not met, faced with a hostile public opinion and isolated. The likely effects of this were not difficult to guess, he said.

In the same issue appeared a letter from J. F. Green who claimed the right to express his feelings in view of his 'long services to the cause of Russian freedom.' He deplored 'the pro-German attitude of several Russo-Jewish refugees in this country.' It was 'hardly decent' at a time when Britain was 'fighting for our national existence' that those who were allowed to live in the country with a 'fuller enjoyment of liberty than any other country' should be denouncing the war with Germany – 'they might at least preserve a discreet silence.' A postscript added that since writing the letter, Green had read Plekhanov's statement. This confirmed his impression that 'the real Russians – i.e. those of Slav race' – supported the Allied cause. It was only 'some of the Jews who, for some unfathomable reason' were 'pro-German.'

A response was not long in coming. L. Lubert, in a letter the following week (12 November) regretted that Green, who was 'well-known as an internationalist,' should now reveal that he was 'only one of the John Bull type – simply good old England!' Of course Germany was the aggressor but how could it be expected that people who had 'for decades been inhumanly oppressed by such a country as Russia to have that hatred for Germany which we Englishmen might have.' Lubert deplored 'the attitude of Mr. Green such and similar utterings.'

Le Vin returned with a letter on 19 November. Green had attacked 'what he pleases to call the "pro-German"' attitude of 'several Russo-Jewish refugees,' but what was 'the attitude of the

"Labour Leader" and a good many Liberals and Radicals in this country?' Green made no mention of them. Instead he singled out 'the Jews, some of whom, as he put it, are "for some unfathomable reason, pro-German."' He then made his 'most emphatic protest.' *Labour Leader* and those who shared its view had made a strong case which 'must be met with arguments and criticism but it is hardly decent to turn round and instead of argument fling at them a "shut up, you foreigner."'

He continued, 'Comrade Green, informs us in his post-scriptum that Plechanoff's letter confirms his experience that "real Russians – i.e. those of the Slav race – are glad that Russia is fighting for freedom (sic) side by side with Britain and France."' In talking of 'Real Russians,' Green, whose experience was 'obviously very meagre,' had, said Le Vin, without knowing it, 'actually borrowed the notorious watchword of the Black Hundreds.'[150] In fact even those Green called 'real Russian' socialists were 'divided on this question.'

> Against the 'real Russian' Plechanoff (the latter will not be thankful to comrade Green for this new epithet), and his followers is ranged the 'real Russian' Lenin with a larger following still. Everybody who has watched events both here and abroad knows perfectly well that everywhere the Socialists, whether Jew or Gentile, are hopelessly split on this very subject.

The following week (26 November) a letter from an otherwise unnamed 'Russian-Jewish Socialist' noted that in the same issue of *Justice* that carried Green's letter there had been a report of 16 London BSP branches passing a resolution condemning the war. 'May not,' he asked, 'a Russian-Jewish Socialist agree with that resolution without being ungrateful or indecent?'

This was followed by another letter, signed 'One of Them' which,

---

[150] The Black Hundreds were ultra-nationalist organisations whose intolerant chauvinist propaganda led to pogroms and murders of political opponents.

expressed shock and disappointment at Green's view – 'which caused me to rub my eyes in dismay.'

> Surely it is impossible to forget the tortures inflicted on us by the Russian Government not so long ago. The horrible pograms and butchery systematically organised and supervised by high officials under the guidance of the Tsar himself, who decorated the members of the 'Black Hundreds' for their noble work. 'Unfathomable reason,' indeed!

Green's attempt to defend himself in a letter to *Justice* on 3 December would have done little, if anything, to conciliate.

> I did never said that all Russian-Jews were pro-German: and when I spoke of Slav-Russians as real Russians, I meant no offence to our Jewish friends. Surely they recognise that they belong to a separate race, and that if a visitor from the Continent wished to obtain a typical English view on any subject he would not go to Lord Rothschild, or Sir Felix Schuster, or a Jew of humble birth in Whitechapel but to a real Englishman.

# CHAPTER 8

# An Unwanted Enemy.
# Germany and the British Left.

## Germans: Which ones are the Enemy?

For opponents of the war, whether the increasingly large proportion of the BSP or the majority of active ILPers, Germans – above all the German working class – were fellow victims of a hideous war that should never have been inflicted on the world. The charge they had to contend with was that of being unpatriotically 'pro-German.' For those socialists who supported the war – with varying degrees of reluctance – the question was how to regard this unwanted enemy. Were *all* Germans to blame, or was it just the 'Prussian militarists' or even just Kaiser Wilhelm II himself?

It may seem strange – or perhaps not – that some of the most vehement denouncers of Germany were people with considerable experience of and connections with that country. A. M. Thompson, the son of much travelled theatrical parents, had been born in Germany and his first language had been German. Also on the *Clarion* team was A. Neil Lyons who had gone to school in Germany. Ernest Belfort Bax of the BSP had studied music in Germany as a sixteen-year-old and a few years later had returned to immerse himself in the philosophy of, especially, Kant and Hegel. He had published *A Handbook to the History of Philosophy* in 1886. Bax was a prolific writer for the rest of his life and several of his books were historical accounts of parts of the German past including works on Germany at the end of the middle ages, the Peasants' War, and the Anabaptists.

Writing on 'Germany and Prussian Domination' on the 10 September Bax told *Justice* readers that Prussia was 'the least German of all the German States' The original Prussians were Borussians – a Slav tribe. Others on the British Left had less profound but nonetheless very real ties with Germany. Tom Groom, the virtual founder of the Clarion Cycling Club, began his 'Cyclorama' on 4 September, 'But for the misfortune of the war it is probable that two or three members of the C.C.C. would be journeying by this time towards Frankfurt-on-Main to take part in the Second Annual Conference of the International Association of Socialists for Physical Education.'

On 18 September the *Clarion's* 'Cockpit' included a letter from Gustav Susieck headed 'A German Socialist.' Claiming this title, the writer expressed a desire to 'go with the English army on the battlefields of France' to 'see with my own eyes the vandalism of Prussian warfare.' An Allied victory would be one for 'Liberty and Democracy' and Prussian militarism would be defeated. 'The German people did not want the war and were driven into it by the brutal military laws and iron discipline. Through the destruction of the German military force we German Socialists hope to go an important step towards the Socialist State.'

But not everyone whose views appeared in that paper were as ready to acquit Germans in general from responsibility for the war. A week later (25 September) R. Kanthack's letter complained of 'a persistent effort to discriminate between a Germany' as represented by the Kaiser and 'his military camarilla and a peaceful, industrial, and intellectual Germany with which we have no quarrel.' This, Kanthack said, was not justified. He had recently lived for two years in a German university town and had travelled throughout the country meeting people of the widest possible variety. All seemed to have a 'firm conviction of the political, intellectual and moral superiority over all other people of the world and of their mission as universal bearers of culture.' He had meet thousands of Germans and had known hundreds well and found them all to be 'aggressively patriotic and imbued with an offensive national conceit.' It might be 'Kaiserism' that was to blame for the war but there was 'an essentially approving nation behind it, educated into approbation during the last forty-four years and longer.' The 'much vituperated Kaiser' was 'merely an exaggerated victim of Germany's hallucination.'

Thompson gave *some* editorial support for this view in the same edition. He blamed, especially, the influence of Treitschke, Bernhardi and Nietzsche.[151] 'In Nietzsche's eyes the founder of civilisation was 'a magnificent blonde brute ranging about and *lusting for booty and victory.'* It was these 'magnificent blonde brutes who have lately burnt Louvain and Reims.' He also cited Prince von Bülow, the German chancellor from 1900 to 1909 who, Thompson said, regarded 'the Prussian creed of Force and Grab as the universal religion of mankind.'

But quoting von Bülow's statement that 'the Social Democratic movement is the antithesis of the Prussian State,' he commented, 'That is why we, loving the Germany of Goethe, Heine, Beethoven and Wagner, applaud the war against the brutal, domineering, bombastic Prussia of Bismarck, Nietzsche, Treitschke, Bernhardi and Attila II'. [152] At this point, at least, Thompson was still going along

---

[151] Heinrich von Treitschke, 1834-1896, was a nationalist and anti-Semite. He was a professor at Humbold University, Berlin, and a member of the *Reichstag*.

Friedrich Nietzsche, 1844-1900, was a philosopher and many-sided intellectual, the interpretation of whose work remains controversial. He is mainly remembered for his statement 'God is Dead' and the concept of a 'superman' in *Also Sprach Zarathustra (Thus Spoke Zarathustra)*.

[152] The responsibility for presenting Wilhelm II as 'Attila' rests in its origin with the man himself. On 27 July 1900, during the Boxer Rebellion he gave the following order to the German contingent of the international force opposing the rebels: 'Mercy will not be shown, prisoners will not be taken. Just as a thousand years ago, the Huns under Attila won a reputation of might that lives on in legends, so may the name of Germany in China, such that no Chinese will even again dare so much as to look askance at a German.' The British habit of calling Germans 'Huns' in both world wars derives, ultimately, from this. The *Clarion*, 25 September 1914,

with the notion of a 'good Germany' betrayed and dragged into war by a gang of Prussian militarists.

One of the most comprehensive instances of anti-Germanism in the *Clarion* grew out of a long debate between A. Neil Lyons and his 'old friend and convive, Dr Harry Roberts'. It began in the issue of 28 August when Roberts complained that 'The Austrian Emperor, Mr. H. G. Wells, the Grand Duke Nicholas, and Mr Neil Lyons are tumbling over themselves in holy enthusiasm for this war.'[153] Given rival national ambitions Roberts believed the war was unavoidable. 'But what business we Socialists who believe these ambitions to be based on the utter fallacy of materialism, have in this gallery passes my comprehension.'

Lyons replied in the next edition of the paper on 4 September. 'I detest the ideas and deeds by which the Pan-German spirit expresses itself,' he declared. 'If I can't have Socialism I'll have Englishism. And I know that having Englishism is a necessary prelude to having anything which approaches even in a minute degree to the Socialism which I want.' He was at pains to point out that, born in Kimberley in South Africa, he was not English himself. Later (25 September), rather confusingly, he would say that while he was 'English by birth' and 'by conviction'. He was 'not of English descent; I am not racially English.'

In his response of 4 September Lyons was able to quote – in his own support as he deemed it – from Roberts' own 1911 book *Towards a National Policy.*

In some circles, to refer to the defence of England otherwise than with a sneer is to mark oneself down as a renegade and traitor to all the principles of the 'free wee kirk' of politics. The narrowing effect of

---

included a poem by A. M. Thompson with the title 'Creed of Attila II'.

[153] Harry Roberts, 1871-1946, was a medical doctor and socialist. The Harry Roberts Nursery School in Stepney, Tower Hamlets, is named after him. David Jeffery's biography *Dr. Harry Roberts – a Petersfield Philanthropist* was published in 2009.

sectarianism are nowhere more obvious than where this question is concerned. The mere thought of a man *fighting in defence of his country, or his country's honour* fills the old-fashioned Socialist or Radical with pious horror. *"Dulce et decorum est pro patria more"* is regarded either as a catchword of the Yellow Press or as a capitalist dodge. This is one of the many reasons why Socialists have not been more popular with the average Englishman. An increasing number, however, are freeing themselves from the vague, cosmopolitan, 'well-intensionedness' of the earlier apostles of Socialism.

Lyons said he agreed and then added, in language that is now bound to sound more shocking than it would have done at the time, 'Further more, cockie, I hate Germans. ... The way they behave to horses, niggers and women, and all other non-military objects is not a way of which I can bring myself to approve.'

Roberts returned on 11 September with a very long 'open letter to Mr. A Neil Lyons' headed 'Socialism and Sobriety.' He agreed that his views had changed since 1911. He defended his utter abhorrence of the war and ended by quoting the whole of Thomas Hardy's poem 'The Man I Killed'. Over four consecutive weeks, 25 September to 16 October, Lyons then responded with a series of his own 'open letters' to Roberts headed 'Confessions of a German Hater.'

He appreciated, he said, in the first letter, 'very keenly the dignity, the restraint and the honesty' of Roberts's previous letter. But he insisted that contrary to what the latter seemed to believe, he really did hate Germans; 'I hate them utterly and bitterly, and what is more, I hate them logically.' He found that his 'Socialistic convictions, which are very strong and very sincere, have an absolutely national foundation. Internationalism is a sentiment that I simply do not understand.' His hatred of Germans was based partly on his experience of being sent to Hanover for eighteen months at the age of fifteen and spending fifteen of them in a *Real Gymnasium* which he was able to contrast with his previous experience of Bedford Grammar School.

In his second letter Lyons wrote that when Roberts claimed that 'the sort of thing expressed by General von Bernhardi is "common enough in England" I simply open my mouth and gape at you. I stand aghast.' He characterised Roberts as 'a singularly insular person' who had never been to Germany and had met few Germans. As a result he failed to see that 'the lowest English vices are a mere pale parody of that which passes for gentlemanly spirit among Germans.' In Britain 'pot house patriotism' reached 'its apotheosis in that immortal anthem about the boys of the bulldog breed.' But 'such drivel is not often sung (except in a spirit of pure mockery) by English people who are neither very illiterate or very drunk.' In contrast, 'educated people in Germany sang songs or recited poems 'compared to which the poem to which I refer is a model of quiet, good taste.'

The final two 'letters' of Lyons's series again drew on his experiences as a schoolboy in Hanover – seeing a 'tradesman's boy' who had accidentally collided with an infantry lieutenant viciously beaten by the latter with his scabbarded sword and the experience of Lyons himself as a 'rather nervous and stammering little boy' being constantly held up by form teachers as 'an example of British decadence.' In giving an account of his school days he 'wanted to show how the national spirit of bumptiousness and brag had penetrated even to the form-rooms of the public schools.' He did, he insisted 'hate Germans.' He believed them to be 'a people of strong and vigorous character who have been thoroughly perverted by fifty years of evil teaching. I think that they are at present the most worldly, greedy, boastful and cruel people in Europe.'

Roberts's final retort on 23 October conceded that he had not visited Germany. But he had, he said 'been a member of a Board of Guardians, and have met quite a number of Borough Councillors, solicitors, vicars' wives and members of the Charity Organisation Society' a good proportion of whom corresponded 'so exactly with your account of the Germans you have met that I am quite convinced of the accuracy of your report.' The 'essential grouping of mankind' could not be made on a national basis. Both 'the people who make us sick' and 'the sort of people we enjoy' were pretty evenly distributed among the nations' Roberts insisted.

## A 'Nation of Spies'?

By this time Blatchford's attitude had hardened considerably. Writing on the front page of the *Clarion* on 23 October under the title 'Things That Matter', he responded to a letter from Cunningham Graham which had appeared in the paper the previous week.[154] The veteran Scottish socialist had admitted that he had been wrong before the war to dismiss Blatchford's 'German menace' warnings.

Blatchford chose to reciprocate.

I have a confession to make also and will make it now. Before this war began, and for a little while after, I thought, and said, that we must blame only the military cult of Prussia, and not the German people. I was wrong. The German people are as mad as their Kaiser. They are full of a brutal lust of lordship, they are as blind to the claims of humanity as he, and they hate and envy Britain and the British with a mean rancour which he has never surpassed. The whole German nation seems to have contracted homicidal mania.

Three weeks previously, on 2 October, in another front-page article, Blatchford had declared 'The fact is that Germans are a nation of spies. Great Britain, Belgium, France and Holland have been infested with German spies for a dozen or twenty years.' He claimed he had been

---

[154] Robert Cunningham Graham, 1852-1936, was a well-known Scottish socialist who would, two years before his death, become the first president of the Scottish National Party. In his younger days he led an adventurous life which included a spell as a cattle rancher in Argentina from which was derived his affectionate nickname, 'Don Roberto'.

warned by French and Russian people years before that 'an attack on railways and bridges in this country had been organised.' This was all part of what the German general staff had 'planned with a boldness and a minuteness which the British public cannot realise.' If Blatchford's critics wanted any further evidence of what they must have regarded as his total paranoia they could find it in this article with its extremely unlikely claims; 'I have seen spies in our quiet village: two cavalry officers came to Lowerison's cottage one day selling boot-laces.[155] A Prussian officer waited on me and Thompson one day in a café in the Strand.' He was prepared for doubters; 'Do you think I am an alarmist? Who put the iron chair on the Dover line?'

A *Labour Leader* response arrived swiftly the following week (8 October) with 'An Open letter to some Germans' by 'Casey'. The article began by quoting the end of Blatchford's diatribe. The only safe plan, the *Clarion* editor had insisted, would be to 'deport *every* German' even those who had been 'long naturalised British subjects' some of whom had been 'amongst the most treacherous and dangerous of spies.' Addressing the *Leader's* editor Casey asked ironically, 'I hope that *you* will not advocate the deportation of all Germans, or Royalty may all be a minus quantity in England.'

This final point was not lost on the writer of *Justice's* 'Critical Chronicle' on 22 October who attempted to take a measured view of 'The Attack Upon Germans.' It was not surprising, given events in Belgium and France where 'beyond all question, Germans have used their position as friendly citizens to betray their hosts in the most terrible way' that there should be an outcry against Germans in Britain. The government should 'run no risk of treachery on the one hand, or of a rush to Lynch law on the other.' The article went on: 'After all, we have got to remember that our Royal Family, the confidential advisors of the Government in finance, the owners of

---

[155] Henry Lowerison was a teacher, educationalist and socialist. He was an occasional *Clarion* contributor and a neighbour of Blatchford.

more than one influential newspaper, etc., etc., are all Germans. Are they all to be put in concentration camps? And what is to become of our First Sea Lord, H.S.H. Prince Louis of Battenberg, G.C.B., G.C.V.O., K.C.M.G., A.D.C.?' Within a week Battenberg, under strong pressure from anti-German public opinion, had been more or less forced to resign.

*Justice* (5 November) believed the government was giving way to 'irresponsible journalistic clamour.' It returned to this theme on its editorial page on 19 November. It protested against the internment of 'Germans' who were naturalised British citizens, some of whom had lived all their lives in the country and in some cases could not speak a word of German. If naturalisation was to count for nothing – 'If a man is not qualified on the score of German descent to be to occupy the post of a Lord of the Admiralty' – should not the same rule be a disqualification for the monarch? It poured scorn on the panic about spies. 'Supposing that all the German waiters in London were spies, how can they accumulate even a tiny fraction of the information possessed by the big armament firms.' Yet German banks had been among the investors in the latter.

Even in the *Clarion* there were those who resisted the trend towards hatred of Germans. 'I like Germans,' Hilda Thompson confessed in the 27 November issue. She was 'dead against this Britishness which is exciting hatred of the German people in the breast of the British people.' She was convinced that the war had been unavoidable since 'Germany meant sooner or later to fight us,' and she hoped that Germany would be soon beaten. 'Not because I hate them but because an autocratic head of State and an iron militarism as supreme guiding power seems to me as the insurmountable bar to the better civilisation we all hope for.' But if how to regard Germans in general was a problem for British socialists it was a great deal less complicated than deciding how to regard their political counterparts in Germany.

## German Socialists

Prior to August 1914 it was reasonable to assume that if Left-wing organisations were going to have a role in preventing the outbreak of war the lead would be taken by the SPD, the largest party in the German *Reichstag* and the biggest and best organised socialist party in the world. As we have seen, there had been reports of great demonstrations against the war before its outbreak. Some seemed to have been on an enormous scale. So the support given to the German government by the SPD deputies voting for war credits seemed – at best – very puzzling and disappointing.

At first the emphasis was on the violent suppression of socialist opposition by what *Justice* called 'the Prussian military caste which dominates the German Empire.' On 13 August it repeated the claim of a *Manchester Guardian* correspondent in Paris that a French socialist deputy had been told of anti-war demonstrations in Berlin and that Liebknecht and other socialists had been shot. But on 20 August the paper was 'heartily glad' to be able to confirm that the latter reports had been false. However, reporting the war credits vote on its front page it added: 'We must confess that ... the attitude of the Social-Democratic Party in the Reichstag appears to us only explainable on the assumption that martial law having been declared in Germany the Reichstag outside of the governing circles was ignorant of the real position of affairs.' *Justice* conceded at as regards the threatened attack by Russia the vote was 'perfectly justified.' But, it went on:

> The declaration of war against Russia was made by Germany on August 1, but on that day German soldiers also seized the railway station at Luxemburg, concentration of troops having already taken place at Aix-la-Chappelle. On the following day the ultimatum to Belgium was delivered, and the declaration of war against both Belgium and France on the 3rd. All this was done before the voting on the war credit in the Reichstag on the 4th.

The Reichstag had been adjourned till late November but when it resumed, the BSP paper declared, 'We are sure that then the 110 Social-Democratic deputies will follow the noble example of Liebknecht and Bebel during the Franco-Prussian war.'[156]

As we would now anticipate, *Labour Leader* took a very different line. Its interpretation on 20 August was a contrast with that of *Justice*. The German movement, it said, had probably protested 'more vigorously' against the war than elsewhere in Europe. It blamed the mobilisation of Russian forces on the German frontier. 'The Socialist Party of no country,' the *Leader* declared, 'could stand aside and allow the tyrant Tsar of Russia and his barbaric hosts to attack their homes without protest, and it was under these circumstances that the Parliamentary Party decided not to oppose the Government's various War Bills.' It quoted from a German paper the speech of Hugo Haase who chaired the SPD deputies.[157] While attributing the war to imperialism Haase had said that it was now a question 'of the means whereby we can defend our frontier.' Germany was 'threatened with annihilation by Russian despotism and to prevent this danger the Government could count on the support' of SPD deputies as long as efforts were made to restore peace.

On the same page under the title of 'The Martyrdom of Our Comrades' Bruce Glasier tried, as it must have seemed to those

---

[156] Wilhelm Liebknecht, 1826-1900, and August Bebel, 1840-1913, were founders of the SPD. They opposed the Franco-Prussian War in 1870/71 and at one stage were charged with high treason though later convicted and imprisoned on a lesser offence. Wilhelm was the father of Karl Liebknecht.

[157] Hugo Haase, 1863-1919, had chaired the SPD since 1911 and when war broke out also the party's Reichstag group. A 'revisionist' like Bernstein, he had attempted to persuade his parliamentary colleagues to vote against the war credits but as a matter of party discipline voted for the loans the following day. Later, in 1915, he would become one of the leaders of the USPD – *Unabhängige Sozialdemokratische Partei Deutschlands* (Independent Social-Democratic Party of Germany) – which broke away from the SPD in 1917. As such he played an important role in the German Revolution until shot and severely wounded in October 1919 which led to his death the following month.

taking a position similar to that of *Justice,* to have it both ways. On the one hand he praised the 'valiant attempt on the part of a considerable section of the Social-Democrats in Berlin to withstand, at the utmost risk of their own lives, the war policy of the German rulers.' On the other he placed the blame for the war on the British government.

> But for the sickening horror in the bosom of every German Socialist at the thought of the descent of the Cossacks on his Fatherland – a peril for which our British alliance with Russia is mainly responsible – the rifle shots which slew Karl Liebknecht and Rosa Luxembourg (sic) would have ere now turned the war into a revolution.

An editorial note – clearly written later than the article – said that there was still some hope that the reports of such murders would prove to be false.

*Justice* too, retreating at least a little from its earlier criticism of the SPD, claimed to have learnt from a Copenhagen source that reports of SPD deputies cheering and shaking hands with the Kaiser were false. That was on 27 August. A week later (3 September) Lee devoted much of the front page to explaining that it was clear that the German people had been misled about the war. News of the German declaration of war on Russia on 1 August had not been announced until 4 August when it had been accompanied by the statement that both the Russians and the French had already crossed the German frontiers. 'In common justice to the mass of the German people,' Lee wrote, 'this should be made known as widely as possible. It explains also how the Social-Democratic Party in the Reichstag came to vote for the war credits.' But if the Germans – including the SPD – had been conned into seeing the war in terms of 'national defence,' he was sure 'that once the truth has been established our action will be approved and joined in by the Socialists of Germany.'

Fred Jowett added his authority as ILP chair in *Labour Leader* on 3 September to the interpretation that foreign socialists, including those in Germany, had not necessarily abandoned their ideals but had been 'obliged to acquiesce.'

> Faced with the awful fact of a Cossack invasion, even a German Socialist may well conclude that there is nothing for it but to fight. If it is argued against him that he is striking France and not Russia, the answer is that France had bound itself to Russia, and war with one involved war with the other.
> Where it has been distinctly clear that the nation has been in danger of invasion (whoever has been responsible) the Socialist has regretfully accepted the situation and actively supported the necessary measures for the welfare of the state to which he belonged.

The following week (10 September) in a *Justice* editorial Belfort Bax blamed the 'Revisionists'[158] Bax mentioned three members of the SPD who he regarded as such though, rather oddly, not the great theoretician of revisionism, Eduard Bernstein. One of the three was 'Dr. Frank, one of the chief Revisionist leaders'. But the following week (17 September) both *Labour Leader* and *Justice* reported his death. *Justice* gave front-page coverage to the death of Frank, the deputy for Mannheim. He had volunteered on the outbreak of war. He had been, the paper said, 'a most capable man, full of ideas, who could ill be spared. A bullet took him away near Luneville. Who fired the shot? Perhaps the very French comrade whose hand he warmly grasped but a short while ago. O, the sadness of it all.' The *Leader*

---

[158] By far the best known and most important 'Revisionist' was Eduard Bernstein, 1850-1932. The positions he took from the 1890s argued against many aspects of what was considered 'orthodox' Marxism. He rejected the need for revolution, taking the view that progress towards socialist goals was what mattered. His major work was *Die Voraussetzungen des Sozialismusund die Aufgaben der Sozialdemokratie* (*The Prerequisites for Socialism and the Tasks of Social Democracy*) of 1899. The merits or otherwise of Revisionism became a major debate particularly in the SPD where his opponents included Rosa Luxemburg and Karl Kautsky. But although Bernstein voted for the war credits in August 1914 he became an opponent of the war a year later and in 1917 was one of the founders of the short-lived USPD, the Independent Social-Democratic Party of Germany.

believed Frank 'destined to be the leader of the Social-Democratic Party of Germany and to play a part in Continental Socialism equal to those played by of Bebel and Jaurès.' It noted the 'noble tributes' paid to Frank in the French socialists press.

Unlike the *Labour Leader, Justice* had no time at all for the idea that for German socialists the war was 'against Tsarism,' declaring that the 'naïvete of Vorwärts is almost incomprehensible.' The following week (24 September) it featured a statement by Liebknecht describing the notion that the SPD had voted unanimously for the war credits as an 'inadmissible legend.' That week too, *Labour Leader* included a piece by Dr Alfred Salter.[159] It was sub-titled 'What is the Duty of the Christian Citizen?' In it he argued a pacifist case, declaring, 'I say deliberately that I am prepared to be shot rather than kill a German peasant with whom I have no conceivable quarrel.' Turning to the SPD, he went on: 'If the Socialists of Germany had felt able to take this line there would have been no European War, many of them, doubtless, would have been executed by the Kaiser, but there would have been no war for over two-fifths of the German army consists of Socialists.'

*Justice,* so critical of *Vorwärts* two weeks earlier, had a much more

---

[159] Alfred Salter, 1873-1945, was a medical practitioner, Christian, socialist activist and pacifist whose primary field of activity was in Bermondsey which he would later represent as a Labour MP. Salter was the first contributor to *Labour Leader* (7 March 1918) to denounce the dissolution of the Constituent Assembly and other actions of the Bolsheviks at a time when most of the Left was carried away by the euphoria arising from an apparently successful socialist revolution and even future implacable critics like MacDonald and Snowden were much more equivocal. Fenner Brockway would write a biography of Salter published in 1949, *Bermondsey Story: the Life of Alfred Salter.* Salter, like his equally remarkable wife, Ada (see note in chapter 2) won respect and admiration from a wider spectrum of political opinion than most Labour MPs – above all in Bermondsey. When a bronze statue of Salter sitting on a park bench was stolen in November 2011 from Cherry Garden Pier, Simon Hughes, Liberal-Democrat MP for Bermondsey, 1983-2015, expressed outrage in his blog of 21 November 2011 and described Salter as 'the greatest of our MPs in the last century.' The statue was replaced together with one of Ada Salter, as well as of Joyce Salter, their only child who died of scarlet fever at the age of eight, and the family cat, by the artist Diane Gorvin, in November 2014 after a local campaign raised about £60,000 and which was matched by Southwark Council.

positive view when it reported on 1 October that the German paper had been 'suppressed.' It showed, it said, that 'our contemporary' was 'doing its best under all the difficulties of martial law.' *Justice* concluded that 'The suppression of "Vorwarts" vindicates its honour more than anything else could have done.' It also gave a summary of Karl Kautsky's *Neue Zeit* article on 'Preparations for Peace.'[160] This was also quoted extensively and praised in *Labour Leader* the following week (8 October).

By then *Justice* was less friendly towards *Vorwärts* than it had been the previous week. It noted that its critical attitude to the war had not been reflected in some of the local SPD papers which had taken up the cry of 'the danger of Russian despotism.' On 15 October the *Leader* and *Justice* had contrasting attitudes to the reappearance of the German socialist daily which had, as the former put it, 'once more survived the Censor's blow.' But *Justice,* noting that in order to be allowed to reappear *Vorwärts* had had to agree 'that no reference should be made to class hatred or the class struggle' for the duration of the war, asked, 'Would not suppression have been better?'

On 22 October *Labour Leader* carried a report from the American Dr. Nasmyth of the World Peace Foundation.[161] Bernstein, said Nasmyth, was being denounced as pro-British just as MacDonald was of being pro-German. An interview with another American socialist,

---

[160] *Die Neue Zeit* was the SPD's theoretical journal, edited by Kautsky having been founded by him in 1883. Kautsky, 1854-1938, was regarded as the leading exponent of 'orthodox' Marxism – as contrasted with Bernstein's 'revisionism'. He would leave the SPD for the USPD in 1917, returning in 1920. By this time his trenchant criticisms of the Bolsheviks, in, particularly, *The Dictatorship of the Proletariat* of 1918, had led to him being denounced as a 'renegade' by Lenin.

[161] The World Peace Foundation had been founded and largely financed by Edward Ginn, the wealthy Boston-based publisher of educational books. He had died in January 1914. Ginn had also been closely associated with Tufts University from which he had graduated in 1862 and later served on its Board of Overseers and as a trustee. The WPF is affiliated with the Fletcher School of Law and Diplomacy at Tufts University.

Dr. George Herron, was published in *Justice* on 5 November.[162] Herron declared that Britain was 'fighting for the preservation of all that is worthwhile in civilisation,' while the German Social-Democrats had shown an 'utter lack of moral force as well as well as its lack of fidelity to freedom and to international Socialism.' The following week (12 November) *Justice* included in its front page a letter, dated 10 September, in which Karl Liebknecht, Rosa Luxemburg, Franz Mehring and Clara Zetkin dissociated themselves from the pro-war position of other members of the SPD.[163] *Labour Leader* also noted this the following week (19 November) while *Justice*, referring to Zetkin as 'our esteemed comrade' published a summary of an article by her on 'The Duty of Working Women in War-Time.'

The *Clarion* during these weeks had relatively little to say about German socialists. On 2 October it did quote, in addition to several pro-war comments from by other members of the SPD, Liebknecht's statement that 'the state of Belgium is a disgrace to the German nation.' On 27 November it included a pro-Ally article by George Herron who, it said, had resigned from Idaho University 'because of hostility of wealthy patrons to his advanced views.'

In the same edition A. M. Thompson considered the failure of the SPD – or its majority – to oppose the war.

> The voting strength of the German Socialist Party has always been a cause of deception to uninformed observers of German politics, who have mistakenly regarded it as the count of a democratically enlightened, compact band of brothers, united in clearness of understanding and definiteness of purpose. But those who have had opportunities of more

---

[162] George D. Herron, 1862-1925, was a Congregationalist minister who became a Christian socialist advocate of the 'Social Gospel' movement. He would remain a supporter of the Allied cause throughout the war.

[163] Franz Mehring, 1846-1919, and Clara Zetkin, 1857-1933, would later leave the SPD for the Spartacist League. Mehring, who died of illness soon after the murders of Liebknecht and Luxemburg, is well known as a biographer of Karl Marx. Zetkin became a prominent member of the German Communist Party.

intimate acquaintance with the elements of the Party, have realised that its collective showing at the polls was entirely misleading, that its individual members were for the most part unpregnant of their cause, and that instead of representing the explicit and sublime creed of its highest teachers, the Party represented at bottom nothing more than a vague and confused chaos of discontent.

Rather than simply attracting support from a mass of convinced socialists the SPD garnered votes from 'all who were dissatisfied with their wages, their working conditions, their military service, their taxes, the growing wealth and influence of the Jews, or any other cause, large or trivial.' This 'swelled the ranks of the Social-Democrats, not because they understood the ideal, but because it was "agin the Government".'

But even so Thompson found what he called 'A Change of Tone in Germany.' Haase's response to the 'Imperial Chancellor's vaunting speech' at reopening of Reichstag suggested 'that the penitence demanded by Professor Herron is awakening.' Meanwhile, while the British socialist weeklies had been debating their undesirable ally and unwanted enemy – the Russian Menace and the German Menace – the horrors of war had been accelerating.

# CHAPTER 9

## The Horrors of War

### The German Invasion of Belgium and France

The holy veil of friendship is all rent,
And broken are the bonds of brotherhood;

So ran the first line of 'August 1914' by May Westoby which appeared in *Justice* on 13 August. The same day *Labour Leader's* headline was 'The Horrors of War, Ghastly Scenes at Liège.' Based on a *Times* report, it told how 'The unhappy German soldiers … were marched to death almost shoulder to shoulder.' It continued, 'During the whole day, Tuesday 6 August, the attack continued with unabated force. The scenes were fearful, carnage heaped upon carnage, thousands of broken human bodies massed together in fields ploughed up by a terrific cannonade.'

But the Belgian fortresses at Liège and then Namur soon fell to the implacable German assault with its massive siege guns. Soon both *Justice* and the *Clarion* were complaining about being misled by official sources and most of the press about the strength of Namur. 'Up to the last moment the entire Press was maintaining that the fortress could hold out for weeks,' said the former on 27 August while in the *Clarion* Thompson made the same point the following day. 'For a fortnight past we have been lulled with flattering fictions: the experience of my boyhood when Paris was being soothed with news of victories while the enemy advanced nearer and nearer the capital, has been precisely repeated in our late joyful tidings from Belgium.' He believed that the previous Monday had been 'the blackest day recorded in the History of England.' It presaged 'the unthinkable world-calamity of the Empire's break-up.' He compared the situation to that facing the French Republic in 1792.

But soon he had better news to share with the readers. On 11 September, as the German retreat from the Marne began. Thompson felt that the positions taken by himself and Blatchford had been vindicated.[164] 'Above the smoke of war one fact shines clear;' he began the editorial, '*the Prussian plot has failed.*' The British contribution had been decisive.

> Let this be quite clear to the amazing persons who still criticise Sir Edward Grey for intervening in this war. The help of our little expeditionary force has been invaluable to the French in the desperate fighting of the last fortnight. The stranglehold of our Navy at the throat of Germany has been an incalculable advantage. Without this help ... the German plan would have succeeded.

He continued, 'Thanks to a few men like Robert Blatchford ... We have saved France, we have saved Belgium, we have saved Holland, we have saved Switzerland, we have saved the British Empire, we have saved our honour.' Then, no doubt with Hardie, MacDonald and the *Labour Leader* in mind, he attacked 'smug sentimentalists who have unquestionably caused this ghastly war by their ostrich-like refusal to look plain, ugly, facts in the face.'

Blatchford himself was cock-a-hoop. His front page *Clarion* article on 18 September bore the title 'Reasons why the Germans will never

---

[164] The Battle of the Marne, 5-12 September, was one of the decisive battles of the war. It may not have ensured that Germany would not eventually emerge as the victor but it did mean that the German blueprint for the defeat of France, the Schlieffen plan, had failed and that it would not secure the decisive early victory in the West that had been confidently planned.

take Paris.' He was able to quote a piece he had written for the *Weekly Dispatch* on 6 September. Disclaiming any military expertise, he had written, 'I will hazard the guess that the German Army near Paris is in a very dangerous position and will never get into Paris at all.' He went on to give a fairly accurate account of the German invasion plan and its failure emphasising his astonishment that France had not anticipated the German attack via Belgium. He predicted, with some accuracy as things eventually turned out, that since 'unemployment and starvation are at work in Austria' there would be a revolution there and 'the dual Empire will fall to pieces.' Germany would lose 'every inch of her colonies and most of her trade.'

Blatchford was not alone in having his contributions to the 'bourgeois' press quoted. On 1 October extracts from a long letter Hyndman had written to the *Morning Post* appeared in *Justice*. In it, the BSP paper said, he had exposed 'the ridiculousness of many of the things now being urged to "capture" German trade.' Hyndman stressed that German economic strength was based largely on the superiority of its compulsory education system, the application of chemistry to industry and other factors where Britain lagged. The following day in the *Clarion* Thompson quoted from the official organ of the Pan-German League,[165] 'There are two kinds of races, master races and inferior races, Political rights belong to the master race alone and can only be won by war. This is a Scientific Law, a law of Biology.' Thompson commented, 'We might have been more effectually convinced of this "law" if the Battle of the Marne and French's contemptible little army hadn't turned out so unexpectedly.[166]

---

[165] The Pan-German League (*Alldeutscher Verband*) was an ultra-nationalist organisation founded in 1891.

[166] Sir John French, 1852-1925, was the commander of the British Expeditionary Force (BEF) which had made a fighting retreat from Mons. It was rumoured that the Kaiser had dismissed the BEF as 'Sir John French's contemptible little army.' This would lead to veterans of the force being known as the Old Contemptibles.

## Blatchford and Thompson in France

By the following week (9 October) both Blatchford and Thompson were reporting from France. Blatchford was keen to bring the reality of war home to his readers – 'we islanders do not know what war means.' He went on – echoing his colleague's comment the previous week, 'Paris is not an island. There is nothing between Paris and the infuriated Germans but a French army and Sir John French's contemptible little force.' In his 'Notes from Paris' in the same issue, Thompson was more upbeat, reporting that according to 'a relative with the British cavalry, German soldiers were so worn by privations and broken in *morale* they are only too glad to be made prisoners.' The 'Great Hope' among the Allies and the sympathetic American military *attaché* was that von Kluck, the commander of the German First Army, had surrendered.

Thompson ended with another hope; 'If only Antwerp can hold out another week!' But it was not to be. The following week (15 October) the first item in *Labour Leader's* 'Review of the Week' was 'The Fall of Antwerp.' The piece began with the statement that 'From the beginning of hostilities we have sympathised with the Belgian people no less sincerely than those who have disagreed with us in our views as to warfare in general and this war in particular.' It denounced the 'crime which Germany has committed' while declaring that 'The cant which has been uttered in an attempt to prove that Germany's invasion of Belgium was the cause of Britain's intervention has, we confess, nauseated us.'

Of all the prominent figures in British socialism in the period before 1914 Blatchford was by far the most unequivocally in favour of British participation in the war. On 28 August he had predicted that 'the time is not far distant when the papers begin to print heavy casualty lists and the meaning of war will come nearer to us.' The

German plan was 'to make war "with the utmost violence."' and Britain must do the same. The war must be 'fought to a finish.' He rejected any 'foolish clemency to Germany.' There should not be 'any kindly willingness to stop the war while Germany is still unconquered.' He concluded this front-page article reiterating this view: 'We have been obliged to fight in our own defence, and in our own defence we shall be obliged to fight to a finish. If Europe is wise this will be the last great European war.'

Many on the Left, both at the time and subsequently, were critical of Blatchford's whole-hearted support for the war effort. Yet he cannot be accused of in any way playing down, let alone attempting to glorify, the horrors of the war. In his 'Paris in War Time' front-page article on 9 October he gave an account of several horrifying incidents. There was the Coldstream Guard soldier who described to *Daily Mail* reporter Valentine Williams 'how he had seen a shell explode under the feet of four Zouaves.[167] The men were blown into the air. Three of them were blown to pieces, their heads and limbs torn off.' Then there was the German prisoner who had been bayoneted and then trapped under the French colonial soldier that had wounded him when the latter's head was almost immediately hit by a stream of bullets from a machine gun 'that literally cut his head to pieces.'

Blatchford asked:

What is to be done with the savages whose vanity causes things like these? In one action our British battalions lost six hundred killed and wounded in an hour. In another a German cavalry brigade was caught in a narrow street and mowed down by machine guns. A thousand dead and wounded were left in that street: men shattered and cut to pieces, men horribly gashed and mutilated...

---

[167] Zouaves were members of French light infantry regiments whose origins went back to the French takeover of Algeria in 1830. By 1914 they were largely recruited from metropolitan France but retained – until the following year when the circumstances of the Western Front led to the adoption of khaki – a colourful uniform of North African style.

A British force during the great retreat dug lines of trenches. When the Germans were driven back over that ground the British went to open the trenches again to cover their advance and found them full of the corpses of Germans killed a week before. 'I tell you,' an English Tommy said to me, 'it was the worst time I ever had.'

Blatchford said he did not want to 'dwell on such horrors. This is not the time. But the bare facts of this war are too terrible to speak of.' He expressed considerable pride in the British troops he encountered.

Yet this did not mean that he was uncritical of the British officer class. On 16 October his article on the *Clarion's* front page had the title 'British Snobs and Indian Princes. Things I have seen in France.' After an army captain he met in France told him that he knew Blatchford disliked his, the captain's, class but insisted 'we are not all blackguards' he was at a loss to know why he was presumed to be so hostile. He had, Blatchford insisted, 'always liked and respected British officers.' But their one great fault was snobbery; 'They are splendid chaps, but snobs.' He then gave an example of this. Arriving at a hotel five hours south of Paris Blatchford was told 'with some pride' by the hotel staff that they had an Indian prince staying there who had 'come to fight for the Empire.'

That evening at dinner he and a friend were able to observe from a nearby table. The prince came in with a British general who managed not to speak to him or even look at him throughout the meal. The following evening he saw a group of British officers ignore him in the smoke-room. Blatchford's, unidentified, 'young friend' thought 'he had never seen anything so caddish and brutal in his life.' And Blatchford agreed. 'He had come all the way from India at his own expense to fight our battles, and he was subjected to the most horrible snub by the officers of the army of the King to whom he was so strangely loyal.' Blatchford's army captain was not present. 'He had gone to the front. Had he been there he would have joined in the infliction of that bitter insult on a brave man.'

This struck a chord with *Justice*. On 22 October much of the 'Topical Tattle' column was devoted to Blatchford's article. 'Whatever some of us may have thought of certain aspects of our friend Robert Blatchford on the European war, we can all agree that he has done excellent service in calling attention to the manner in which English officers behave to Indian princes.' The paper's 'Critical Chronicle' was equally supportive. 'Robert Blatchford has done much good service for many years, but we doubt if he ever did a better bit of work for his own country and humanity at large than by his exposure in last week's "Clarion" of the incredibly caddish behaviour of "English officers and gentlemen".' The paper thought the prince's action in coming to fight was 'very foolish of him,' but the officers' rudeness – or as we would now see it, racism – was inexcusable. 'How silly from the "Imperial" point of view, as well as how blackguardly.'

Reporting further on his 'Trip to France,' on 30 October. Thompson attempted to describe something of what he had seen near the front.

> The cottages of ploughboys and shepherds are inhabited by troops, the farmhouses by colonels and generals. The fields are monstrous gipsy encampments, with artillery instead of hawkers' vans. Costly motor cars without wheels are scattered along the roadside, with here and there a dead horse. The highways and the country lanes are thronged with a never-ending movement of military transports and soldiers – not soldiers like the dapper Tommies of the Horse Guards' Parade or the shining cuirassiers of Longchamps but disorderly swarms of slouching, slovenly scarecrows, dirty as hounds returned from otter-hunting in muddy burrows, and dragging their feet like weary tramps.

'Incidentally,' Thompson added, 'I myself enjoyed the adventure of being arrested by French officers as a German spy.' *Justice* the following week (5 November) also reported the incident adding, 'Fortunately there were no casualties.'

## Atrocities

By the beginning of September the reports of German atrocities committed in Belgium were being reported in the socialist weeklies. On 3 September *Justice* published an interview with Emile Vandervelde, by this time a member of the Belgian government which by then controlled only a tiny strip of the country around the Yser. He had been sent on a special mission to the UK and the USA to 'make known the brutalities' which some of the German troops had committed in Belgium. Asked whether it was true that Louvain had been completely destroyed he said that it was true in the main but they had left standing 'our beautiful old Hotel de Ville.'

On the same day the *Labour Leader* noted that 'Horrible atrocities are reported as having been committed by the German soldiers in Belgium and by the Russian soldiers in Eastern Prussia; the German papers are as full of accounts of the latter as our papers have been of accounts of the former.' And it added, 'We are glad to find *Vorwärts* protesting against the burning of Louvain; it was a crime inexcusable even in time of war.'[168]

The next day the *Clarion's* Julia Dawson added her own denunciation.[169]

The excuse for the destruction of the very best works of the hands of man (when men's hands that were meant for good work were allowed to do it) in lovely and loveable Louvain was some 'devilish women' pouring boiling oil on some German soldiers. If all the women of Louvain had

---

[168] The burning of Louvain (now Leuven) in late August 1914, and especially of the university and its library founded in 1426, quickly became a potent symbol of German brutality.

[169] Julia Dawson was the pen-name of Mrs D.J. Myddleton-Worrall who ran the paper's 'women's page.' She was also credited with the idea that led to the Clarion Vans.

been real devils and had drown in boiling oil all the brutes masquerading as men (a pity they didn't), it would not have been the slightest excuse for the demolition of one brick in any one of the beautiful buildings of Louvain, which will never now, alas, stand on top of another.

A week later (10 September) the *Leader* warned against efforts 'to inflame the passions' by 'unconfirmed reports' of German atrocities. It conceded that 'It is possibly true that the atrocities that are reported to have been committed by the German army have aroused more feeling against Germany than all the arguments of Sir Edward Grey.' But 'in time of war stories of this kind are exaggerated beyond recognition.' There were atrocities in all wars, on both sides. There had been reports of Russian atrocities in East Prussia, atrocities on both sides in Russo-Japanese war and in the South African war there was the burning of Boer farms by the British and 'the horrors of the concentration camps, where Boer women and children died like flies.'

*Justice* made the same comparison with the British burning of farms and 'the shameful treatment meted out to Boer women' on 24 September in raising 'an emphatic protest against certain of the British Press with the tacit approval of the British Press Bureau to inflame the passions of the British public by circulating unconfirmed reports of alleged German atrocities in Belgium and France'. It instanced a totally baseless report of a British nurse whose breasts were supposedly cut off at Vilvorde. Like the *Labour Leader* a fortnight before it insisted that 'There never was a war in which excesses did not occur or an army that was guiltless of them.' It concluded, 'Louvain, Termonde and Rheims are bad enough in all conscience without the addition of imaginary horrors.'[170]

Clearly, *Labour Leader* tended – reacting no doubt to the way such

---

[170] At Termonde (Dendermonde) about half the houses of the town were destroyed. At Reims the medieval cathedral was badly damaged by German shellfire on 20 September. The building was not fully re-opened until 1938.

stories were seized on by much of the press – to play down the atrocities committed by German troops. Its 'Review of the Week' on 24 September included a long quotation from a letter, dated 3 September, by a number of American journalists who stated, 'We were with the German columns at Landen, Louvain, Brussels, Nivelles, Binche, Buissière, Haurtes Wiherie, Merbes-le-Chateau, Soire-sur-Sambre and Beaumont without being able to substantiate a single case of wanton brutality. Numerous investigated rumours proved groundless.' On 8 October the same paper reported that press reports which had claimed that Reims cathedral had been 'destroyed beyond repair' were exaggerated; only the roof had been damaged. It quoted the Paris correspondent of the *New Statesman* who agreed that German claims that the towers of the building had been used as observation posts for French artillery were correct. How differently these events could appear is illustrated by a letter in the following day's *Clarion* from John Dory deploring the lack of international indignation at 'the destruction of Reims Cathedral.'

The most startling suggestion related to atrocities came in the lead item of the 'Critical Chronicle' of *Justice* on 22 October. Under the heading 'A Life for a Life' it attacked the German tactic of 'dropping bombs from airships and aeroplanes on unfortified towns.' This constituted a 'distinct breach of the international rules governing "civilised" warfare.' It proposed that captured German officers should be held as hostages and 'one of them – the higher rank the better' – should be shot for every civilian killed as a result of such bombing. 'The officer cast have relatives among the German governing class. Thus and thus only can these outrages against civilians be stopped.'

## The War at Home

A sense of how the war had taken over everything comes through vividly in the account in his regular feature – 'Cyclorama' – by Tom Groom, in the issue of the *Clarion* of 21 August. It is an account of the conversations he had with those he met during a cycle ride 'The war. Nothing but the war,' he began. 'From Slush Lane to Worcester, from Worcester to Hereford and back again to Slush Lane, one heard nothing but war talk.' He stops at a 'wayside inn' and joins locals on the bench outside listening to the peaceful sound of the reaping machine in the field opposite – and talking about the war. 'Serious talk, too. There was none of that empty blether that one heard when the war was a few thousand miles off. There were tales of horses commandeered whilst taking produce to market, of wagons left on the roadside to take their chance of being hauled away, of men called from reaping to take their places in the ranks, of villages almost depleted as reservists and recruits had marched away.'

By 5 November *Justice* was complaining about 'The Real Danger of Darkest London.' The 'vast metropolis' was being turned into a 'city of dreadful night for at least thirteen hours out of the twenty-four' by an 'edict issued by no one knows whom.' The paper thought it 'too silly and too contemptible for words to express.' Flying experts believed that 'the danger from Zeppelins is of no account.' Inflicting 'Egyptian darkness' on the civilian population would lead not only to 'danger to life and limb.' It saw what would later be called the 'blackout' as particularly unfair to the poor who were far less likely to be able to enjoy themselves during daylight than the non-working rich. The following week (12 November) repeated its contention that the result was that 'the dangers we run just now are not from Zeppelin bombs but from street accidents.'[171]

---

[171] Nevertheless the first Zeppelin raid on Britain came soon enough. In January 1915 several civilians were killed by raids on Great Yarmouth and Kings Lynn on the east coast. Raids on London began in May 1915.

We saw in an earlier chapter how the recruitment campaign had split the Left and particularly the BSP. The *Clarion* was very critical of the way it was conducted and the poor provision provided for recruits but was otherwise supportive. *Labour Leader* advised ILPers to have nothing to do with it and in the BSP it became an early issue over which the divisions which were to culminate in the 'split' of 1916 manifested themselves in the pages of *Justice*. Some on the Left took more nuanced positions. The manifesto of the Women's Labour League appeared in the *Leader* on 15 October. It blamed the war on 'the past actions of Governments and the inaction of the people' and demanded proper provision for soldiers and dependants. It protested against recruiters trying to 'use the helplessness and affections of women as a weapon to compel enlistment. We feel strongly that a woman who is herself unable to bear arms has little feeling for the honour of her sex when she brands a man who will not fight as "a coward".'

Almost from the start there were fears that the government would introduce conscription – already in force in all the other belligerents but unknown in Britain. Both the *Labour Leader* and *Justice* predicted it on 27 August. On the front page of the former Keir Hardie warned that a speech by Kitchener had made it quite clear that if the voluntary system failed to raise enough recruits then 'sufficient compulsion will have to be applied.' The editorial added that it was 'quite clear that within a few months Great Britain will be a conscript country.' [172] *Justice* commented on the same speech by the Secretary of State for War under the heading 'Is it Conscription?' It urged consideration of an alternative. 'A Citizen Army was one of the watchwords of the old S.D.F. Is it too late to urge its necessity now?'

---

[172] Conscription was introduced by the Military Service Act in January 1916 which specified that single men aged 18 to 40 years old were liable to be called up for military service unless they were widowed with children or ministers of a religion. In June 1916 conscription was extended to married men and eventually the upper age limit was raised to 51. Military Service Tribunals adjudicated on exemptions including cases of conscientious objection.

Hyndman would return to the citizen army theme in a *Justice* editorial on 19 November arguing that it was the acceptable alternative to conscription. It would ensue that 'No citizens could then shirk their duty as soldiers: all soldiers would retain their full rights to speak and act as citizens.' What was needed was a 'modification of the Swiss system on more democratic lines.' The same day *Labour Leader* referred to the campaigns of the National Service League which had been agitating for conscription since 1902. It commented that on the Left the idea 'found Harry Quelch to be kind to it.' The following week's *Justice* was indignant. It insisted that Quelch, who had died in 1913, had not supported 'national service.' He had supported 'the Citizen Army – the nation armed – just as did Jaurès.'

Given its greater acceptance of the necessity of the war – one could hardly say its enthusiasm for it – it might be expected that the *Clarion* would support conscription. But at this stage it did not, Writing on 'Patriotism and Pay' in the 11 September issue, R. B. Suthers noted that 'Our blood-and-iron professors are already calling for conscription.' Recalling the aftermath of other wars he went on:

> We know what will happen. There will be one-armed men selling matches in the gutters, with insulting labels on their chests informing the inheritors of Freedom that the wearer of the label lost his arm in the Great War and cannot subsist on the pension provided by his fellow-inheritors. Insulting labels which will not insult. There will be widows and children struggling to live on the mere pittance due to them as relatives of a warrior and hero who helped to save the Empire from the Iron Heel of German Oppression.

Many who would otherwise enlist, he believed, 'have these pictures in their mind's eye.' If proper provision was made for servicemen and their dependents conscription would be unnecessary.

> If conscription does come, it will not be because British men are slackers or shirkers, but because British shopkeepers and British

landlords and British manufacturers and British financiers and British newspaper proprietors are too mean and stingy to pay the insurance premium on their property which war demands, because they are too mean and stingy to pay those who would risk their lives in their country's defence a living wage. If conscription comes and the death of Liberty, it will be because of an unholy alliance between the spirit of the German War Lords and the spirit of the blackmailers and bloodsuckers of British commerce and industry.

Blatchford made clear his own position on 13 November with a front-page *Clarion* article with the title 'The Government Plot for Conscription.' He did not believe that conscription was necessary and 'not until proper provision is made for the men that fight for us, will I admit that conscription is just.' With a £1 a week separation allowance recruitment would shoot up.

> If this war establishes the principle that property is not more sacred than life; if it brings home to the whole nation that the wealth as well as the blood of the people belongs to the nation, then the war will have proved a blessing to our people. If it is to be waged on compulsion by a class that is to pay as well as fight, while another class does neither, then it is a war not worth the winning.

And, he concluded, 'If the people insist upon justice this war will have done more than anything else in our time to help the realisation of a free and sane Socialism in this country.' Thompson's editorial took up the same theme.

On 12 November the *Labour Leader* gave its view that 'At the moment the fears of conscription are exaggerated.' But it urged those determined to resist it to organise themselves.

> Already many correspondents have written to us declaring that, whatever be the consequences, they will not take up arms against their fellows, and, whilst we appreciate the attitude of those who think that,

whatever the cause of the war, now we are in it they must defend their 'hearths and homes,' we think it would be well for those who intend to resist conscription should it come, to enrol themselves for united action.

A week later (19 November) a letter from Brockway in the *Labour Leader* reported that he had received 150 letters in the previous six days many urging the formation of such an organisation and that with this in view he was getting in touch with 'representative men who share this attitude with us.' Then, a fortnight later (3 December) another letter appeared announcing the formation of the No-Conscription Fellowship. It was signed by W. H. Ayles, Clifford Allen, the Rev. Leyton Richards, A. Sutherland Campbell, and – as its 'Hon. Sec.' – Fenner Brockway himself.

For some, reactions to the experience of being at war took unusual turns. In her *Clarion* 'Passing Show' column of 20 November Hilda Thompson questioned the propriety of the revival, replete with 'martial spirit and the clash of arms of *Henry IV Part One*', by Sir Herbert Tree.[173]

My personal feeling during the battle scenes was one of intense unrest and irritation. In fact, it revolted me. To see an audience, of men and women in evening dress, calmly watching stage fights, listening to speeches discussing the deaths of a few thousand men, while so close at hand the real thing is happening – well it is incomprehensible to me. Have we people no imagination, no sense of proportion?

---

[173] Sir Herbert Beerbohm Tree was an actor and the manager of His Majesty's Theatre in which he lived. Notable for Shakespeare productions, he was the father of the film director Carol Reed and the grandfather of the actor Oliver Reed.

## The Wider War

As one would expect, the attention of all three socialist weeklies was mainly focussed on the domestic situation and the events in nearby Belgium and France. But other theatres of war were not entirely neglected nor the way that the war was expanding beyond what was still mainly referred to as a European war. *Justice* was far from pleased with Japan's entry to the war on the Allied side. It saw this as a totally opportunistic move, believing its promise of 'eventual restoration' of territory in China to be on a par with British undertakings after the occupation of Egypt. The paper thought that Germany could only respond to the occupation of the territories it controlled in the East 'as Belgium did the German ultimatum.' Japan's action had been made 'under the Anglo-Japanese treaty, another of these "agreements" which tend to make the European conflict a world-wide one.'

On 18 September the *Clarion* was scathing about the British government's postponement of Irish Home Rule until after the war at a time when both Liberals and Tories claimed to be fighting Germany in defence of the rights of small nations. It described as a 'fanatical outburst' the recent statements of James Connelly in *The Irish Worker.* He had written, 'I rejoice with all my heart at English reverses, and acclaim German victories as the victories of the most enlightened nation in Europe – the nation whose democracy is most feared by the cunning capitalist rulers of the world.' Thompson professed 'not to be hugely surprised' at such sentiments given the government's postponement of Home Rule.[174]

Later (10 December) *Labour Leader's* 'Notes of the Moment' was sorry to see that James Larkin, the leader of the Irish Transport Workers' Union, had 'identified himself with the pro-German group

---

[174] James Connelly 1868-1916, was a founder of the Socialist Labour Party, which broke away from the SDF in 1903 under the influence of the American socialist theorist Daniel De Leon. Connelly would be executed by firing squad following his participation in the Easter Rising of 1916.

in America.' [175] It reported that at a Philadelphia meeting featuring some sort of military formations of 'German Uhlans and Irish volunteers' Larkin had appealed for gifts of guns with which to fight 'for the destruction of the British Empire and the construction of the Irish Republic.' The *Leader* declared itself 'wholeheartedly with Larkin in his desire for Irish freedom, but that freedom will not be won by the policy he is advocating, Civil war in Ireland can only retard Ireland's salvation.'

Still closer to home, at a time when some in Britain were looking forward to decisive Trafalgar-style naval battles, *Justice* declared 'full confidence' in 'The Silent Victories of the British Navy.' It needed to 'keep this island safe from attack and the commerce of the Empire secure from capture.' Taking a swipe at the press barons, it concluded, on 22 October, that the 'real workers' were not 'eager for great sea battles, in order that they may sell their papers and get steps in the Peerage.'

A little later (5 November) it reported the admiralty had closed the North Sea, apart from some specified routes. This had been done because of the 'reckless sowing of German mines.' *Justice* equated those killed in the sinking of neutral vessels with 'the killing of non-combatants by Zeppelin bombs.' The same day *Labour Leader* was concerned about Turkey which, it reported had recently had the Dardenelles bombarded by a combined British and French naval squadron. As usual with the *Leader,* the focus was on Russian machinations. 'It does not seem possible that Britain can now fail to join Russia in engaging in a war with Turkey, but the circumstances strongly suggest to us that Russia, with her eyes on Constantinople,

---

[175] James Larkin, 1876-1947, was the Liverpool-born founder of the Irish Transport and General Workers' Union in 1908 and came to great prominence in the seven month long (and ultimately unsuccessful from the union's point of view) Dublin Lockout of 1913. The British TUC gave financial support but refused calls for sympathy strike action in Britain This was a major blow which hastened the defeat of the workers. Larkin, had left for the United States sometime after the end of the lockout.

has been anxious to create a cause of hostility with Turkey and that, once more, Britain is playing her game.'

The next day (6 November) Thompson's *Clarion* editorial took a broad look at the progress of the war. Three developments meant that the overall situation had 'decidedly brightened.' First, the 'Prussians' had suffered 'a smashing blow on the Vistula.'[176] Secondly, the German 'frantic dash on Calais' had 'cost them staggering losses and yielded not an inch.' Thirdly, their 'intrigue' in South Africa was fizzling out. The optimistic Thompson even found a positive aspect to Turkey's entry to the war on the side of Germany and Austria-Hungary. The arrival and handover to at least nominal Turkish control of the German cruisers *Goeben* and *Breslau* might 'cause some mischief in the Black Sea' but Turkey's participation in the war would see the end of the Ottoman empire.

As the war spread so did questions about what should happen after it had ended. What should the post-war Europe look like? What of the British empire and the rest of the world? What principles should a peace settlement, when it finally came, be based on?

---

[176] This refers to the initial successes of the Russian invasion of East Prussia which began in mid-August.' But by the time Thompson wrote Hindenberg and Ludendorff had won the Battle of Tannenberg which together the Battle of the Masurian Lakes changed the situation completely in favour of Germany. Thompson's information was out-of-date.

# CHAPTER 10

# Beyond the War

## Can the War be Stopped?

From the outset there were those, particularly in the ILP and around *Labour Leader*, for whom the overwhelming priority was the restoration of peace. To varying extents they found themselves at odds with those reluctant supporters of British participation in the war who were persuaded that only a decisive defeat of 'Prussian militarism' would ensure that the conflict was not simply renewed at a later date. Women played a major role in efforts to bring the war to an end. In *Labour Leader* on 8 October Katharine Bruce Glasier began a front page article recalling how, at the start of the war, 'in writing to my sisters in the Women's Labour League I pleaded for a resistance to the last breath of the spiritual poison of war.' Her plea was now 'tenfold more necessary.'

A letter in the same edition from another prominent ILPer, Isabella Ford, gave a brief account of a message she had received from Rosika Schwimmer of the International Women's Suffrage Alliance.[177] The

---

[177] Isabella O. Ford, 1855-1928, was a founder member of the ILP and prominent trade unionist. She came from a Quaker background.

Rosika Schwimmer, 1877-1948 was a Hungarian-born campaigner who would found the Women's Peace Party in the USA in 1915 and the Campaign for World Government in 1937. The International Women's Suffrage Alliance became, after the war, the International Alliance of Women for Suffrage and Equal Citizenship and in 1946 it took its current name, the International Alliance of Women.

latter had had a meeting with President Woodrow Wilson urging him to offer US mediation to bring the war to an end. Ford suggested that ILP branches should send messages to the government asking that 'when the suitable moment arrives the idea of America's mediation be considered and accepted.'

In *Justice* the same day there was a lengthy statement from the Socialist Party of America's executive calling for a conference of the Socialist International in either a neutral country in Europe or in Washington. It offered financial support to delegates and pointed out that the resolution adopted at the Stuttgart conference of the International had pledged not only 'every effort to avert the outbreak of war' but also 'to strive with all our might to bring the war to a speedy end!' In his editorial, 'Peace!', H.W. Lee congratulated the American party but questioned whether such a conference was 'really feasible at present.' Yet he ended by asking, 'Is it too much to hope that we can join together in a common effort, with our comrades in all other countries, to secure a lasting peace at the earliest opportunity?'

The idea of meeting in the USA was ruled out by *Labour Leader* (22 October). It would be impossible for European socialists to get there. Switzerland was a more practicable possibility but the paper was opposed to any suggestion that only socialists from one side of the conflict should meet.[178]

The same day J. Hunter Watts in *Justice* professed the belief that if the German people 'threw off the yoke of Prussian Kaiserdom and proclaimed a Republic of the United States of Germany peace could

---

[178] Two of the conferences that would constitute what came to be called the 'Zimmerwald movement' of socialist opponents of the war were held in Switzerland, the first in September 1915 at the village of Zimmerwald and the second in April 1916 at Kienthal. The third was held in Stockholm in September 1917. No British delegates were able to attend though Bruce Glasier and Jowett, for the ILP, and Fairchild for the BSP had been selected to represent their organisations. They were denied passports by the British government and were unable to do more than send messages of support for the general aims of the Zimmerwald conference.

be brought about within a fortnight.'[179] But failing this he could see no prospects for ending the war quickly. A statement from Jean Longuet reprinted from *Humanité* in *Justice* on 29 October came to the same conclusion; 'we must continue the struggle until a definite result has been obtained.'[180] A week later *Labour Leader* hoped that Longuet did not speak for the 'entire French party' in opposing an International conference. It pointed out that 'With magnificent courage, Herr Edward Bernstein pleaded for an early peace at a public meeting in Berlin' the previous week. Longuet would agree, so surely it was desirable that he and Bernstein should be able to express their 'common thought from a common platform.'

Both *Labour Leader* and *Justice* reported on 26 November that an international conference of socialists from neutral countries was being organised to take place early the following month in Copenhagen. The latter said that neither the Swiss nor the Italian parties were prepared to take part, while the *Leader* regretted that what was proposed did not include representation from the belligerent countries. Nevertheless it might be, it thought, of some use if the socialists in neutral countries were able to plan united action to bring pressure to bear on their governments to intervene to 'secure an early and lasting peace.' A week later (3 December) the paper reported that the conference had been postponed and that the Italian and Swiss parties wanted to meet in Switzerland. It emphasised that *'Its only task will be to look for a basis on which Socialists can take action to secure peace.'* Meanwhile, some were already attempting to address the question of whether – if the war could be stopped or when it eventually came to an end – it would be the last of its kind?

---

[179] J. (John) Hunter Watts, 1852-1923, was another member of the 'Old Guard of the SDF' who would follow Hyndman and Co when the BSP split in 1916.

[180] Jean Longuet, 1876-1938, was a prominent French socialist. He was a grandson of Karl Marx.

# A War to End War?

As we saw in Chapter 7, H. G. Wells's 'pro-war' *Nation* article had generated considerable controversy in *Labour Leader*. Another participant in the debate was introduced to readers as the 'Hon. Bertrand Russell' on 10 September.[181] The headline to his article summed up its argument: 'Will This War End War? Not Unless the Democracy of Europe Awakes.'

There was no reason to believe, he argued, that those in power would think like Wells and that they would agree to, or wish to, 'forgo part of the fruits of victory' and pursue a very different kind of diplomacy in future. Russell, after considering the possibility of a victorious Russia looking for further 'triumphs' and conscription being introduced in Britain 'for the defence of the north-west frontier of India,' turned to Germany with what turned out to be all too much prescience.

> And if Germany is defeated, why should German militarism cease? Why should not Germany wait, like France after 1870 for the opportunity of revenge in some still vaster war hereafter? Prophecy for prophecy, this outcome seems as probable as that foretold by Mr. Wells.

In Russell's view two conditions were necessary if anything resembling Wells's hopes for a peaceful aftermath to the war were to come true. Humiliating the defeated would have to be avoided, and secondly there would need to be 'genuine popular control, by men with traditions quite different from those of the Chancelleries of the international relations of those countries which have Parliamentary

---

[181] Bertrand Russell, 1872-1970, was already a distinguished philosopher and mathematician. A determined opponent of the war, he would be sacked by Trinity College, Cambridge, after a conviction under the notorious DORA (Defence of the Realm Act) and was later imprisoned for anti-war activities. He inherited an earldom in 1931 and remained a prominent political activist for the rest of his life.

government.' This would happen only if there was an 'overwhelming popular upheaval' in Germany, France and Britain brought about, not by reason or humanity, or any of the temporarily extinct ideas of Liberalism, but 'by hunger the one force for peace which is strong enough to cope with the forces of war.'

He went on:

> Suppose – to adopt what appears to be Mr. Wells's hypothesis – that famine produces in Germany a revolution against the government of the Kaiser. Would the Tsar, or even Lord Kitchener, regard this as a reason for offering milder terms to the Germans? Would they not rather see in the resulting loss of military efficiency an opportunity for exacting an even more galling submission? The way the powers treated attempts at Liberal revolution in Turkey, Persia and China affords little ground for optimism. Unless such a movement in Germany is accompanied by a similar movement here and in France it will have, I fear, but a slender chance of success.

Only a war to 'repel actual invasion' was just. British participation in the war might be defended if it was 'limited to the expulsion of the Germans from Belgium and France.' But Germany was also being invaded and there was every reason to believe the government wished it 'to develop into a war of conquest, in which we shall seize German colonies and assist Russia to wreak barbaric vengeance upon the populations of Prussia and Austria.' Russell concluded, 'All wars are thought to be righteous, and all are fought in the interests of peace, but no war hitherto has put an end to war.'

The same page carried a letter from MacDonald.

> The difference between Mr. Wells and myself is this: that when he finds himself in a war that might have been avoided, that is a danger to European democracy, and that even in some respects is a blow to European civilisation, he is willing to believe any false excuse given by the authors of the war, and to whitewash any Power that may be our

ally in the conflict. Whereas I do not.

For many in the ILP even Russell's limited notion of what constituted a 'just war' was unacceptable. Their position was a consistently pacifist one. 'Never again must Socialists fight,' declared Ada Salter in the *Leader* on 29 October. 'We must insist,' she wrote, 'that war itself is an atrocity and must never again have the backing of Socialist either individually or as a party.'

A. A. Watts in *Justice* on 19 November asked, 'Will the War be a Final War?'[182] He believed that wars would continue 'until Socialism is established in some form.' The current war, therefore, would 'be the final war only on the assumption that the peoples will be educated in Socialist principles.' On Christmas Eve, *Labour Leader* included the text of an address on 'The Tragedy of Hate' given by E. D. Morel at the Friends' Meeting House in Manchester.

Morel saw in the 'council chambers of the nations' many manifestations of the 'spirit of hate.'

It finds expression, on either side, in the talk of 'crushing,' of annihilation, of reducing the foe to everlasting impotence.
That way madness lies. If hate is to be the last word in this unholy business; if hate is to be the dominating inspiration of the terms of settlement than the settlement will be no settlement, the peace will be no peace.

There was general agreement on the British Left, whatever position was taken on the war itself, that any prospects for the current conflict being 'a war to end war' depended entirely on the nature of the peace that followed.

---

[182] A. A. Watts, 1862-1928, was a prominent member of the SDF and BSP who opposed the war and would later join the Communist Party.

## After the War. Terms of Peace.

Even those most sceptical about the causes of the war and the justification of British participation could try and glean some comfort from past conflicts. In *Labour Leader* (13 August) 'Casey', a regular contributor, voiced the usual condemnations of 'The Vampires of War' but ended on a more optimistic note. 'The war of 1870, so mercilessly outlined by Zola in "The Downfall," placed an Emperor at least in the waste-paper basket. As sure as the sun rises history will repeat itself. The outcome of this may mean that more than one war-lord will be broken for ever.' [183] This view was echoed in a Hyndman editorial on 20 August. The hope was that just as the war of 1870 gave France a republic 'the war of 1914 may secure for England the beginnings of a Co-operative Commonwealth.'

One *Clarion* correspondent, 'J.B.' (14 August) was as fervent a believer in the rightness of Britain's war effort as Blatchford himself. 'We are at war and cannot draw back,' he wrote and then continued, 'What is to be the outcome of it? Let us assume that Germany will be defeated. On what terms will peace be made?' If a democratic government in Germany could be secured it would be 'a step onwards for humanity, another guarantee for peace in Europe, and a sweet gift from comrades to our German cousins. It will be something worth having as a result of this ghastly war.' He went on:

> Our German comrades have long struggled for constitutional reform. They are not likely to get it without a fierce, perhaps bloody, effort, possibly many years hence. They have not a fair representation in the Reichstag; and it is notorious that their work there is nullified by the German Constitution. And against them is the bigoted, insolent army caste.

---

[183] *La Débâcle* (*The Downfall*) was the penultimate novel by Émile Zola, 1840-1902, in his Rougon-Macquart series. It gives a graphic account of the Franco-Prussia War, the overthrow of Napoleon III and the Paris Commune and its violent suppression

'German comrades' notwithstanding, 'J.B.' insisted on the most vigorous prosecution of the war.

> Britain and France, now that the war is thrust upon them, ought to strain every nerve and muscle to triumph emphatically. The British Fleet ought to account for and sink every German ship afloat. And our armies should aim at capturing the German armament factories and destroying the utensils for armament making.

He also believed that Blatchford's ideal of 'a future alliance between England, France and republican Germany is next to the Socialist ideal of universal brotherhood the noblest that it has entered the heart of man to conceive.' With the overthrow of the German autocracy, 'there would be a prospect for the three great democracies – Britain, France and the United States – coming to an agreement concerning armaments at the next Hague Conference. We could impose peace and disarmament on the world. A way could be found to deal with navyless Russia if she refused to come into line.'

'J.B.' would return to the 'Clarion Cockpit' on 4 December with his own brief version of what should be the 'Terms of Peace.'

> Sir. The simplest solution of war would be:
> - As you have already hinted, that such provinces as Alsace, etc., should decide by plebiscite as to which nation they should attach themselves
> - An all-round arbitration treaty for all the States of Europe. Part of the executive for this exists in the Hague Tribunal. Armaments would automatically reduce themselves.
> - The abolition of all secret diplomacy
>
> Heartiest appreciation of the present high standard of the Clarion.

MacDonald, in the *Leader* (27 August) thought notions of the war bringing an end to militarism and a lasting peace were 'moonshine.' A 'new military despotism in Europe' was far more likely. The war was 'the beginning of a dark epoch dangerous, not merely to democracy, but to civilisation itself.'

For F.J. Gould in *Justice* (3 September) the key to peace in post-war Europe was what he called 'racial nationality.' This should be generally the basis for nation states. *Labour Leader* (24 September) sought three main things from a future peace settlement, a radical reduction in armaments, a 'more cumbrous and more democratic' mobilisation procedure, and 'open diplomacy.' It cautioned, 'All these things can be secured after the present war if the democracy is insistent; none will be secured if the negotiations are left in the hands of the men who made the war.'

In the same issue a letter appeared announcing the formation of the Union of Democratic Control [UDC].[184] It was signed by Ramsay MacDonald, Charles Trevelyan, Arthur Ponsonby, Norman Angell and E.D. Morel. With 'the turn that the military situation has happily taken,' the signatories urged, there was a need to think about peace. It suggested four principles which the British government should pursue during the peacemaking. No 'province' should be transferred 'without the consent by plebiscite of the population,' there should be 'adequate machinery for ensuring democratic control of foreign policy, Britain should pursue not alliances but the creation of a 'Concert of Europe' whose business would be conducted publicly, and Britain should propose a 'drastic reduction of armaments.' To facilitate this it advocated 'the general nationalisation of the manufacture of armaments and the prohibition of the export of

---

[184] The story of the UDC was first told by Helena Swanwick in 1924 – H.M. Swanwick, *Builders of Peace. Being Ten Year's History of the Union of Democratic Control*, London: Swarthmore Press – and much later by Marvin Swartz, *The Union of Democratic Control in British politics during the First World War*, Oxford: Clarendon Press, 1971.

armaments by one country to another.' Brockway welcomed its formation in the paper the same week.

A large advertisement for the UDC appeared on the front page of the Christmas Eve edition of *Labour Leader*. It began with a statement of aims:

> The Union aims: (a) at the concentration of all national forces with the object of ensuring that when the right moment occurs, public opinion may be in a position to demand a settlement which shall conduce to a durable peace; (b) to promote the growth of a desire in our country and, eventually, in other countries for such changes and modifications in the existing system of intercourse between States as may be calculated to remove the fundamental causes leading to war.

It then listed as 'those associated with the General Council the Union' the Liberal MPs Charles Trevelyan, Arthur Ponsonby, and R. D. Denman,[185] and the Labour MPs Arthur Henderson, Ramsay MacDonald, and F. W. Jowett. Also listed were a number of others including Bertrand Russell, Norman Angell, H. N. Brailsford, E. D. Morel, Marion Phillips and Vernon Lee. Pamphlets by Angell, Brailsford, Ponsonby and Russell were advertised.

Much earlier A. M. Thompson had offered a very detailed account of how he hoped Europe would be reshaped after the war in the *Clarion* of 18 September. Where possible, there should be 'neutral buffer states' – such as Poland – between, in that case, Germany and Russia. Their neutrality should be guaranteed by all the 'Powers' including the USA. He foresaw 'the inevitable break-up of the Austrian empire' with an independent Hungary, the restoration of the' Kingdom or Republic of Bohemia' while 'Serbo-Croatia would probably elect to join the Slav countries of Servia, Montenegro,

---

[185] R. D. (Richard Douglas) Denman, 1876-1957, had been elected as a Liberal in 1910. He stood down in 1918, joined the Labour Party in 1924 and was elected as Labour MP in 1929. In 1931 he sided with MacDonald's National Labour and remained an MP until he retired in 1945 being subsequently made a baronet.

Bosnia and Herzegovina,' though he admitted his limited knowledge of south-eastern Europe. He proposed assigning 'the narrow strip of Lorraine bordering the Rhine to Belgium and the German strip of Alsace to Switzerland' and assumed that German losses of Alsace and territory to Poland and Denmark would be more than made up by the addition of German Austria.

When there were demands for what he called 'a vindictive smashing of German unity' after the war and 'even worse' in the *Daily Mail,* Thompson hastened to reject them. He did this in the *Clarion* (2 October) along with 'the infamous suggestion that Britain should, as a price for victory, establish her alien rule over German territory by annexing Hanover.' Anything of the sort would not end war it would simply 'begin it all over again.' On 6 November he added that since it would take 'a very long time to create such a body of public opinion and such machinery of democratic expression' needed to influence the ultimate settlement, it was important that this get underway at once. For *Labour Leader* (22 October) the peace terms should include security for Belgium, a democratic choice in Alsace and Lorraine to remain German, return to France, or achieve independence from both, self-government for Finland and the revival of Poland.

One of the more interesting, and prescient, articles about the future peace settlement and the post-war role of socialists appeared in *Justice* on 12 November under the title 'Conditions of Peace.' It was by F. W. Wibaut who was introduced to readers as 'our Dutch comrade' who had 'attended the dinner to Hyndman on his 70th birthday as the representative of the Dutch Social-Democratic Party.' The paper was 'gladly' publishing the article 'without necessarily endorsing all the views to which he has given expression.'

The article began by asking what could be done to end the war given that in most belligerent countries 'the Social-Democrats have placed them behind the Governments, in accepting the war.' And, while 'our Russian comrades' had refused to support war credits that did not mean that 'the Russian nation' had not backed the war. Posing the question, "How will it end?' Wibaut speculated that it might come about through 'exhaustion of the means of carrying it on' most likely 'exhaustion of fightable men, or weapons, or munitions.'

Would 'International Social-Democracy' have real influence on the peace? Would the peace be 'the starting point for a new war' or could social-democrats 'make the character of the terms of peace a guarantee against further wars?' Positions taken by socialist parties did not 'justify over-sanguine expectations.' If at the end of the war they 'continue to feel at one with the nation at large' this did not augur well for the peace. Nationalism in both Germany and France had 'proved many times stronger than we supposed that it would.' If 'unweakened nationalism dictated the terms of peace,' it would 'contain the germs for later war.' The peace would be 'nothing more than an armistice if it does not prepare for the abandonment of armaments.' In Wibaut's judgement the war had already shown 'that wars cannot be prevented if they have come near at hand. The lesson is that wars must be stopped by preventing their preparation, by directing all the force of the proletariat against national armaments.'

He turned his attention to the policy to prevent war that the Left should pursue questioning the validity in modern conditions of the 'armed nation' – or 'citizen army' – policy which had been pursued by socialists hitherto. 'The present war is a "war of machines"' which 'kills in accordance with the rules of technical science.' This was bound to cause the 'armed nation' policy to be questioned and almost certainly abandoned in the future. A better policy was one of 'fighting all systems of national armaments.' The socialist movement was not yet powerful enough to end capitalism but capitalism 'no longer necessitates wars between competing nations.' As evidence for this Wibaut cited how 'the huge organisations of capitalists of various countries have well started international combination, and have thereby achieved in several instances, in Morocco, in Asia Minor, in South America, in China the same extension of capitalist exploitation which warfaring Imperialism could have obtained.' This meant that wars were no longer inevitable under capitalism and strengthened socialist demands for the 'abandonment of armaments.'

It is clear that however much conflict there might be within the British Left about the war, there was very little disagreement that the peace should be just and non-vindictive and that 'secret diplomacy' should be abandoned. Democracy and, as far as possible, socialism, should replace authoritarian rule and the national boundaries should be determined by democratic choice. The danger of a future war should be countered by mutual disarmament. One idea about what should follow the war and ensure future peace that had a very wide support among British socialists appeared very early in the war. It was the call for a United States of Europe.

## The United States of Europe

As we saw in chapter 4 the ILP manifesto looked forward to the possibility of a United States of Europe on 13 August. The following day the term featured in one of A. M. Thompson's *Clarion* editorials. 'The German War Lords,' Thompson wrote, had 'scorned Sir Edward Grey's "Utopian" offer of a British guarantee against French or Russian attack on Germany which would have formed the basis for the establishment of the United States of Europe.' He used the term again in the editorial on 18 September outlining the ideas for a peace settlement in Europe already noted. The following week (20 August) saw *Labour Leader* hoping that 'the black night of fratricide' would give way to the 'dawn of fraternity' and when the 'scheming Chancelleries of Europe' were replaced by 'a permanent federation of interdependent states.'

Then, again in the *Leader* (17 September), the Cambridge philosopher G. Lowes Dickinson contributed an article on 'The War and the Way Out. Preparing the Path to Peace.' [186] He rehearsed the necessary objectives of an equitable peace settlement – no vindictive deprivation of German territory and no nations under 'alien rule,' concluding, 'We must aim at a permanent League of Europe which will control and limit national armaments while leaving every nation free to accomplish its own internal development.'

At the beginning of September all three papers mentioned the celebrations of Edward Carpenter's 70th birthday. [187] *Justice* (3 September) devoted only a paragraph to it mentioning the congratulatory letter that had been sent by the BSP and the 'cordial letter' with which Carpenter had responded. But both *Labour Leader* (3 September) and the *Clarion* (4 September) quoted extensively from the poet's speech at the event. It was not impossible, Carpenter maintained, that 'when the nightmare of war was over the states of western Europe would 'consolidate their democracies and the establishment of a great Federation on a Labour basis.'

Brockway took up the call on the front page of the *Leader* on 24 September in the second of two articles under the headline 'After the War – What? II. Towards a United States of Europe.' Peace, he insisted, must 'denote the triumph not so much of the Allies or of Germany as of Europe.' A 'League of Europe' should be able to grow into a United States of Europe. 'The United States of America is composed of the peoples of every nation in Europe. Why should not those peoples, before they cross the Atlantic, form a United States of Europe?' Perhaps it was the wider perspective of someone born in India – and who would in the then distant future (1954) chair the Movement for Colonial Freedom – that accounts for the way Brockway then went on. Beyond a Europe with a 'European

---

[186] G. (Goldsworthy) Lowes Dickinson, 1862-1932, known to friends as Goldie, was a Cambridge political scientist and philosopher who soon after the outbreak of war in 1914 became the passionate advocate of a League of Nations.

[187] Edward Carpenter, 1844-1929, was a poet, greatly influenced by Walt Whitman, and an early advocate of gay rights.

Parliament' and a 'European police force' he caught a glimpse of 'a federation of nations in which America and the British Dominions are part, and, more dimly, of a still larger federation including the peoples of Asia, Africa and South America.'

These ideas were developed in greater detail in the *Leader's* 'Review of the Week' on 8 October which suggested a six-point 'United Platform for European Socialists' which it summarised as follows:

I. Frontiers should represent nations and not annexations.

II. Subject peoples should have self-government and decide by plebiscite whether they desire to be under the suzerainty of any Power.

III. These 'natural' nations should constitute a League of Europe, and all quarrels should be submitted to arbitration.

IV. The political machinery of all nations should be democratised. Foreign policy should be brought under control and women's claim to citizenship recognised.

V. The armaments industry should be taken out of private hands.

VI. The goal ever before us should be a United States of Europe (ultimately of the world), in which national armies and navies are replaced by International Police Force.

A simpler 'programme for Peace' in the same paper on 19 November comprised 'no forcible annexation of territory,' or 'War Indemnities', a 'people's right to determine their own fate' and 'A United States of Europe, without dynasties, secret diplomacy, feudal castes, or standing armies.' With both the 'pro-war' *Clarion* and the 'anti-war' *Labour Leader* promoting the idea of a 'United States of Europe' after the war it is again clear that while divisions within the socialist movement in Britain were serious with regard to attitudes to the war and questions of the responsibility for it, there was something approaching unanimity on the question of the principles that should inform the eventual peace settlement and the future of the post-war world and especially post-war Europe. In any case, just *how* divided was the Left during these first months of war?

# CHAPTER 11

# Division or Unity?

## The Labour Party and Ramsay MacDonald's Resignation

It was not until 1922 that the Labour Party acquired a formal leader – in the shape of Ramsay MacDonald. There is a tendency to read this later situation back to the early years of the party and credit Hardie and later MacDonald as 'Leader' at various times in the years leading up to the war. Both were certainly leaders in the more general, informal, sense, but the formal position that existed in 1914 was that of Chairman of the Parliamentary Labour Party [PLP]. It was from this position that MacDonald resigned after the majority Labour MPs voted in support of war credits on 5 August.

The next day Labour's NEC passed a resolution which was reported in *Labour Leader* the following week (13 August). It began by dissociating itself completely from the foreign policy of maintaining the balance of power pursued by Grey and the government prior to the war with its 'understandings' with France and Russia. These had been undertaken, it said, 'without the knowledge of our people,' which endangered 'good relations with Germany.' The party's object was now to 'secure peace at the earliest possible moment.' As agreed the previous day (5 August) at a conference of Labour movement organisations, energies should now be concentrated on the measures to 'mitigate the destitution which will inevitably overtake our working people.' This was to be done 'without in any way receding from the position the Labour movement has taken to our engaging in a European war.' When Labour MPs decided to vote in support of war credits MacDonald had resigned from the chairmanship of the parliamentary party – while remaining treasurer.

If MacDonald was at odds with the majority of the PLP he could count on the support of the ILP and the *Labour Leader*. On 13 August its 'Review of the Week' noted that 'Some of the Labour members of Parliament, even, have not been able to withstand the wave of militarist feeling that has swept over the country,' and consequently MacDonald had resigned. The paper's 'Gallery correspondent' added, after noting the efforts of the PLP to 'prevent distress' that 'On the question of the war itself the Labour Party are unhappily divided, and the momentous protest in which under different circumstances MacDonald would have signalled to the Socialists of the Continent was not made.'

At special meeting of the ILP's NAC a resolution 'of deep appreciation of the attitude that he has adopted' had been carried. It was not 'necessary to assure Mr. MacDonald of the sympathy of the members of the I.L.P. will feel for him at this moment nor the pride and admiration his magnificent stance has evoked.' The same issue reported resolutions supporting MacDonald's stance and regretting that of the PLP from the Warrington, Blackburn and Ferryhill branches. At a meeting in Leicester, MacDonald's constituency, representing, the paper reported, the ILP, the local Labour Party, the Women's Labour League and the Trades Council, the MP had 'fully explained' his position and 'was accorded an unanimous and enthusiastic vote of confidence.'

A more unusual kind of support came when, on 15 October the *Leader* published 'Two Sonnets to J. Ramsay MacDonald' by Violet Spender.[188] The first two lines of each give a fair idea of her view of

---

[188] Violet Spender, 1890-1921, was a poet and painter. She was married to Harold Spender, a well-known journalist. One of their sons was Stephen Spender, the poet and writer. A volume of her poems, *The Path to Caister and other poems* was published

her subject.

You sought to lead us to the Promised Land,
Where souls and minds and bodies should have food
and
Hope on, brave man and true, nor ever yield
To doubt, or think that all you gave is vain.

Given their stance on the war MacDonald and the ILP were able to draw on support from pacifists – notably Quakers – who did not necessarily share their socialist convictions. This was, on the whole, a more prosperous segment of the population than the pre-1914 ILP membership and in time, especially during the chairmanship of Clifford Allen in the 1920s, it would become an important source of income for the party. [189] The foundations of this alliance were already being laid in 1914. On 5 November *Labour Leader* reported under the headline 'MacDonald with the Friends' that 2,000 members of the Society of Friends had attended a meeting at Manchester's Free Trade Hall at which MacDonald was the main speaker.

However, the dominant view in the wider Labour movement – in the unions – was far less supportive of the position taken by MacDonald and the ILP. A *Justice* editorial by John Stokes – 'Organised Labour and the War' – claimed on 29 October that opinion among both leadership and 'the so-called rank and file' was 'unmistakably definite.' There was 'no hesitation in calling for the overthrow of 'Prussian militarist domination.' But fraternal feelings remained towards 'German, Austrian and Hungarian comrades' and 'the sentiment of international solidarity' was as strong as ever. No-one blamed German workers for 'this horrible and bloody war of conquest.'

---

posthumously in 1922.
[189] See, especially, Chapter 5 of *Under Siege.*

There was much criticism of the PLP from both those 'anti' and 'pro' the war. In its 'Parliament Day by Day' feature on 26 November *Labour Leader* praised 'the excellence of speeches made from the Labour benches' but regretted that the party should 'appear to demand only a few shillings extra for the victims of war when our quarrel is with nothing less than war itself.' The same issue reported that the Eastleigh Labour Representation Committee had written to Arthur Henderson, now chairing the PLP, explaining its refusal to take part in the recruitment campaign and objecting to the party 'throwing the whole of its energies into the business of persuading the manhood of the nation to join the militarist forces.'

Yet even *Labour Leader* could find things to applaud in a speech in the Commons by Henderson reported on 19 November. He had pledged the Labour movement 'to safeguard the interests of true nationalism and democracy when the time came to settle the war.' He had made a strong protest against the Home Office's behaviour towards soldiers' wives and 'the general harrying of these lonely women by the well-intentioned busybodies who now everywhere beset them' and he had secured promises of improvement of soldiers' pay by the War Office.

At the very end of the year (31 December) *Labour Leader* was able to report a Labour electoral success. W.C. Anderson had been elected at a by-election in Attercliffe, Sheffield. He was 'the chairman of the Labour Party, but he has remained true to the international faith of Socialism and has served our cause far more effectively than is generally known,' the *Leader* reminded readers. Meanwhile, though differences within both the PLP and the movement in the country grew there were still those who tried to emphasise unity of purpose rather than conflict of opinion.

## Agree to Disagree?

Although, as we have already seen in earlier chapters, there was a great deal of conflict within the British socialist movement over the war, there were also many areas of agreement. The aspirations for a just and democratic peace settlement and the unanimity with which a fair deal for those fighting and their dependants was demanded have already been noted. There was *relatively* little accusatory name-calling. Keir Hardie's comment on the *Labour Leader* front page on 27 August that 'Some British Socialists are, unfortunately, ranging themselves on the side of militarism' seems mild enough given the literally life and death nature of the situation.

In his reply to Wells and Ensor that we looked at in the context of attitudes towards the alliance with Russia, Hardie made the usual attack on 'knavish secret diplomacy and backstairs understandings,' but, equally, he pledged that the ILP would 'insist that the State shall pay adequately for the soldiers and sailors who do its fighting.' On the same page of the *Leader* (10 September) Katharine Bruce Glasier made a plea that 'Socialist comrades who possibly can find a way to serve the community usefully at home.' But she added, 'Let those go to the war first, at any rate, who can honestly persuade themselves that they are fighting their country's enemy on the field of battle.' Similarly, W.C. Anderson, after making it clear that the ILP should have nothing to do with recruiting, went on: 'I hope we shall try to be quite fair to those who differ from us, remembering that they, also, have opinions and convictions sincerely held.'

The following day (11 September) A. Neil Lyons – who we met earlier as a 'hater' of Germans – defended Hardie against an attack by the novelist W. J. Locke. [190]

---

[190] W. J. (William John) Locke, 1863-1930, was a successful novelist and playwright. He was particularly successful in the USA where his books featured in the *Publishers Weekly* list of best-selling novels in 1909, 1910, 1914, 1915, and 1917. Many of his works were later filmed including his 1916 short story *Ladies in Lavender* which was

God knows that we of the CLARION are pretty far removed from Mr Hardie in our way of living, our outlook on life, our artistic and spiritual impulses, and our ultimate political ideas. But we should no more think of calling Mr. Hardie and his followers 'the scum of uneducated thought' as we should think of applying to Mr. Locke and the thousands of languishing young ladies who read his novels the epithet that some coarse and unreflective 'bus driver might perhaps apply to these phenomena of our civilisation.

Hardie was, he went on, 'an old gentleman' – he was actually 58 – 'whom we believe to be wrong-headed and stubborn but we know to be honest and sincere.' He represented 'a considerable body of soured opinion but he does not represent it through all these years, by virtue of being "uneducated."' He was a man who had 'thought deeply and piously about the matters which constitute his faith; he has worked hard and read much.'

The following week's *Labour Leader* (17 September) included a letter from Beatrice Webb in which she supported Anderson's 'plea for courtesy and good feeling, and even for mutual respect, among members of the Labour and Socialist movement who hold different views on this complicated and most tragic question.' She found it hard, she went on, to understand anyone in the Labour Party who could not 'appreciate the disinterestedness and the long-standing conviction which have led Mr. J. R. MacDonald to give up the chairmanship of the Labour Party; or the honourable and courageous patriotism which has induced Mr. Arthur Henderson to help the Government in its work of recruiting a new army.'

She was concerned that those 'criticising each other's convictions on the foreign policy of the Government' would not have the time, energy or perhaps even the 'kind of temper' necessary 'for energetic action to keep the Government straight on its home policy.' She

---

the basis of the 2004 film of the same name.

pleaded for 'a truce in mutual recriminations.' The announcement made 'To our Readers' in the *Leader* on 8 October could hardly have been less recriminatory: 'Many of the I.L.P. have been 'called to the colours. The good wishes of their comrades go with them and the hope that they may return safely to our ranks.'

Yet anyone doubting the existence of the recriminations Beatrice Webb had warned against had only to turn to some of the other pages of the edition in which her letter appeared (17 September). Among the other letters they would have found H. G. Wells's long and angry response to Hardie's equally dismissive criticism of the writer's views on Russia. Hardie, said Wells, had clearly read nothing that he, Wells, had written on the war crisis. If he had then he was 'either drunk or mad to say that I am "shouting with the multitude." I am working with all my being for Socialism and the peace of the world.' He objected to Hardie's 'whining – confound it! he whines!' Hardie, he went on, accused him of 'taking a mean advantage of those he does not like.' His own hostile reputation, Wells maintained, was owed 'to the spiteful lying chatter of the shabbiest scum of Socialism.' The editorial 'Review of the Week' defending Hardie and MacDonald professed to be amused by 'the colossal conceit and condescension of this letter.'

Wells, however, was not very closely associated with either the ILP or the BSP. H. W. Lee was in a very different situation. In *Justice* (24 September) he declared his belief, or at least hope, that the divisions among socialists were more apparent than real. In an editorial on 'The War and the Socialist Movement' he concluded that the international socialist movement had always been for peace but having 'completely failed to prevent the outbreak of European war, or to interfere in the slightest degree with its operations' it now had to 'face the situation as it is not as we would wish it to be.' He went on to criticise both the Labour Party and the TUC for failing to 'force the Government to grant something like reasonable conditions for those enlisting' before 'throwing in their lot entirely with the Government.'

The ILP manifesto, Lee argued, might appear to be 'a definite declaration against recruiting' but read more closely and with the explanations given by Jowett, MacDonald and Hardie it seemed rather to be the case 'that the I.L.P. is not against recruiting for the war, but only the company in which it may be advocated.' This was not so very different from the position taken by BSP, said Lee, and suggested that the Joint Socialist Council – on which both ILP and BSP were represented – might be able to reach a common agreement on this question.

Yet very soon after (1 October), *Justice* was far less kind to MacDonald. Under the title 'Ramsay and MacDonald' it quoted apparently contradictory extracts from his speeches and articles on the war. In a *Labour Leader* article now being reprinted and circulated by the ILP he had characterised the government's claim to have 'vindicated' Belgian independence as 'a pretty little game of hypocrisy.' Later, in the *Leicester Pioneer*, he had written that 'We could not afford, either from the point of view of honour or of interest, to see Germany occupy Belgium.' On the eve of the war, on 3 August, he had told the House of Commons that 'the country ought to have remained neutral' while in a letter to the mayor of Leicester read at a recruiting meeting he had announced 'Victory must be ours' and gone on to call for 'serious men' of the movement to 'face their duty.' *Justice* thought this was indeed a 'pretty little game of hypocrisy' and asked, 'What are we to think of Ramsay MacDonald after this?'

This did not deter Lee, in a *Justice* editorial (15 October) under the title 'The Duty of British Socialists,' from renewing the call for the convening of the Joint Socialist Council – something that had been put forward as a consequence of the BSP's decision to affiliate to the Labour Party. It was to bring about 'unity of purpose and co-ordination of effort.' The 'calamitous upheaval' of the war was bound to bring about differences of opinion. These could be argued 'thoroughly, even heatedly if necessary.' But there was no room for 'the imputation of motives, the distrust of comrades, and the breaking away of members.'

The ILP's NAC report in *Labour Leader* on 29 October noted a letter from the BSP requesting a Joint Socialist Council meeting but 'was unanimously agreed that the moment was not opportune to inaugurate any new departure.' Clearly, there was considerable support among socialists – irrespective of positions taken on the war – for tolerance of disagreement even on such a fundamental issue as the war, and for attempting to maintain unity. Equally clearly, this was very difficult to sustain. Nowhere was this more evident than within the BSP.

## Growing Conflict in the BSP

We saw in Chapter 4 how, as reflected by the debate on the war in *Justice,* revolt against the 'Old Guard' was growing in the BSP. The 'Manifesto' on 'Recruiting for the War' led to protests and growing dissent was reflected the success of Fineberg, an 'anti-war' candidate, in the election to fill the London vacancy on the executive.

Opposition to the recruiting manifesto was by no means confined to the BSP stronghold, relatively speaking, of London, but it was clearly very strong there.

On 15 October *Justice* reported some reactions from BSP branches to the executive manifesto. It was a mixed bag. Bethnal Green branch repudiated the executive's statement with 'no uncertain voice.' Another London branch, Tottenham, objected to the 'tone of the manifesto' and wanted the BSP to 'take up a neutral position.' The Plymouth branch was critical of the executive for taking a position on such an important matter as army recruiting without 'first ascertaining the feeling of the whole Party.' The East Liverpool branch's letter concluded with a recommendation to the workers 'to husband their physical and intellectual resources for the only war that matters – the war of the classes.'

However, the executive could count on the support of the Central Branch, which had 'unanimously approved' of the manifesto, while the Carlisle branch recorded its 'cordial appreciation' and agreement. Likewise the management committee of the Burnley branch expressed its 'entire agreement' and added a comment that 'To express a desire "to see the prosecution of the war to a speedy and successful issue," and at the same time to refuse the only possible means whereby success can be assured seems to us to be the extreme of fatuity.'

The following week (22 October) the BSP paper reported that at a meeting at the Chandos Hall delegates of eighteen London branches had passed a resolution, supported by fifteen of them, calling for the withdrawal of the statement on recruiting. The same day the meeting was reported in *Labour Leader* with the heading 'The B.S.P. Revolt'. It appeared on a page listing the widespread, if not quite unanimous, support by its own branches for the line taken by the ILP. There was little need to spell out the contrast in the degree of unity to be found in the two socialist parties. A letter from R. C. Fletcher Woods in *Justice* on 12 November underlined how divided the BSP was becoming. 'The deplorable Executive's manifesto,' he wrote, 'was the work of men who had forgotten an essential principle of their own Socialism.'

## Greater Unity in the ILP

While the BSP was faced with considerable dissent concentrated in, but by no means confined to, London, the ILP, though far from reaching complete unanimity, enjoyed a greater degree of internal agreement. *Labour Leader* on 15 October was able to report that there had been three party conferences in Scotland – at Clydebank. Falkirk and Paisley. They had all been addressed by Bruce Glasier and James Maxton and all three conferences had endorsed the NAC's manifesto.[191] A week later (22 October) it announced 'OVERWHELMING SUPPORT FOR N.A.C.', listing 95 branches, federations and divisional councils in support of the NAC and only seven opposing its position. It also reported that sixteen local Labour Parties and Trades Councils had passed motions dissenting from the Labour Party Executive's position or opposing participation in recruiting while 'Many branches of the British Socialist Party and one District Council have passed resolutions either endorsing the I.L.P. attitude or repudiating the attitude of their own executive.'

On 29 October it reported that a local socialist monthly paper in Bournemouth – *The Worker* – was 'uncompromisingly against the war.' The *Leader* said it had now so many new readers that it was necessary to re-state the principles of the paper and the ILP. 'We are opposed to warfare in general and this war in particular.' It did not believe that any single 'Power' was responsible for starting the war.

> Now that the disaster is upon us each individual must obey the dictates of his own conscience as to how he shall act. Some of our members, believing our national existence to be threatened, will take up arms in self-defence; others will not feel justified in killing a fellow man under any conditions. That issue, we feel, is one for the individual to decide; and not for the Party. It is in essence a religious and spiritual issue of a peculiarly personal nature, and in such questions the Party has never felt it right to interfere.

Of its own position on the war Brockway's editorial summed it up like this. 'We are not pro-German. We are not anti-British. We are anti-War.'

---

[191] James Maxton, 1885-1946, was at this time a Glasgow teacher and already a prominent ILPer. He would be a conscientious objector and become one of the leading figures in 'Red Clydeside'. He would be imprisoned in 1916 for sedition. Elected as a Labour MP in 1922 he would become the left-wing scourge of Ramsay MacDonald's minority governments and a key figure in the decision of the ILP to disaffiliate from Labour in 1932 remaining an ILP MP until his death.

The same issue reported that Emily Hobhouse had joined the ILP.[192] Hobhouse was the outstanding campaigner against what the Liberal leader, Campbell Bannerman, later called 'methods of barbarism' in the concentration camps employed by the British in the South African War of 1899-1902. *Labour Leader* published her letter in which she said that she had 'never belonged to any party but now I feel constrained to join the I.L.P. through its National Branch.'

There was something of a mixed bag of resolutions reported in *Labour Leader* that week (29 October). The Lewisham branch reported that it was 'equally divided on the attitude of the N.A.C. to the war, but there will be no split.' There was support for the NAC from the Crewe ILP which also recorded 'its admiration for the stand taken by the LABOUR LEADER during the crisis.' But a 'specially convened' meeting of the Richmond ILP reaffirmed its decision not to endorse the NAC's position on recruiting. By taking part, it urged, it could have drawn public attention to the 'inadequacy of the provision for combatants and their dependents and the unjustified methods adopted in some quarters to obtain recruits.' Clearly, though division was more apparent in the case of the BSP with opposition growing particularly in London neither of the British socialist parties was entirely united in its attitudes towards the war.

## ILP versus BSP

There was still some hope that the degree of unity so recently secured between the ILP and the BSP might yet be somehow maintained though there was already much resentment to overcome. 'Tattler', in

---

[192] Emily Hobhouse, 1860-1926, had gone to South Africa on behalf of the South African Conciliation Committee in Britain. She exposed the appalling conditions in which mainly women and children were living in the concentration camps at Bloemfontein and other South African locations. She would remain an active opponent of the 1914 war.

*Justice* on 19 November, was 'a trifle astonished' to see that *Labour Leader* had referred to 'the crime which Germany has committed against Belgium.' This was language *he* was happy to use but had he done so in the recent past it would have been regarded as exemplifying the "jingo' and 'pro-British' attitude of *Justice*. He concluded, 'Well the war may do one good thing for the Socialist movement here. It will test, not only the zeal, but the readiness of comrades of both the B.S.P. and the I.L.P. to stick together, in spite of differences that were bound to arise in such a crisis as we are now going through.'

Calling for 'Clearing our Thoughts' in *Justice* (3 December) F. J. Gould began, 'The truth is that the war has made as much havoc in Socialist thought as the Germans have made in Belgian life and industry.' Socialists had been unable to prevent the war because 'no nationality has enough Socialists, and ... International Socialism consists only of a sentiment and has no really international machinery.' In years of reading the 'capitalist Press' he had 'never yet detected unmistakable signs of fear of the Socialist factor. There has been some uneasiness, not fear.'

In December one issue arose which did little to advance the cause of socialist unity. The BSP remained keen to make constitutional changes within the Labour Party to allow candidates – *their* candidates in particular – to run as 'Labour and Socialist' rather than simply 'Labour.' This had been rejected, it will be recalled, in July before the outbreak of war. At a London Labour Party meeting on 28 November – reported by A. A. Watts in *Justice* on 3 December – it was again rejected by 162 votes to 120. Several ILP delegates and one trade unionist had spoken against it. But Watts was very critical of those BSP members who had wanted to leave the Labour Party if the proposal was rejected.

Watts's account of the meeting was challenged a fortnight later (*Justice* 17 December) in a letter from G. R. Rowbotham, the mover of the unsuccessful BSP amendment. He denied ever saying that the BSP should withdraw from Labour if the proposal was rejected. His branch, Southwark, was definitely staying in the London Labour Party. But he had a dig at the ILP delegates who had opposed the amendment; 'it does make one think seriously when one knows that the amendment was not opposed by a non-Socialist or anti-Socialist vote, which could be converted in time; but by the action of the majority of I.L.P. branches voting against it.' Another issue that had showed the divisions in the broader British Labour movement and clear undertones of ILP/BSP antipathy also arose in December.

## 'Paid Emissaries'

On 3 December *Justice* took as its lead story on the front page a report headlined 'Keir Hardie & Paid Emissaries of the British Government.' It claimed that in a recent edition of the *American Socialist,* the weekly paper of the American Socialist Party, Hardie, writing about the war, had charged 'the British Government with paying two leading trade unionists to travel through the United States and Canada to influence working class opinion in favour of the war.' Who were these 'paid emissaries' *Justice* wanted to know? It quoted 'Comrade Max Hayes' in the *New York Call,* a socialist daily linked to the American Socialist Party, who suggested that the two 'emissaries' must be James A. Seddon, who he described inaccurately as 'one of the leaders of the Labour Party in Parliament' – he was no longer an MP – and A. Bellamy the president of the main rail union, the National Union of Railwaymen.'[193]

---

[193] James Andrew Seddon, 1868-1939, was active both as a member of the TUC Parliamentary Committee, the predecessor of the General Council, and, in the Labour Party which he had represented as an MP from 1906-1910. Later in the war he would leave Labour for the NDP or National Democratic and Labour Party and serve as one of its handful of MPs from 1918 to 1922. Albert Bellamy was President of the National Union of Railwayman, formed in 1913 by the amalgamation of earlier rail unions and a key part of the 'Triple Alliance.'

It was, said Hayes, 'hinted' that they were in North America to rouse support for the Allied cause, but the truth was that they had been sent 'by the British working people to assure the officials of international unions that, although the war was being waged fiercely' there was 'no actual feeling of hatred among the organised workers of the United Kingdom towards the organised working people of Germany and Austria.' *Justice* ended by asking whether these were the two that Hardie meant. 'If not, who are they? If so, why have they not been exposed in this country?' The same day, in the context of criticisms of the Labour Party for its uncritical collaboration with the government, Brockway in the *Labour Leader* was clear that the government was 'footing the bill' for Seddon's and Bellamy's trip which was being made, he said, 'supposedly as representatives of the British working class.'

Hayes' account of their mission might not have seemed to many to rule out the sort of thing with which Hardie was charging the two trade unionists. But *Justice* was clearly not disposed to let the matter go. The following week (10 December) it returned to what it called 'the mystery of the "paid emissaries."' For both their own sakes and that of the British trade union movement this needed to be 'cleared up at once.' It hoped that either Hardie or the TUC would produce 'something definite.' Another week passed and *Justice* on 24 December was still insisting that the 'mystery' still needed to be cleared up in the interests of quelling the 'amount of suspicion ... prevailing in trade union circles in the United States and in Canada.' Seddon, now in Canada, had apparently said that he and Bellamy were there to 'stimulate assistance for the Belgian refugees' and had held meetings in Montreal and Toronto for that purpose. 'If that is so, all well and good. But why the mystery?' asked *Justice*. The BSP paper was careful not to rule out the charges made against Seddon and Bellamy while at the same time leaving the suggestion that Hardie had made an accusation he was not able, or not prepared, to substantiate.

## Bernard Shaw on the War

George Bernard Shaw was no stranger to controversy, especially controversy with Blatchford, whether it concerned contrasting views on human evolution, as we saw in the first chapter, or on socialism and Labour politics. So it was not very surprising that when the *New Statesman* published his pamphlet *Common Sense About the War* as a supplement Blatchford's reaction was entirely hostile – in spite of Shaw's essentially 'pro-war' conclusion.

It was, said Blatchford from his usual platform of the front page of the *Clarion* on 20 November, the latest example of 'Mr Shaw's egregious vanity and shallowness.' The war was 'the most awful tragedy in history.' But it was a war 'which *must* be fought out to a dreadful finish, which must entail a bloody carnage never perhaps equalled in this terrible world.' All that was clear. 'And here comes Bernard Shaw in his fool's cap brandishing his bladder of dried peas and trying to impress the world with his irony and cleverness. It makes one deadly sick.' Blatchford accused Shaw of trying to use the 'stale one' of trying to show that the war was 'six of one and half dozen of the other,' a subheading the playwright used in the pamphlet. He thought Shaw's effort would be 'joyfully received' in Germany.

In *Common Sense About the War,* Shaw had presented 'the Junkers and Militarists of England and Germany jumping at the chance they have longed for in vain for many years of smashing one another and establishing their own oligarchy as the dominant military power in the world.' However, he concluded that the Germans had made 'their dash and put themselves in the wrong at every point morally, besides making victory humanly impossible for themselves militarily.' This left Britain in the role of 'the responsible policeman of the west. There was nobody else in Europe strong enough to chain "the mad dog."'

On 26 November *Labour Leader* carried a letter from Shaw sent initially to the *Times* which had, it claimed, 'suppressed' it. Shaw argued that just as MacDonald's visits to India had 'probably helped to gain us that popular support as against Germany which we certainly do not owe to the utterances of his political opponents,' MacDonald's opinions on Germany would be useful 'when we have finished our fight with Germany' and 'unless we are utter cads' would 'shake hands with her.' It would then be important for the Germans to know that when 'British organised Labour' rallied to the war they were not supporting 'the proceedings of our Foreign Office.'

Shaw was again featured in the *Leader* the following week (3 December). This time it was in response to a letter he had sent to the soon-to-be defunct *Daily Citizen,* the short-lived Labour Party and TUC paper. He had appealed for a distinction to be made between support for the war and support for Grey's policy that led up to it. Commenting in his *Leader* editorial, Brockway accepted that such a distinction was possible and that had Labour done so clearly 'we should have found far less ground to complain.' But, he went on, 'unfortunately many Labour leaders have out-Jingoed the Jingoes and out-militarised the militarists.' He excepted Henderson and Clynes from this criticism, 'But the Party as a whole has failed to voice the democratic view.' Brockway then followed this up with several instances of Labour's uncritical collaboration with the government.

The 'declaration' signed by twenty-five Labour MPs and the Parliamentary Committee of the TUC had been sent out for signature in official 'O.H.M.S.' envelopes under the auspices of the Parliamentary Recruiting Committee.[194] 'It would be interesting to know who paid for its publication and distribution.' At least one TUC manifesto was 'printed (at a non Trade Union firm) by the Government and posted on the hoardings at its expense.' It was time that the 'rank and file' of the movement was made aware of what was going on.

---

[194] On Her/His Majesty's Service is used as official franking for correspondence from government departments.

Two *Labour Leader* letters that week also responded to what Shaw himself called his 'many-sided' take on the war. One from Herbert Bryan began by mentioning Shaw's quoting of the Labour NEC resolution of 6 August and the *Citizen's* citing in response 'a statement justifying Britain's intervention in the war' signed by 'a somewhat imposing list' of Labour MPs and trade union officials. Bryan rejected the *Citizen's* claim that this conclusively proved that the British Labour movement 'was convinced of the justice of the Government case.' Signed by a 'miscellaneous collection of people in their individual capacities,' the omissions were more significant, said Bryan. Shaw had 'quite properly refused' to sign. So had eleven members of the Parliamentary Labour Party, including Hardie, MacDonald, Jowett and Snowden. The chairman, Anderson, and deputy chairman, Alex Gordon Cameron, treasurer, MacDonald and four other members of the Labour Party Executive were also non-signers. Bryan also mentioned several notable trade union leaders including Robert Smillie of the miners' union and Mary Macarthur of the Women's Trade Union movement.[195] No officer of the ILP, BSP or National Women's Labour League had signed. It was hardly necessary for Bryan to spell out further why the statement could not be regarded as being anything like as representative as the *Citizen* was claiming.

The second letter was from T. Mactavish who explained that 'like Mr. Bernard Shaw' he and his colleagues had been making recruiting speeches. He praised Shaw's 'brilliant contribution to the *New Statesman*' but dissented from the latter's view that Britain's role was to be that of a 'policeman.' If Britain wanted to act in this way

---

[195] Mary Macarthur, 1880-1921, was secretary of the Women's Trade Union League. She was an 'adult suffragist', opposing the idea of campaigning for votes for women on the existing terms for men – which would keep many working-class women disenfranchised - and she was an opponent of the war though she served on the Ministry of Labour's national committee on women's employment during the conflict.

it should have begun it before 'we occupied Egypt, chummed it with France and financed Russia.' The 'devil' let loose in Germany was 'Junkerdom, steeped in militarism.' The part played by the Foreign Office in unleashing this devil was 'a matter for serious consideration' but the immediate imperative was to destroy that 'devil.' It was the island nature of Britain that made it possible 'for our N. A. C. to issue its manifesto and for Mr. Shaw to write letters to the *Times*. They couldn't do it if they were Belgians.'

But Mactavish's own position was not a simple one. 'I am glad the I.L.P. has taken up the position it has, for it is not strong enough to affect our resisting power to the triumph of Junkerism while at the same time it keeps untarnished its faith in Internationalism. England is the only country in the war where a Socialist organisation could take the stand the I.L.P. has taken.' He applauded this while regretting that his participation in recruiting meant he had 'quarrelled with some of my comrades.' He hoped that they would 'realise that both jobs have got to be done' and would 'forgive me and other backsliders like me.' An editorial note followed pointing out that 'Russian and Servian Socialists' had also 'refused to participate in the prosecution of the war.'

The same day (3 December) 'Tattler' noted in *Justice* that the arguments in Shaw's pamphlet, *Common Sense About the War* were able to be used by both *Labour Leader* and the *Daily Citizen* in support of their 'different and divergent views.' 'Tattler' professed to be 'one of those who do not take Shaw seriously' but nevertheless endorsed his view that Germany could have confined itself to attacking Russia and, quoting Shaw, 'entrusted the security of her western frontier to the public opinion of the west of Europe and to America.' If France had insisted on going on the attack that would have led to the strongest protests and even armed intervention on the side of Germany.

The next day (4 December) Thompson, in the *Clarion*, announced that Shaw's lengthy arguments had been 'boiled down by the New York 'World' to five points:

- That Great Britain was abundantly justified in making war against Germany.
- That the explanation given by the British Government for making war against Germany was stupid, hypocritical, mendacious and disgraceful
- That he alone is capable of interpreting the moral purpose of the British people in undertaking this necessary work of civilisation.
- That the reason the British Government's justification for the war is so inadequate is because no British Government is ever so clever as Bernard Shaw.
- That even in the midst of the most horrible calamity known to human history it pays to advertise.

Thompson confined himself to commenting that 'Various patriots have various ways of serving their country. Some go to the firing-line to be shot, others stay at home to be a source of innocent merriment to the survivors.'

Though Shaw laid himself open to such comments they hardly did justice to the arguments in his pamphlet. Evidently Shaw's take on the war was satisfactory to neither 'pro' nor 'anti' war socialists, though both could endorse parts of his position. But he had at least one defender among the letters in that edition of the *Clarion*. J. F. Horrabin set out to explain why he and many others preferred Shaw to Blatchford. 'We prefer Mr Shaw's views to Mr Blatchford's because Mr Shaw is a Socialist first and a "patriot" afterwards; because he believes and asserts it at the right time, that 'your Union Jacks and Tricolours and Imperial Eagles are only to keep you amused, and that there are only two real flags in the world henceforth; the red flag of Democratic

Socialism and the black flag of Capitalism.' He added, 'And we prefer Mr Shaw to Mr Blatchford (the present Mr Blatchford) because Mr Shaw has not been afraid to speak the truth.'

# CHAPTER 12

## December.

## The end of the first five months of war.

### THE DRUMS OF ARMAGEDDON

The drums of Armageddon roll:
Press forward the attack!
Through hell to heaven, man's destined goal;
There is no turning back.
Earth's sturdiest sons these valiant ones,
Who brave the battle brunt;
To the last breath fight to the death,
Bear freedom to the front.

The drums of Armageddon roll:
Through hail of shot and shell
The men of might fought for the right:
Mourn not for those who fell:
Undying fame shall bless their name;
Triumphant to the last,
Their flag unfurled waves o'er the world – 'War's tyranny is past.'

The drums of Armageddon roll;
Through flood of blood and tears,
The sons of men shall rise again
In fairer, happier spheres.
Purged of the vile, the earth shall smile;
War's wild alarms shall cease;
Man shall be kin to brother man ,
Blessed in a world-wide peace.

ARTHUR LAYCOCK
One of a several poems that appeared in the *Clarion,* 4 December 1914

## The First Christmas of the War

For everyone December posed the question of how one could mark the season of peace and goodwill in the midst of the horrific war. The *Clarion* produced its Christmas supplement early, on 4 December. Its contents were not very seasonable. They included a translation by Alex Thompson of Alphonse Daudet's story 'The Last Class,' Edward Carpenter on the 'Roots of the Great War' and Rowland Kenny on 'Soldiers' Dependents.'

*Labour Leader* devoted its front page on 17 December to 'On Earth Peace. A Christmas Message' and the following week on 24 December, Christmas Eve, Clement J. Bundock attempted on its front page to rename the season more appropriately – as 'Marsmas 1914.' The paper's editorial declared that 'To the irony of a warring Christendom is for us added a warring International. We bow our heads in sorrow at the thought that Socialists who had sworn allegiance to the world-wide solidarity of the common people of all lands should be lifting their guns against each other.' But it drew some comfort from the fact that 'Karl Liebknecht is still free' and some members of the Duma were 'now suffering the horrors of the Russian dungeons because they have remained faithful to the two great Christmas truths… the sanctity and unity of human life.' The paper also contained much poetry including several pages of 'Labour War Chants' by Albert Allen.

The same day *Justice* ran again Herbert Burrows's mock Christmas sermon, 'that the Bishop of London has been asked to preach', from 1887. This ended with the cleric abandoning bishopric, palace and income to preach to the unemployed in Trafalgar Square. The editorial by Louie Scarlett 'On Earth Peace, Goodwill Toward Men' concluded with a plea to 'work together towards the goal of Socialism.' There was an exposé of 'Christmas Catering for the Wealthy' which featured details of expensive dinners and entertainments for Christmas Day at the Ritz and other similar venues. *Justice* also gave a big headline – TO OUR COMRADES AMONG THE ENEMY. GREETING! – to a letter from John Helston in which he predicted that 'when this bloody madness has gone from the earth, we, as common men, shall have learnt many things to our sorrow,' and hoped that 'some of you must already be convinced … of that vile and insidious fraud perpetrated on you by your war lords which slowly but surely is being revealed in the pages of diplomatic correspondence.'

The final *Labour Leader* of 1914 on 31 December which featured greetings from Karl Liebknecht, Rosa Luxemburg and Clara Zetkin included a letter from J. M. Nuttall which began 'This is the one of the saddest, nay, *the* saddest, Christmas days I have ever spent.' It should be a time 'when even old gold-cased Scrooges melt in the presence of the Christ Child, the incarnation of love and peace.' The one 'ray of light' was the messages 'flashed across the battlefields' There were also several 'Cartoons for Christmas 1914.' 'The International Juggler' showed Death playing with the nations of Europe, while 'Repairing the International' showed a lineman up a pole and included a reference to the planned Copenhagen conference. Others had a definite religious overtone with titles such as 'The Forgotten Christ' and 'Christ or Mars?'

In contrast Thompson's editorial which came out on Christmas Day saw the war as presaging the end to religious belief; 'No creed can stand against such reeling subversion of its foundation.' When the war was over 'and reason resumes its sway our dogmas shall be found scored through forever. Meantime, we will not mock you with any "seasonable greetings."' That edition of the paper would include news of an event that would bring home the horrors of the war perhaps more vividly at this stage than anything that had to that date appeared in the socialist press in Britain.

## The Horrors of War Come Home; the East Coast Attacks

On 16 December German battleships bombarded the East Coast towns of Scarborough, Hartlepool, West Hartlepool and Whitby. There were nearly 600 casualties, mostly civilians, including 137 fatalities. An eyewitness account by Thomas Beckett, headed 'Bloody Murder' appeared in the *Clarion,* with terrible irony, on Christmas Day. He began by referring to the reassuring statements from the Admiralty about the 'entire absence of panic.' But what did they know? 'We others know. By God we do!' He continued, 'We poor civilians who are so brave, and whose murder is to be regretted, we have no trenches or dugouts in which to seek shelter,' and he then gave the following graphic narrative.

> I saw a man hurrying along the street holding a girl by the arm. She was bespattered with blood from head to foot. The man was holding her arm to stop the gush of blood. I saw a thing on a flat cart driven at a gallop; it had a bloody flattened mass where the head should be. I picked up a shrieking woman… she had seen her sixteen year old boy shattered by a shell.'

He went on:

> Yes, our demeanour was everything to be desired. It was. The self-sacrificing way in which the helpless civilians assisted each other stands for ever as a crushing reply to the immutant law of self-preservation. Here a poor mother with five naked children flying before the murder; and here people turning back to get clothes for these poor naked bodies and to comfort the demented mother. And all the while the very atmosphere rocking with the blood-dry of hell-hounds let loose.

On the same page Hilda Thompson criticised the slowness of the press in bringing out 'specials' on the East Coast bombardment. It was, she said, 'an event which so far as England is concerned is unparalleled in the history of generations' Blatchford believed that fewer men had joined up than expected because 'they have not realised that this war is a real war.' They would now.

A letter from a 'Subaltern' who had joined the army as a trooper but was now a first lieutenant made a similar point, if a great deal more brutally. 'The episode of Scarborough etc. will do a lot of good. I lament the women, and especially the children; but their lives will not have been given in vain if it leads to the destruction of that pusillanimous spirit which only desires peace because war interferes with profit-squeezing.'


**Blatchford claims vindication. Retreating from 'The Movement'.**


In the same edition in which the other reactions to the East Coast bombardment appeared, Blatchford himself did not resist the temptation to make a sally against the Christianity he had caused some scandalised horror in rejecting in his 1903 *God and My Neighbour.* How could a good Christian explain that the great service at St Paul's Cathedral asking God 'to help us lick the Germans' was barely over before the latter shelled the East Coast with so many casualties? Nor could he resist the temptation to say – once again – 'I told you so!'

He had, six or seven years before, made the point that even with the most powerful navy imaginable it would not be possible to protect the whole of the East Coast and therefore he had 'urged the nation to construct defences armed with heavy guns for the defence of the big open towns and ports.' But he had been 'laughed at and reviled by the wise comrades who have made such a brilliant success of misleading the Labour Parties.' But had his advice been followed, the 'massacres at Hartlepool and Scarborough would have been prevented.'

When the war had broken out he had urged the deportation of Germans and warned of spies only to be accused of fomenting 'spy mania.' Now after spies had made the East Coast attack possible the government were beginning to talk about 'arresting German residents.'

> Listen comrades! I live on the East Coast. Any morning a German cruiser may lay to on the sea within a few miles (say three) of my house and blow it to matchwood in ten minutes. And I'm rather fond of my country cottage, which is all I have to show for a life of crime And then there is the village. It's as good a village as any village in Norfolk which is no better than it, and I don't want the Methodist Chapel and the post office destroyed, nor do I want to see a lot of little children murdered its streets.

Blatchford had been such a crucial figure in the British socialism movement that his distancing himself from the movement he had such an influence in creating is well worth careful consideration. In explaining Blatchford's support of the war much is rightly made of his years in the army in the 1870s. When his early memoir *My Life in the Army* was re-issued his colleague and first biographer, A. Neil Lyons, commented (*Clarion,* 18 September 1914), 'Anyone who has ever spoken to Mr Blatchford knows how strongly his outlook and personality have been affected by his time in the Army. Just as a man who has been to Oxford remains an Oxford man for the rest of his days, so an Army man remains an Army man.' He added, 'He went to a poor man's university and took the best which it had to offer him.'

But Blatchford's army had been a peacetime one. As Thomas Beckett pointed out as a preface to his account of the horrifying East Coast shelling:

> R. Blatchford has never been under fire of any sort, and A. M. Thompson who has had experience of the Commune, even he cannot conceive what a shelling by naval gunfire is like. We others know. By God we do!

Yet it would be wrong to ascribe Blatchford's acceptance of the need to support the war *entirely* to his military background. There were, clearly, other factors. One was the fatalism, noted in Chapter 1, that Blatchford seems to have sunk into based on an acceptance of a very deterministic version of Darwinian evolution. He had warned of the danger of war and when it broke out, having, as he said, agonised about it over a week, reached the conclusion that it had been inevitable and determined by forces way beyond the influence of himself or the socialist movement, domestic or international. The perceived inevitability of the war did nothing to lessen its horror for Blatchford. 'Who could have believed war was so near?' he wrote on 2 October. 'And war so terrible, so terrific a war of the nations, spilling blood over every part of the globe.'

The same front-page *Clarion* article demanded the deportation of all Germans and gave an account which even sympathetic readers must have found hard to take seriously of encounters with alleged German spies. It was also where he claimed to have dropped all interest in politics four years previously. 'The scene changed in a flash. Someone seemed to shout the ugly word "War" and I started up wide awake.' As noted in Chapter 1, correspondents were concerned about 'Blatchford's gloom' in July when war, at least war involving Britain, still seemed a fairly remote possibility. In part this was a consequence of his sense of having failed to 'make socialists' – at least on the scale that he had wished. No doubt the hostility he had encountered from large parts of the Left over his 'German menace' warnings contributed to this. Even before the war began he was retreating from the movement he had done so much to create.

By October 1914 this was becoming very clear, even though so many of his friends and most loyal supporters found it hard to accept. On 23 October the following appeared on the front page of the *Clarion* under the headline 'Things that matter.'

I have before me as I write a letter requesting me to take the chair at a meeting. The ideas strikes me as grotesquely funny. Take the chair at a meeting! I? I should as soon think of going on as a music-hall turn in a white hat and a suit of draughtboard check. The 'Labour Movement'. Take the chair?

I have not changed my religion. I am still a Communist Socialist, as I was when I wrote 'Merrie England,' but one must face the facts, and it is a fact that I have done for the Movement all I could or can do. I cannot go back to it, even if I wanted to. It is too late. I am too old.[196] Whether the Movement succeed or fail I am past my youth; my blood is cooler. I know quite well that the future is with the young. To the young I leave the Movement with my blessing and best wishes. I have done my share, I hope. But if I have not done my share it is too late to remedy the failure.

He did not want to be, he insisted, 'a Labour leader', nor a war correspondent, nor a public person, preferring to 'potter about in my garden.'

What is to be will be. Perhaps the Movement will learn wisdom! Perhaps the young girls and boys will put new life in it. For my part, I am past all that. Besides, I am deeply interested in the war. This war is very much the most tremendous event that has happened during my lifetime. It may last for years. After that it may take more years for the nations to readjust themselves. All that will keep me absorbed, and may perhaps keep me busy. Not until that is all over and men have time to think again in peace will the Movement get a chance and when it does the chance will be for the young.

Yet however much Blatchford protested and announced his retirement from 'the Movement' his friends were reluctant to accept that he really meant what he said. 'Never has the name of Blatchford stood so high,' proclaimed Harry Lowerison in the same issue of the paper as he urged readers to make 'a concerted effort to get the paper into homes where it has never been admitted. Leave a copy of The

---

[196] Blatchford was in fact 63 at this time. He would live until December 1943 having published an autobiography *My Eighty Years* in 1931.

War that was Foretold and a CLARION at each house.'

Tom Groom, the founding figure of the Clarion Cycling Club who presided over the paper's 'Cyclorama' was another who refused to believe that Blatchford had really withdrawn from left-wing politics. On 30 October he asked what this 'Movement' was that Blatchford had 'renounced' and gave his version of the course of the *Clarion's* politics since its foundation.

> Some of us once joined the I.L.P. and thought that that was the movement. But the I.L.P. joined the Labour Party and the Labour Party joined the Liberals; so we came out. Then we joined the B.S.P, and thought that this was the Movement right enough. But the B.S.P. headed straight for the morass of politics, wasted a lot of time in 'perfecting the irregular verb,' passed a lot of impossible resolutions; and we came out of that.

Groom then went on to give a succinct summary of the distinctly *Clarion* approach to socialism. The work of 'the Movement' was 'to convert thousands and then still thousands more' to a desire to live in a socialist society. 'When that desire is great enough the professional politician will supply the goods, whether he calls himself Liberal, Tory or Labour Man. Our work is to create that desire.'

In the *Clarion* cockpit on 11 December 'One of the Fellowship' defended Blatchford against 'this carping criticism, the anti-Blatchford, this anti-CLARION feeling.' Readers should think of 'what he has done for Socialism in the past,' compare the *Clarion* to other papers and 'consider all the cycling clubs, dramatic societies, vocal unions, Fellowship clubs, etc., up and down the country,' and 'all the fine chaps and nice girls' in these organisations.

In the same issue as Groom's piece was a column by Fred Hagger of the National Clarion Fellowship comprising a letter he had written in response to Blatchford's statement the previous week. He regretted that the latter had refused the request that he chair twelve demonstrations in different parts of the country aimed, primarily, at bringing pressure to bear on the government over the 'inadequate pay' of servicemen and 'beggarly provision' for their dependents. These would also serve to promote the *Clarion* and to rally the Fellowship. He appealed to Blatchford: 'You are one of the most talked-of and, certainly, one of the most widely-read men in the Empire. Your name is a household word.'

Blatchford included a brief response in his diatribe against 'Bernard Shaw's Latest Impertinence' on 20 November.

> I want to point out to old friends like Groom and Hagger that I do not propose to abandon the cause of Socialism, nor when I speak of the Movement, include in my thoughts as part of the Movement the Clarion Fellowship. Anything I can do for Socialism or for the Fellowship – after the war, I will do. For the great Democratic Movement I feel I have done all I can.'

But the key phrase was clearly 'after the war.'

Meanwhile, Blatchford had been ill. On 30 October Thompson told readers, under the title 'Illness of the Chief' that 'R.B. is suffering from the worst breakdown he has had for many years.' But the following week (6 November) Blatchford was back on the *Clarion* front page, explaining that he had been in bed for a fortnight with 'a severe and serious attack of gout.' He was, he said now 'only half-way out of the wood.' There was, he wrote at the end of the month (27 November) no way of getting away from the war and its horrors; 'The war is a kind of Aaron's rod which had devoured all other subjects.' But what could 'a poor crock of a non-combatant say, worth reading, on the subject of Armageddon?'

Blatchford decided his role should be to address the 'humdrum unromantic side of the war.'

What are the soldiers being paid? What pensions do their widows get? How are we to raise the army we require? Who is going to make clear to the man in the street the reasons why Europe is at war? Who is to pour cold commonsense on the delirious nonsense which the pacifists talk about 'Militarism'? Why don't you help to kick the Cabinet Ministers into a proper frame of mind? In short, get a move on.

If the common sense of national defence was to be brought home to the nation and 'sorry cant about international Socialism' was to be silenced 'an organised and steady effort was needed; We have before us the phenomenon of pacifists and cosmopolitans applauding our enemies and blaming their own countrymen.' This was clearly aimed chiefly at the ILP and the *Labour Leader.* Little wonder that by this time hostility towards Blatchford was growing on the Left.

On 4 December Blatchford reminded *Clarion* readers of 'an effusion of Keir Hardie in which international Socialism was credited with power to perform the marvellous feat of killing the war spirit before it was born.' He had never, he said, 'had the smallest atom of faith in the will or the power of the German Socialists to stop or hinder a war between Britain and Germany. The fine promises of the Socialists at their meetings and congresses did not harmonise with their conduct in the Reichstag.'

But he responded a correspondent 'H J.L' on 11 December who asked, 'Whoever thought that your ideals of a Socialistic future were bound by frontiers?' A plea followed: 'Robert, you are out of place in the limelight of this carnage. Your business is Socialism. You made it your business, and war is not Socialism.' An editorial note insisted that 'R B has never in any of his works expressed faith in Internationalism. His attitude has always been, as it is to-day, reluctantly sceptical.'

Another correspondent, R. Hay, made the point in the 25 December *Clarion* that 'the very title of R.B's books, "Merrie England" and "Britain for the British" make us think the author is a stronger patriot than internationalist.' But Hay added, 'The present war is not only a war for patriots but internationalists: if it is carried out as we hope it will increase the bond between the Allied Powers.' The first part of this assessment had been more or less confirmed by Blatchford himself on 11 December when he wrote, 'I am not a Party man. I wrote about the German Menace as an Englishman, not as a Socialist or a Tory.' Some letters, such as the one from T. H. Ferris on 11 December, were much more dismissive; the *Clarion* attitude to the war was 'intolerable' and 'Blatchford and Thompson *never have* believed in Socialism, nor yet in their fellow-men, nor yet in themselves.'

Another thing that further alienated those on the Left who did not share Blatchford's view of the war was that he was now writing not only in the *Clarion* but also in the 'capitalist Press,' as to a lesser extent was Thompson. On 20 November the paper carried an advertisement for a piece by Thompson on 'Why We Hold our Empire.' Then on 27 November it was the *Daily Mail* that was advertised including 'The Prophecy Which came true; Germany and England' by Robert Blatchford.' This was said to be 'An amazing forecast of the present War, laying bare the German plot to dominate Europe.'

The last page of the final edition of the year on 25 December drew attention to more of Blatchford's writing this time in the *Weekly Dispatch*. It probably cut very little ice with his critics that one of his defenders, Bilsborough, reminded readers – this time of *Justice* (24 December) rather than the *Clarion* – that 'A goodly number of years ago this same Blatchford was in receipt of a handsome salary writing for a well-known weekly journal. He sacrificed that salary and forsook that journal rather than betray his Socialist principles, when those principles were rather less popular than now.' The *Clarion* would survive until 1931, but it would never enjoy the same kind of influence on the British Left that it had done before 1914. Partly this was because the influence of Bolshevism at the end of the war went far beyond the minority of the Left that joined the Communist Party. But the decline had begun before the war with those who took exception to his stance on the 'German menace' and was greatly intensified by

Blatchford's wholehearted support for the British war effort.


## The Shape of Things to Come. Conflict continues in the BSP.


On 19 November *Justice* carried an article by 'our esteemed comrade Clara Zetkin'. It had originally appeared in the New York version of *Vorwärts*. Entitled 'The Duty of Working Women in War Time', it began by declaring that the 'international proletariat' had shown itself 'powerless' to prevent the war. Martial law, said Zetkin, made it impossible to answer the question 'Was it necessary?' But while the 'shrivelled, merciless hand' of hunger knocked 'at the door of each family whose breadwinner is in the field,' there was a 'wide field where the Socialist women' could 'fight battles which at the same time are battles for their rights as human beings.'

Margaretta Hicks picked up on this a fortnight later (3 December) in her regular Women's National Council report.

> The letter from our comrade Clara Zetkin emphasises the same line we have taken in England. We protested against the war as long as possible, but when war had been declared further resistance was futile. We save our breath and set about checking some of the horrors.

The BSP Women's Council might have been prepared to save their breath but if this meant going along with the still dominant leadership view of the war they were out of step with much of the party.

The divisions in the BSP between the 'Old Guard' of ex-SDFers and those who regarded themselves as 'internationalists' went back beyond its foundation. Even before its formation in 1911 there had been tensions between those who regarded the warnings of, especially, Hyndman about the 'German menace' as bordering on, if not lapsing into, chauvinism and jingoism, and those who saw them as realistic and designed to head off the threat of war. As we have seen, the internationalist opposition was particularly strong in London. Some of its proponents, but by no means all, were émigrés from the Russian Empire. Prominent among these was the formidable Zelda Kahan.

There were demands for a special conference to debate BSP policy towards the war. According to the announcement in *Justice* on 3 December the BSP executive had consulted branches and found that 'the overwhelming opinion' was in favour of a conference. But 'Owing to the prevalence of unemployment and short time, a large number of branches, whilst being in favour of the Conference, were not in a position to send delegates if the Conference were held any considerable distance away from their respective localities, and it was impossible to select a central point to which it was certain that anything like a majority of branches could send delegates.' It was therefore decided to call instead six divisional conferences with 'a common agenda' to take place on Sunday 7 February 1915. The venues would be announced later. A timetable was given for the receipt of motions from branches, a preliminary agenda, proposed amendments and final agenda. The first of these had to be received by 28 December and the final agenda issued on 23 January.

There probably were genuine reasons for adopting this unusual procedure; many branches may well have expressed concerns about not being able to send delegates. But, equally, Walter Kendall's judgement that it 'served to atomize the uncoordinated opposition to the advantage of the firmly established bloc supporting the war and severely restricted opportunities of the left to unite upon a common programme and make a clear sweep of the old guard' seems almost certain to be true.[197]

The stand-off between the two factions of the BSP – with the opposition quickly becoming far less 'uncoordinated' – would remain until 1916 when the 'Old Guard' would leave the BSP to form the

---

[197] Kendall, 91.

very unfortunately named National Socialist Party which retained control of *Justice*. They would later revert to the old name of Social-Democratic Federation. It would be a most uncompromising critic of all aspects of Bolshevism while the BSP itself would, in 1920, form the overwhelming majority of the newly-formed Communist Party of Great Britain.[198]

## More Unity – and More Ambiguity in the ILP

It is tempting to see the ILP and the 'internationalists' of the BSP as 'anti-war' and the 'Hyndmanites', *Justice,* the *Clarion* and the Labour Party apart from the ILP as 'pro-war'. But to present the situation of the British Left in 1914 in this way would be to oversimplify to an extent that distorts the reality of the positions taken. No-one was 'pro-war' in the sense of welcoming the conflict that broke out in August 1914. And the extent to which the ILP was really 'anti-war' can be, and often was, exaggerated.

On 17 December *Justice's* 'Critical Chronicle' asked, 'Where is the I.L.P.?'

This is a question we may well ask some of our friends who seem to imagine that the I.L.P. is pursuing a clear and definite policy in respect to the great war. We dealt with the I.L.P. manifesto and the utterances of certain of its prominent members some weeks ago. Since then the following statement by Keir Hardie in the 'Merthyr Pioneer' has been widely quoted: 'I have never said or written anything to dissuade our young men from enlisting; I know too well all what there is at stake.' Objection has been taken, very naturally, to so much publicity being given to this particular statement without reference being made to the context; but taking the article in the 'Merthyr Pioneer' as a whole, we fail

---

[198] For *Justice's* unequivocal rejection of Bolshevism see Ian Bullock, *Romancing the Revolution*, 125-35.

to see that the quotation which has been published so widely is greatly affected by the rest of the article. Take the following: 'None of them [the I.L.P. pamphlets] clamours for immediately stopping the war. That would be foolish in the extreme, until, at least, the Germans have been driven back across their own frontier... 'Quite so' but what do some say when we say so?

We must take into account when considering such comments the desire of *Justice* to score points against a rival. But we should also be aware of the frustration and indignation of those who were upset by being accused of Jingoism when, apparently, Keir Hardie was reportedly saying much the same thing.

As we have seen much of the *Labour Leader* discussion of the origins of and responsibility for the war revolved around a rejection of 'secret diplomacy' in general and specifically the policies pursued by Grey, the foreign secretary. This often involved a very detailed analysis of the documentation available – sometimes going back as far as the treaty of 1839 guaranteeing Belgian independence and territorial integrity. But this was an area where there was little or no disagreement. Everyone – or virtually everyone – on the British Left wanted greater transparency and accountability in foreign affairs and especially in any international agreements or 'understandings' in future.

All wished that such a path had been taken long before the war. All believed that had successive British governments done so the war might well have been avoided. There was, of course, a fundamental difference between those who thought that the publicly avowed and conducted policy should have been one that sought peace by refusing to get involved in Continental alliances and alignments and rejecting any notion of the traditional 'balance of power,' and those who believed that making it clear to Germany that Britain would oppose it militarily if it was the aggressor and strengthening naval and military forces sufficiently to make this credible was the stance required. But on the need to end confidential dealings in international affairs – 'secret diplomacy' – there was a something very close to unanimity. But some believed that this was of little relevance to the question of what Britain should do once Germany had invaded Belgium and France.

For example, Fred H. Gorle in a letter *Justice* 26 November had little time for what he regarded as the equivocations of an earlier letter which, Gorle maintained, drew 'some very doubtful conclusions from diplomatic correspondence concerning Belgian neutrality.' He asked, 'What does it matter *now* if questions of other concern came into the minds of some of the people intimately connected with the affairs leading to the war?' Mixed motives were always present. But for Gorle at least these did not alter the crucial question.

> The actual facts to-day are that we are fighting for Belgium's independence; we are fighting against Prussian militarism; we are fighting for political democracies that are, politically, in advance of German political democracy.

But if there was a general commitment to see an end to 'secret diplomacy' it is true that it was the ILP that pursued this most relentlessly. The Union of Democratic Control [UDC] brought together Radical Liberals like Charles Trevelyan and Arthur Ponsonby and leading ILPers such as MacDonald, Snowden and Jowett. The ILP would account for a substantial segment of the UDC's membership and support throughout the war. The first historian of the UDC, Helena Swanwick, wrote in her 1924 account: 'The Independent Labour Party from the first needed no conversion. It had the root of the matter, and from I.L.P. members the Union received some of its best support.'[199]

The position of the ILP on participation in the war was, essentially, that it was a matter of individual conscience. Not all members of the ILP were pacifists though many were. There were very few advocates

---

[199] H. M. Swanwick, 50-51.

of Leninist 'revolutionary defeatism' in the ILP. But there remained a certain degree of ambiguity about the ILP'S position.

The approach of the ILP meant that while it did not prevent internal conflict and personal animosities it did do something to minimise them. Clement Attlee had joined the Stepney ILP in 1907. He volunteered in 1914, was badly wounded, and reached the rank of major by the end of the war. Clifford Allen, one of the founders of the No-Conscription Fellowship was, like Attlee's brother Tom, a conscientious objector. Allen contracted tuberculosis in prison and came close to death on more than one occasion. Yet by 1921, he and Clement Attlee, both active once more in the ILP, were the joint promoters of the 'Allen-Attlee' version of what became the 'guild socialist' constitution of the party the following year.[200]

## Changing Perceptions and Changing Circumstances. The Years that Lay Ahead.

At the end of the war, in the 'khaki election' of December 1918 most ILP MPs, particularly those like MacDonald who were seen as opponents of the war and lacking in patriotism, would lose their seats. But within a few years MacDonald, the ILP and Labour made a considerable comeback and by 1924 MacDonald was prime minister – admittedly of a minority government and in very particular circumstances. For a growing number of people by then the war was coming to seem to have been not only horrific but pointless. How much this turnaround was a product of the disillusionment caused by the failure of Lloyd-George's 'homes for heroes,' the poor economic circumstances and a peace settlement which was far from bringing about anything approaching the pacific harmony many had looked

---

[200] See Ian Bullock, *Under Siege*. Chapter 5.

for is uncertain. Would a settlement more equitable than Versailles and a more promising future seeming to lie ahead have made the war seem necessary and worthwhile? It is impossible to say.

But some on the British Left had already anticipated by the end of 1914 with quite reasonable accuracy the likely state of the post-war world. Perhaps the most surprising example – because of its seemingly inappropriate setting – appeared in Tom Groom's 'Cyclorama' – addressed to the cycling club – in the Christmas Day *Clarion*.

When this war is over there will be a greater need than ever for a vigorous campaign on behalf of Socialism. We shall see the inevitable swing-back from foreign to home affairs, and the certain rise of a big unemployment problem. With the return of the troops to civil life the unemployment question will be intensified, and there will be certain attempts to lower wages and continue the suspension of the Factory Acts, on the ground that Capital will be unable to recoup itself except on those conditions. There will be the same old attempts made to shuffle the burdens of the war from the shoulders of Capital to the workers. It is against these things that the Socialists will have to fight, and fight hard. And it will be the duty of the Clarion C C to see that the cause of Socialism is not drowned in a flood of Tariff Reform, Militarism, and Flap-doodleism that will then sweep the country.

By the time hostilities had come to an end and something not too distant from Groom's prediction had begun to come to pass; the Left in Britain – as elsewhere – was radically divided by the coming of Communism. The war had brought about divisions, just at a time when the BSP's decision to affiliate to the Labour Party seemed to promise greater unity, but these were relatively minor compared to what was to come. The socialist movement in Britain in 1914 had been far too small and powerless to do anything effective to prevent the outbreak of war. Divided about the responsibility for the war it was united about much else, including its vision of the sort of just settlement and international co-operation with the beginnings of a

'United States of Europe'. But it did not have the power and influence to bring these things about – and was unlikely to change that while it remained so divided.

Blatchford had likened the war to Aaron's rod which had, according to *Exodus,* turned into a serpent and swallowed all those of the Pharaoh's priests. Certainly the war inevitably tended to monopolise attention. After 4 August there were occasional references relating to the issues – women's suffrage, trade union conflicts and the future of Ireland – that had so preoccupied the three papers and the Left generally in July. One can find a few supportive mentions of the campaign for women's suffrage. *Justice* on 3 December headlined a 'Trade Union Victory' when two workers' representatives were elected to the Committee of the Great Northern Railway Superannuation Fund of which the company had previously 'obstinately refused to give the men a share in the management.' And some of the comments about Larkin's 'pro-German' activities in the United States were noted in Chapter 9, but by and large Blatchford was correct in his assessment of the situation in these first months of the war.

But those questions were to re-emerge long before the war was over albeit not in forms that many in July 1914 would have predicted. 1916 saw the Easter Rising in Dublin. In 1917 there was a massive wave of strikes and the rise of the shop-stewards' movement. 1918 brought the Representation of the People Act, a first step in enfranchising women, albeit one which satisfied the conditions of neither the campaigners for the 'limited suffrage' since women were not given voting rights 'on the same terms as men' nor those who demanded 'adult suffrage,' since many adult women remained voteless.

By the end of 1914 it is clear that the seeds of fundamental divisions on the British Left had been sown – particularly among the membership of the BSP. Yet in 1914 itself it was still possible, in spite of the arguments about responsibility for the war and about recruiting, to believe in *some* sort of unity that would at least give the socialist movement a firm basis from which to expand. We have met

Fred Gorle as a wholehearted supporter of Britain's participation in the war to defend Belgium and France and as achieving a poor equal second place in the ballot for the London representative on the BSP executive. Not, one might suppose, the most likely or the most convincing advocate of unity. Yet that is what he attempted in the final *Justice* editorial of 1914 – 'Peace and Goodwill Through Internationality' – on 31 December.

The previous week (24 December), *Labour Leader* had featured a number of 'Messages of Goodwill from Across the Battlefields.' These included statements of international solidarity from leading German socialists Karl Kautsky and Edouard Bernstein and, among several others the Swedish socialist leader Hjamar Branting.[201] In a short statement, barely two paragraphs long, Branting praised both *Labour Leader* and 'the fact that England alone has sufficient respect for individual liberty that she does not attempt to suppress it.'

Gorle, in his *Justice* editorial the following week welcomed Branting's comments, slightly misquoting the part about the paper not being suppressed because – in Gorle's revised version – the government 'dare not suppress it.' He made some little digs against the ILP paper noting that it seemed that no BSP member had been asked to contribute to the goodwill messages and asking whether any French or Belgian socialists had been invited to do so. But his general thrust was to claim that what Branting said reinforced his, Gorle's, position and then going on to plead for tolerance and conciliation in the British movement. He quoted Branting's enthusiasm for a future 'vast association of a United States of Europe, uniting the different nations, each free and sovereign in its own entire self-government.' The next part of Branting's statement, also quoted by Gorle, went on. 'But I should be lacking in candour if I did not add that so splendid an aim must remain fatally chimerical if we are not determined to put

---

[201] Hjamar Branting, 1860-1925, led the Swedish Social-Democratic Party from 1907 until his death. He became prime minister for three short periods in the early 1920s.

forth against the expansive force of capitalism the force of nationality when threatened and anxious to preserve its entire liberty.'

For Gorle, this was 'an effective endorsement of our position.' As he interpreted Branting the latter was arguing 'that Internationalism is not a vague abstraction, signifying in some far distant time the blending of all nationalities into one nation. It is rather the correlation of nationalities; the giving to every nation the fullest possibility of development.' Such notions would not have gone down well either at *Labour Leader* or among the growing 'internationalist' group in the BSP but this did not prevent Gorle from making a New Year plea for unity. He praised the War Emergency Committee which had 'drawn and kept together all the Socialist factions' and then went on:

We say, then, ourselves, let us have tolerance and respect one to another, and to our comrades of other organisations. We have the right to ask the same of other organisations.

For twenty or thirty years we have been wasting effort, money and, worst of all, enthusiasm through intolerance and uncharitableness. We have an extraordinary though a difficult opportunity. We can only adequately seize it by stopping this waste....

We put it plainly to our fellow Socialists of the I.L.P., the Fabian Society and the 'Clarion' that to do this we have to get into more intimate relations, and to remember that usefulness and knowledge are of many varied kinds , not confined to our organisation...

The Fabian, the I.L.P.-er, the Clarionette and the B.S.P.-er have much to learn from each other...

Workers of the world unite. Yes, let us begin with the Socialists, and begin it with the year that now opens before us.

# ABOUT THE AUTHOR

Ian Bullock worked for most of his career in Further Education where he initiated and ran a very large Access to Higher Education course assisting mature students to access a university education. After retirement in 2003 he was for some years an Associate Tutor and later a Visiting Research Fellow at the University of Sussex.

In 1982 he received a D Phil degree from the University of Sussex for a thesis which explored the relationship in the British context of democracy and socialism in the 1880 to 1914 period.

Subsequently, he edited with Richard Pankurst *Sylvia Pankhurst. From Artist to Anti-Fascist* in 1992 and co-wrote with Logie Barrow *Democratic Ideas and the British Labour Movement, 1880-1914* in 1996. His books published in the current century are *Romancing the Revolution. The Myth of Soviet Democracy and the British Left* in 2011 and *Under Siege. The Independent Labour Party in Interwar Britain* in 2017.

# INDEX

Where people or events are covered by footnotes this is indicated by giving first the page number and then the number of the note (n).

Printed in Great Britain
by Amazon

46283908R00167